When the Theater Turns to Itself

Diego Velazquez. Las Meninas. *Courtesy of the Prado Museum.*

When the Theater Turns to Itself

The Aesthetic Metaphor in Shakespeare

Sidney Homan

Lewisburg
Bucknell University Press
London and Toronto: Associated University Presses

Also by Sidney Homan:

Shakespeare's "More Than Words Can Witness":
Essays on Visual and Nonverbal Enactment in
the Plays (editor)
A Midsummer Night's Dream. Blackfriars Shakespeare
Series (editor)

Associated University Presses, Inc.
4 Cornwall Drive
East Brunswick, New Jersey 08816

Associated University Presses Ltd.
69 Fleet Street
London EC4Y 1EU, England

Associated University Presses
Toronto, Ontario, Canada M5E 1A7

Library of Congress Cataloging in Publication Data

Homan, Sidney, 1938-
     When the theater turns to itself.

     Includes bibliographical references and index.
     1. Shakespeare, William, 1564–1616—Knowledge—
Performing arts. 2. Theater in literature.
I. Title.   II. Title: Aesthetic metaphor in
Shakespeare.
PR3034.H6   822.3'3   80-65453
ISBN 0-8387-5009-5

Printed in the United States of America

To Norma

Let me not to the marriage of true minds
Admit impediments. . . .
                                                      Sonnet 116

Contents

Preface

There is a scene in *Antony and Cleopatra* that seems to charm even the queen's many detractors, and even those critics who see her as some sort of female Vice seducing Antony from his rightful place in Rome.[1] It is Cleopatra's death scene (act 5, sc. 2),* and it is literally a "scene," because this is how Cleopatra thinks of it, even wearing her robe and crown to signify the uniqueness of the occasion. The clown, confused as to why a woman would request a basket of asps, has just departed. With his leering rejoinder, "I wish you joy o' th' worm," the clown may stand for that uncomprehending world, the unimaginative Rome for whom the queen is nothing more than the stimulus for a phallic joke. Then, as Cleopatra takes the asp to her breast something extraordinary happens. By the force of her vision she metamorphoses the disgusting serpent, still dripping the "slime and ooze" (2.7.25) from its bed in the Nile, into a lover. The first bite becomes "a lover's pinch, / Which hurts, and is desir'd" (5.2.299). Fourteen lines later Cleopatra, by her alchemy, changes a second asp into a baby nursed at her breast. Applying another asp to her arm she calls it Antony. In this manner a gruesome occasion is transformed into the rather homey picture of a mother embracing her husband and their sleeping child feeding at her breast. Although it only lasts for a moment, something base and ugly has become something symbolic and lovely.

There are, of course, thematic reasons for Cleopatra's metaphoric encounter with the asp. Moments later the

9

Romans come on stage and in an almost obscene clinical detachment they notice the "vent" of blood on Cleopatra's chest, after searching for more obvious signs of her death. Then they spot the mud that the unclean serpent has dragged over the "tawny front" (1.1.6) of the Egyptian.

This encounter also marks a moment when the theater turns to itself. Here Cleopatra triumphs with bad material in a way that parallels Shakespeare's own achievement in suggesting highly sensual femininity in a character who, on the stage of the Globe theater, would most probably be enacted by an older boy. She is an artist, one given to metamorphosis, no less than her playwright. Properly done, the role of Shakespeare's Cleopatra represents the epitome of mature, amoral sexual love. Surely it dwarfs the portrait in the film version of the Cleopatra story starring Claudette Colbert, complete with fans discreetly hiding the lovers during climax and the phallic beating of the ship's oars. Earlier in the play the actor playing the queen has reminded us of the painful reality behind the stage impersonation when Cleopatra fears that, if she compromises with Octavius and follows him to Rome, she will be parodied on stage. Her prediction is that Antony will be reduced to the caricature of a drunkard, while "Some squeaking Cleopatra [will] boy [her] greatness" (5.2.219–20). Though lacking the thousands of Nubian slaves, special effects, panoramic sweeps of the countryside, pliant actresses, and so forth, which were available to the De Milles of Hollywood, Shakespeare's modest company worked with the "essence" of splendor, sexuality, and drama, rather than with its physical verification. They did so not with money or scrupulous attention to "historic detail," but only with talent and with what I suggest is a use of the theater itself as metaphor.

In moments such as this one in the plays, Shakespeare makes us very conscious of his art. The term "Aesthetic Metaphor" in the title of this book refers not just to theatrical references in the text itself but to metaphors based on all the components of the theater: the act of creation on the playwright's part, the resulting text, the techniques of acting and the delivery of that text, and the presence and function of the audience. Beyond the printed text there is what actors call the "subtext" (stage business and wordless dimensions of a production), and also what might be called the "overtext." This overtext emerges in that marvelous union of perfectly normal men and women paying good money to see an obvious fabrication and actors, with egos enough, subordinating their true selves to fictive roles.

The playwright finds metaphors in the very process of his composition, in our awareness of his role as overseer, in the language itself, in the relation of something as theoretical as words to the physical realities of the stage. At times, the characters themselves, using these aesthetic metaphors, are aware of the larger dimension to their actions provided by the theater. At his end Hamlet speaks of the "mutes or audience" (5.2.346) to the events on stage; his immediate reference to the other characters assembled in the make-believe throne room quickly broadens to include us, the larger audience surrounding the stage. Yet he may also refer to mankind generally, as we ourselves alternate in life between being participant and spectator.

Minutes after the assassination of Caesar, Cassius commands his fellow conspirators to wash themselves in Caesar's blood. Then he has an extraordinary vision: "How many ages hence / Shall this our lofty scene be acted over / In states unborn and accents yet unknown!" Brutus completes the thought: "How many times shall Caesar bleed in sport, / That now on Pompey's basis lies along / No worthier than the dust" (3.1.111–16). For a moment Cassius and Brutus are able to translate their present reality into a play. Speaking centuries before the Renaissance, these Romans anticipate a Globe audience in 1599 watch-

ing a stage representation of their deed. The "states unborn and accents yet unknown" here become Elizabethan
England, the language Shakespeare's. Fictive characters
with origins real but distant, they share by such imagining
of future theatrical production a common bond with the
audience alive and assembled around the stage. One might
legitimately argue that if Cassius and Brutus could retain
this theatrical perspective, they could escape their assigned
parts, escape the world of *Julius Caesar,* which, like all
revenge worlds, will now relentlessly close upon them. For
one moment they see beyond the scene that thematically
defines them. Shakespeare comments here, I believe, on
the mirror function of his stage: it offers us the illusion of
detachment from our reality, even though we in no way
leave that reality when we are present at a performance.

Besides coming from the playwright and the inner
world of his play, aesthetic metaphors also spring from the
very process of acting: the voice, the gestures, the methods
of delivery, the profession in general. No less important is
the other side, the audience. The plays are full of
metaphors based on eyes and ears, on seeing and hearing,
the two senses most engaged in performance. We thus
become part of the larger aesthetic metaphor, and this fact
doubles back on the plays when Shakespeare shows us a
parallel audience in the world on stage, such as the courtiers assembled for Bottom's *Pyramus and Thisby* or
Claudius and his court in attendance for *The Murder of
Gonzago.*

By this inclusive definition of aesthetic metaphors I
hope not to abandon the text—it supplies direct examples
enough—but rather to duplicate what I take to be a
catholic definition on Shakespeare's part. Theatrical words
themselves admit this inclusiveness. "To act" can refer
specifically to the motions of a stage actor, but it also
implies nontheatrical action, life's process of doing and
being experienced by the spectator as well. "Play" de-

scribes the fictitious situation on stage—a mere play, not to be confused with reality. But in our own reality it can be a pejorative term, indicating the sense of acting, of duplicity behind surface appearance. "Role" implies both a character part and one's station in life.

If such words do double service, for events both on- and offstage, Shakespeare's plays themselves challenge an easy distinction between the theater and reality. Indeed, the playwright allows for a delightful, productive "confusion" between the two. If the theater is an art form, a way of creating an illusion, of making the stage's two hours' traffic seem momentarily real and of importance, is not the world surrounding the stage also one of role playing? Is the theater not a place where the art of language can create the reality we wish to project, for ourselves as well as for others? The assumption of the scientist, that the universe is relative and that any belief in the "realness," the substantiality of our world can be questioned, refers to the nature of the theater itself, as well as to the speculations of philosophers ancient and modern. We can balance the Renaissance notion of the world as a stage and the stage as a little world against the existential doctrine of existence and awareness, of one's being not a certainty, but rather a compilation of what one thinks one is and what one is imagined to be by others. Genet argues, persuasively, in *Our Lady of the Flowers* that the theater is "true" in that it is a self-confessed fakery, whereas life is "false" or unreal in that men there act as if they were not actors, forcing themselves and others to take a fiction as a fact. Shakespeare constantly questions just how certain the line is between the world onstage and that offstage. His inquiry can be both terrifying (the reality in which we confided may be only an illusion) and yet comforting (if it is an illusion, then it can have only the fake terror of an illusion). Behind the latter notion is, surely, the biblical injunction that this world, and all those who inhabit it, is vanity. In Plato's sense, we have a mere copy of a truth that is to be found elsewhere and only approximated here.

Because the seeming antithesis between the stage and the world may be illusory, I have often been forced to use words in a double sense. The "world" may refer either to that drawn by the playwright or to the reality surrounding the stage, the world we inhabit exclusive of our time in the theater. "Reality" can have its normal meaning. But in the commentary on Hamlet's distrust of the Claudius-Gertrude world and his subsequent admiration of the players' "reality" (they are at least what they appear to be, actors playing actors), "reality" has a broader meaning when we speak of the theater. Conversely, "illusion" can refer both to what seems substantial and to the conscious product of the playwright.

Along with this double sense of words the precise meaning of some terms shifts with the situation, with the specific moment in the text as well as our changing experience with the performance. The term "art," for example, can refer to a blasphemous challenge to reality, a cheap artifice, or a charlatan's business. The artist seduces us with what is, ultimately, a mere illusion, a fraudulent stage world that at length fades away, leaving us empty-handed. And yet "art" can suggest the larger situation—created by that trinity of playwright, actors, and audience—in which we go further into understanding reality than we could without a play, or further than we could relying on reason alone. Art in this sense can be both a source for sterile illusion and for mind-expanding vision. "Language" may be a way of transcending the specific moment, a way of uniting what is here and now with what may properly be said to have a metaphysical and timeless dimension. Conversely, "language" or "speech" can also be a jumble of words, an arbitrary imposition on reality, a social convenience by which we are self-victimized, in the fashion of Ionesco's couples in *The Bald Soprano,* when we lose sight of what "is" by giving ourselves to clichés substituting sound for meaning.

In effect, the possible sources for aesthetic metaphors can be found in the entire process by which a play is finally received, from the principles of composition (and the materials as well), to its maker, its delivery, and the goal of any performance, the audience. The text referred to is both that on paper and that created by the experience of everyone assembled in the theater. Aesthetic terms themselves, such as "truth" and "reality," have both double meanings and—at a deeper level—a single point of reference when the barrier between the "worlds" on- and offstage is broken. Moreover, the terms themselves have a host of meanings, from negative to positive.

-i-

Along with this definition of aesthetic metaphors, I raise the question of why it is profitable to concentrate on this aspect of the plays. First of all, there is a certain purity about such metaphors in the theater, for they are "created" on the spot, justified by what is happening at the time. These theatrical metaphors may be opposed, say, to a metaphor based on caves, where both playwright at the moment of composition and audience at the performance must rely on memories of experiences that are peripheral to the theater. A man who has no knowledge of what a cave looks like might experience some difficulty understanding "cave" as metaphor in a play. But all men at the performance are on equal grounds when an aesthetic metaphor is employed. Such metaphors are "pure" because they come from the medium itself. And they are "true" since even if the play, as Prospero rightly understands it, is only a baseless fabric, it *is* art and it *is* theater. A play cannot be reduced to anything less than itself, though in the theater the goal always seems to be that of giving an

illusion of the stage world's being more than itself. Because
of this purity, this advantage in the aesthetic metaphor's
appealing directly to the only audience of any importance,
that which is on hand for the production, Shakespeare
often uses such metaphors at the climactic moments of his
plays—as in the example cited earlier from *Antony and
Cleopatra.*

In reminding us of what we are experiencing, aesthetic
metaphors ratify the playwright's art, the existence of his
or her theater. Not subliminal advertisements, metaphors
that come from the playwright, the theater, the actors, and
the audience underscore our giving up for two hours the
seeming certainty of life for a fiction. In entering the
theater we thereby announce, consciously or unconsciously, our dissatisfaction with a definition of reality,
such as Theseus's in *A Midsummer Night's Dream,* which
would exclude the world of the imagination, that world
less given to tangible, rational measurements.

This broadcasting on the part of the theater is even
more blatant in our own time, particularly in a play like
Pirandello's *Six Characters in Search of an Author.* Characters
in various stages of evolution escape from the brain of a
playwright who is incapable of sustaining them and stumble upon a stage manager and his company who are
rehearsing another play of the author. Desperate for a
home for their story, they find the "real" actors unable to
portray adequately what is the only reality to them. All the
while the professional company is conscious of the limitations of the physical stage and unwilling to see as a reality
what is, for them, only a truncated illusion. They simply
cannot accommodate the demands of the visitors, such as
allowing them to talk at moments on stage unheard by the
audience. When a crude compromise is reached, the reality of the six characters leads to the murder of the Son.
Still, the company sees the event only in terms of the stage,
and the play thereby ends in confusion:

The Manager. Pretense? Reality? To hell with it all! Never in my life has such a thing happened to me. I've lost a whole day over these people, a whole day!

A superficial reading of *Six Characters* might find this just another dreary play about plays, the sort of backstage look that has provided the plot for countless Hollywood movies about the "business." We may think of the maudlin screen biographies from *The Al Jolson Story* to Julie Andrews's failure in *Star.* Yet this particular turning toward itself provides not just another instance of theatrical self-indulgence but surely Pirandello's most brilliant indictment of our common human dilemma. The difficulties of the stage, of communication, of "telling our story," become identical with those in life itself. This the father well knows:

Each of us has within him a whole world of things. . . . And how can we ever come to an understanding if I put in the words I utter the sense and value of things as I see them; while you who listen to me must inevitably translate them according to the conception of things each one of you has within himself.[2]

The "credible situations" of the theater are true in that they are contained within a form and are unchanging. But at heart they are only an illusion. The "infinite absurdities" of life are true in that they actually happen, but they are also illusory or false since they are infinite and changing. This meeting of the theater and life, between the six characters and the company, allows for a mirror reflection of a common dilemma. Ironically, Pirandello's convincing illusion of the theater failing to sustain the characters' story only celebrates his own larger achievement as playwright.

If aesthetic metaphors establish a broad definition of what a play can mean, as something beyond the literal text, these same metaphors also remind us that our experience in the theater is just as vital to life as living or dying, doing things constructive or destructive. That experience is normal, natural, unavoidable—an inevitable part of our genetic makeup that leads us to witness a play, whether it be at the lofty level of Shakespeare or at the gross, immediate level of burlesque. Both Shakespeare and burlesque are part of a common human heritage, though, pleasant as the latter can be, there is a world of difference between them.

-ii-

My topic here is hardly a new one, and I find myself particularly indebted in the present study to the important work of Lionel Abel in *Metatheatre*, Anne Barton in *Shakespeare and the Idea of the Play*, Maynard Mack in his influential essay on *Hamlet*, James Calderwood in *Shakespearean Metadrama*, Murray Krieger in *Shakespeare's Sonnets: A Window to Criticism*, Francis Fergusson in *The Idea of a Theatre*, and other critics who appear repeatedly in the notes.[3] The issue of this aesthetic dimension, by which we perceive the theater's role in our common reality, is no less important in the Renaissance. Indeed, any study of Renaissance critical and aesthetic theory would rely not just on clearly labeled treatises, such as Sidney's *An Apology for Poetrie* or Puttenham's *The Arte of English Poesie*, but on the information provided by the works themselves. If the Renaissance seems sparse in critical theory, or at least sparse in theory equal to the task of explaining its most splendid literary and theatrical achievements, far from being so impoverished, the age is rich. However, those riches are perhaps not so easily abstracted as they are in our time. In the Renaissance, talking about art and "doing it" are often the same thing. *Hamlet* is both an important philosophical document about the condition of man crawling between earth and heaven and an aesthetic inquiry into the nature of the theater. These two seeming halves are ultimately one, part of one larger vision.

In the presence of such august critics, both past and present, and the testimony of the plays themselves, the present study is justified on the grounds that I have tried to complement what has been said earlier with an even more inclusive definition of what aesthetic metaphors can mean, of where they can be found, and of their contribution to the worlds within and without the immediate play. I have tried to discuss these metaphors both as a subject matter in the plays and as a living part of the performance of those plays. These insights will, at the most, be new, and, at least, they will be personal.

Morris Weitz reminds us in *Hamlet and the Philosophy of Literary Criticism* that criticism ultimately defines the stance of the individual writer, that we should be concerned with what the critic includes *and* excludes to reach that stance. In speaking of a play the critic thereby tells us about his or her own situation, that of a literate spectator, rather than penetrating the "mystery" of the text.[4] In Marshall McLuhan's words, we are the text of any performance.[5] A response to Shakespeare, using aesthetic metaphors, political metaphors, or metaphors based on honor or on the family, is ultimately a personal critical response, the critic serving as an audience of one. It is the right of the reader to choose and buy, as the critic puts his or her wares forth on the marketplace of ideas.

In bringing together my own responses to the plays I cannot claim to "update" critics such as Anne Barton and James Calderwood. Rather, in incorporating their findings with my own (and thereby absolving them of any responsibility for my deeds), and then adding that indefinite but most important factor of the personality of the individual critic, I can speak, at best, as part of a tradition of response to the play. To speak of the play as a literary document, as a repository for, say, the political or religious thought of an age, is not my way. That is another way, another means, equally valid, whereby a spectator (substitute for "critic") chooses to complement his or her attendance or applause with commentary.

-iii-

If the book reflects the personality of an individual spectator, my concern for moments when the theater turns to itself, or reminds the audience of itself, has been reaffirmed by two recent experiences. Several years ago, under a grant from the Florida Endowment for the Humanities (the state's regrant agency for the National Endowment for the Humanities), I took a company of actors about Florida, playing in ten cities, with a program that combined scenes from seven modern plays and comments from an urbanologist and a humanist. At issue was the FEH topic, "Population Density and the Future of Florida." In our program, titled "Florida's Madding Crowd," we used the theater both as a mirror for the problems of living (in crowded inner cities, faceless suburbs, and declining small towns) and as a source for remarks from the urbanologist and humanist. A scene from Albee's *Zoo Story*, for example, might be followed by observations from the humanist on the playwright's allegory of antithetical and warring halves of the human psyche. Then, after comments from the urbanologist on big-city violence and the pressures of urban living, we would return to the violent ending of Albee's play.

For most of the tour the program was a disaster. Audiences would come either to a lecture or to a play, but not to this "unnatural" combination of the two. On our part we didn't believe—though we would not admit it to our conscious selves—that the "world" of the play could be so opened up, so used for purposes other than a convincing illusion. It was only when we understood that these seven worlds, of as many playwrights, could be both mirrors (a self-contained world, responsible to the laws of aesthetics, satisfying on its own terms) and windows (a way of viewing reality, of looking back out on what surrounds the stage, an art form with public responsibilities and functions) that we began to communicate with our audiences.[6] Breaking down the barrier between actors and audience, seeing the stage world not as something unique but, in Brecht's fashion, as "another" event in the larger world, led us out of disaster. By the time we played in Miami—Florida's largest city, and, appropriately, the last stop on our tour—the evening of theater had become so informal that the audience felt no hesitation in barging into the stage performance, chatting with "characters" (actors still in character) as easily as with the actors and choral figures before them.

A year later I received a second grant from the same agency to take a production of Beckett's *Waiting for Godot* to ten Florida state prisons. By chance we had performed, as a sort of "public service," at Florida State Prison, the state's maximum security prison. The response from the inmates was extraordinary; they were the most eloquent, passionate, productive audience we had ever known. They shouted comments and questions to Vladimir and Estragon, asked Pozzo to step forward to explain himself, curiously berated Lucky in his downtrodden state, talked to guests in the audience during the actual performance, and talked to each other. With little or no theatrical orientation, not having learned that stultifying etiquette that often characterizes Broadway, the inmates assumed that *Godot* was just another experience, a "happening" in which they had no need to remain passive. In the early 1950s, after *Godot* had failed with polite audiences in Miami Beach and later in New York, Beckett's American director, in his inspired anger, took the cast to San Quentin Prison and there received the same wonderful reception that over twenty years later we would find duplicated at all ten Florida state prisons.

One night in particular stands out. We had played at a moderate-security prison on the Gulf Coast. It was two in the morning and we were still "high" from the performance as well as from long conversations afterwards with the inmates and then with the warden and his staff. We were then led by a phalanx of guards from the auditorium and across the gravel-lined prison yard, with cold yellow lights glaring down on us. On the opposite side we could just make out the dark outlines of the dormitory-style cell blocks. As we neared the entrance gate a most wonderful thing happened. In violation of the curfew regulations the prisoners suddenly flung open their windows and began calling out goodnights from the opposite side of the yard. I heard a familiar voice in the darkness, the heavy Brooklyn accent of one inmate who, because of transfers, had seen *Godot* in three separate prisons: "Hey, Sid, that Beckett fellow—he wrote a thing called *Endgame,* didn't he?" I shouted back: "Yes, yes he did," glad to talk with a true Beckett fan. "Well, listen buddy, you bring that *Endgame* here tomorrow night—you hear?" I knew what he meant: the theater was so inseparable from life, so much a part of his own existence while he waited for his personal Godot just as Didi and Gogo waited for theirs, that of course actors didn't need to rehearse a second Beckett play, and we could bring it tomorrow as easily as we could bring ourselves. For my Brooklyn friend, for this unique and precious audience, the theater was nothing more than acting and talking. It didn't matter to him whether one did that on the stage or on the world's stage.

-iv-

There is somewhat of a chronology to the plays discussed in this study; I begin with *The Taming of the Shrew* and end with *The Tempest*. I *am* concerned with general changes in Shakespeare's use of aesthetic metaphors, but this is not a survey; and, therefore, all of Shakespeare's plays are not discussed, even all of the "major" plays. Rather, I am concerned with three general "stages" in discussing this dimension of Shakespeare's work, and, by a purposeful arrangement of nine of his plays, I offer a thematic narrative that moves from chapter to chapter.

The first stage includes Chapters 1 to 3, covering *The Taming of The Shrew, Love's Labour's Lost,* and *A Midsummer Night's Dream.* My focus here is on the relationship between the "worlds" offstage and onstage, and the role of the playwright and actor in bridging whatever gap exists between these two worlds. What happens when we apply the Renaissance commonplace of the world as a stage and the stage as a little world to these three comedies? Of particular concern here is the function of stage language and the audience's role in receiving not only that language but the general stage illusion. In a word, this first stage treats the "basics" of the theater.

In stage two—Chapters 4 and 5 on *Othello* and two late comedies, *As You Like It* and *Measure for Measure*— I continue the subjects introduced in the first stage. But now more attention is given to the controlling figure, the character in each play (Iago, Rosalind, and Duke Vincentio) who manages the action, "plays" a role, and arranges scenes, serving, as it were, as something of a playwright-director. In the tragedy the artist is perverse, whereas in the comedies the controlling figures affirm our reality, bringing the other characters to a certain order and meaning.

In the final stage I turn to Hamlet (Chapter 6), Cleopatra (Chapter 7), and Prospero (Chapter 8) because in their plays we find Shakespeare's own divided attitude toward the artist and his craft. Besides expanding on issues raised in earlier plays, *Hamlet, Antony and Cleopatra,* and *The Tempest* represent extraordinary celebrations of art and, at the same time, serious questionings of the relation between art and life, between the worlds off- and onstage.

This general, three-stage argument frames the narrative argument itself. In Chapter 1 *(The Shrew)* we examine how the audience crosses the line from reality to the stage. Two playwrights, the Lord in the Induction scenes and Petruchio in the inner play, work, respectively, with an audience of one (Sly) and a willing-unwilling actress (Kate). In a sense this chapter looks at how a play "starts." The two successful "plays" of Chapter 1 are balanced with the two unsuccessful plays (the masque and the Worthies' interlude) in *Love's Labour's Lost* (Chapter 2). More than *The Shrew*, this courtly comedy treats the relation between language and successful (and unsuccessful) illusion. Whereas *The Shrew* is playful, literally a series of tricks, *Love's Labour's Lost* charts a sane course for reality, guided by responsible love and responsible language. This wider look at the theater leads to a celebration in *A Midsummer Night's Dream* (Chapter 3) of the artist as one who expands our own definition of reality. As it questions the boundaries of Theseus's Athens, *A Midsummer Night's Dream* shows us the role of love and the imagination in penetrating a world beyond that comprehended solely by reason. But that celebration is balanced by a sober inquiry into the stature of humanity once Athens ceases to be the boundary for reality. In Bottom's company, Shakespeare continues and amplifies his inquiry into the ways in which the theater functions.

Othello (Chapter 4) qualifies the celebration of the artist in *A Midsummer Night's Dream,* for Iago supplants a reality (the marriage of Othello and Desdemona) with a worthless, unproductive illusion. The world of this tragedy is as small as that of the comedy is large. But Iago also introduces the first of three controlling figures—on the wrong foot, so to speak, since his aim is to separate people, to pervert that precious reality that we already have. Still,

Iago is fascinating in his malignancy, and our divided response to him anticipates one of the two major concerns of stage three. In Chapter 5 I try to rebalance the dark portrait of the controlling figure with two positive controllers, Rosalind of *As You Like It* and Duke Vincentio of *Measure for Measure*. Here art is a way of life, and playing is a means of exposing absurdity or evil, of patching up society. The plays are not lighthearted: Rosalind and the Duke are no less knowledgeable than Hamlet about the nature of men and women. But they are controllers who through imagination and theatrics allow us to go on. They celebrate the playwright-director even as Iago seems to confirm the Puritan objection to playwrights and their theater.

In *Hamlet* (Chapter 6) two issues predominate: Hamlet's obsession with the theater (and the effect, both positive and negative, that it has on his being, and on our response to him) and Shakespeare's own divided response to the theater, to the use of aesthetic metaphors as a mirror for life. Here the issue is not just the relation between art and life but the degree to which we can profitably see life through the theater. These same concerns inform *Antony and Cleopatra* (Chapter 7), and yet our response to Cleopatra, and particularly to her death, is different in many ways from our experience with Hamlet. Given to acting, disdainful of reality, Cleopatra, unlike Hamlet, is able to love—however excessively and adulterously. Earlier I consider the relation between love and the imagination: even Theseus contemptuously, but properly, links poets and lovers (and madmen) in his harangue at the opening of Act 5. Cleopatra's passion is therefore the source of her difference from Hamlet.

The Tempest (Chapter 8) surveys the various topics of the other seven chapters. I consider this play as Shakespeare's own summary of a lifelong use of aesthetic metaphors. But his final comedy is also about our release from the theater, just as *The Shrew* treated our induction. With *The Tempest* we experience the movement back to a world of which the theater, that less obvious reality, is no less a part.

As stated earlier, my purpose here is not to provide a catalogue of theatrical self-references or to think of Shakespeare's aesthetic metaphors as a thing in themselves or as some sort of "evidence" of his aesthetic principles. Rather, I want to use these metaphors as a means of interpreting the plays, of showing how inseparable, ultimately, aesthetics and thematics are. By the selection of these plays, and by placing them in a framework of three stages and, at the same time, in a narration extending over eight chapters, I hope to offer some material that may offer a little profit and thereby pleasure to the reader.

Gainesville, Florida   Sidney Homan

Acknowledgments

This book has been in my heart and mind for some years, and I have borrowed some of the ideas and, at times, some of the actual prose from earlier publications. Still, I must confess that it is both pleasant and a little alarming to acknowledge this present child in its earlier years. But I do that here: "The Single World of *A Midsummer Night's Dream*" (*Bucknell Review*, 17 [1968], 72-84), "Poetry and the Object of Love: Shakespeare's Sonnets and *Love's Labour's Lost*" (*Revista de Letras*, 1 [1969], 518-30), "Iago's Aesthetics: *Othello* and Shakespeare's Portrait of an Artist" (*Shakespeare Studies*, 5 [1969] 141-48), "Divided Response and the Imagination in *Antony* and *Cleopatra*" (*Philological Quarterly*, 49 [1970], 460-68), "*The Tempest* and Shakespeare's Last Plays: the Aesthetic Dimensions" (*Shakespeare Quarterly*, 24, [1973], 69-76). I take the title of the book itself and part of the Preface from a piece in *New Literary History* (2 [1971], 407-17), "When the Theater Turns to Itself."

When the Theater Turns
to Itself

1

Induction to the Theater:
The Taming of the Shrew

The Taming of the Shrew concerns the two changes necessary for perpetrating the illusions of the stage. The spectator is drawn from that real world encompassing the
theater to the fictive world within. Yet the new role as
spectator and participant in the illusion only parallels the
old role as observer and actor. The other transformation is
an interior one; the playwright and the director—here
shamefully and subsequently hyphenated into
playwright-director—convert an individual into a character. That character is born of words as well as the flesh of
the actor assigned to the part. The meeting of these two
"shapes," spectator and character, with the playwright-
director standing in the wings, constitutes a "play." Sly and
Kate, spectator and character, are separated by different
worlds. One is a supposedly real man metamorphosed into
an audience of one, a cultured lord with players at his
command. The other is caught in the play-within-a-play,
playing the part of a real woman converted from the
shallow pose of a shrew to the image of a model wife. Yet
though they never meet, they are one, part of the same
vision. The hand of the playwright-director, the Lord in
the Induction and Petruchio in the inner play, manipu-
lates both Sly and Kate. Both are changed from either
what they think they should be or what they pretend to be,

31

from drunken tinker and shrewish woman into spectator and character. Sly observes Kate, and Kate both unknowingly and knowingly, as character and as actress, plays before Sly. Sly's transition is a prerequisite to the transformation of woman to character or, on Shakespeare's stage, of boy to shrew to model wife. And whereas the comedy of Sly playing an aristocrat is clear, perhaps the dominant element in the Induction, I concentrate here on the second dimension of his role, namely that of spectator.

-i-

Scenes involving spectators are common in the plays of Shakespeare, and we look again at such moments: the last act of *A Midsummer Night's Dream* in which Puck and Oberon oversee Theseus and his court in attendance for Bottom's *Pyramus and Thisby;* act 5, scene 2 of *Love's Labour's Lost* where the courtiers watch an interlude of Worthies after having, unaware, been performers themselves observed by taunting ladies; Hamlet's dumb show and the playlet *The Murder of Gonzago,* observed by Claudius who is in turn observed by Hamlet and Horatio; the scene Iago stages for Othello's "benefit" in which Cassio supposedly slanders Desdemona; and the wedding masque in *The Tempest* that even strikes some "passion" in Prospero, its creator. Clearly the Induction in *The Shrew* is related to all of these scenes. Yet it also offers us an extended view of a spectator who probably more closely resembled the majority of Shakespeare's audience than did aristocrats such as the King of *Love's Labour's Lost* or Claudius in *Hamlet.* Now Sly may not be everyone's ideal spectator: he is vulgar, given to drink, and easily duped. In *The Taming of a Shrew,* the anonymous play of 1594 which has been seen as Shakespeare's source or as an attempt by a rival dramatist to imitate Shakespeare,[1] Sly is a bit more refined than is Shakespeare's creation. Nor is Shakespeare's character experienced as a spectator: the Lord tells the visiting actors that he has never seen a play before. As far as Sly knows, a "comonty" (his word for "comedy") is nothing more than "a Christmas gambold, or a tumbling trick" (Ind. sc. 2.140-41). He may represent, then, not just all of us but each of us at his or her first play.

Actually, we do not see that much of Sly. Why Shakespeare's Sly disappears has intrigued commentators on the play.[2] Perhaps he once appeared in later scenes, perhaps even in an epilogue (as the Sly of *A Shrew* does); yet for some reason those scenes were dropped from the printed text. If *A Shrew* was based on *The Shrew*, then either it restores such scenes or offers original material added by a rival playwright.[3] Counterarguments hold that Sly does not appear in the Shakespeare play because of considerations of doubling. Or since there is a marked decline in the use of the epilogue in Renaissance drama, Shakespeare may merely follow a trend. Perhaps having established his point that this is a play improvised as part of a practical joke on a drunkard, Shakespeare did not feel any necessity to repeat his premise. If Sly remains on stage the whole time, with dialogue provided only in the two induction scenes and briefly at the end of the first scene, there is the question of how much attention an audience would give such a silent witness. Would Sly gradually lose his unique status as a character and become one of us, albeit a good deal closer to the action? A thematic argument might contend that not having Sly speak again after act 1, scene 1 enables his character to stretch out to infinity. He is the "reason" for the play, the butt of a theatrical joke, but also larger than the play. He ultimately leaves the little stage world and becomes one with the audience, with us.

The situation here would be much like that in Ionesco's *The Chairs*,[4] in which an old man and woman who are both near death try to justify their lives by inviting an Orator as the evening's speaker. Their hope is that the Orator will reveal the secret of life—a secret that has eluded and frustrated the elderly couple. Ionesco's stage direction allows for imaginary chairs to be used on stage, and the bulk of the play is given over to the old couple ushering in the invisible guests, making small talk with them, and arranging the "chairs." The Orator, however, turns out to be deaf and dumb. Failing to speak coherently to the assembled "guests," he impulsively writes some meaning-less words on a blackboard. As the would-be prophet leaves in despair, the invisible and up-to-now silent audi-ence also leaves. Ionesco's directions call for recorded voices and sounds to come from behind the stage. As these sounds and voices mingle with our own when we too leave the theater, it may dawn on us that all along *we* have been the invited guests. We have been drawn into the illusion by imagining that the guests were confined to the stage. In a way the entire theater is now a stage, and we are, however unintentionally, players. Our suspension of belief in im-agining the chairs to be occupied by a fictive guest, or Sly as a spectator, is miniscule in comparison with our new role as participants in the evening's entertainment. Our own search in life for meaning or, barring that, at least entertainment, is mirrored by that of the guests on what may now be called the smaller stage. Their "bursts of laughter, murmurs, shh's," and "ironical coughs" imitate our own on leaving the theater. If he does remain on stage until the end, then Sly does no more or no less than we do. He watches Kate deliver her speech of matrimonial obedi-ence, and then leaves the theater as we do, if only from a different direction.

If we recall the convention of the dream vision, in which the poet claims to tell us what he has experienced during sleep, then Sly's disappearance might be thought of as a dream vision in reverse. It is quite the opposite of Bottom's situation when he wakes from the forest adventures with Titania and then tries to recount the "bottomless" dream he has just had. In *The Shrew* we move from waking state to dream; the play itself is a dream in the conventional Renaissance sense of the theater being a mere illusion, the insubstantial product of the playwright's vision. Indeed, in the Induction the Lord speaks of how, when Sly awakes clothed as a lord, his past life will seem to him "Even as a flatt'ring dream or worthless fancy" (Ind., sc. 1.44). But since Sly is actually hurtled into the "dream world" conjured up by the Lord with the unwitting assistance of the actors, the ascription seems to work for Sly's life before and after. If a character without dialogue can be said to disappear, Sly ultimately disappears even from that tenuous dream in which the Lord plants him. Now we see Sly, now we don't; he fades from our own vision the way Prospero claims his masque fades once its baseless fabric is supplanted by reality. Sly's disappearance has bothered some modern directors of the play to the extent that they insert additional scenes for Sly taken from *A Shrew*.

The commentary thus far has centered on when Sly is "not," or on times when he is silent. As a positive, rather than a negative spectator he is even more interesting and less theoretical. And if Sly is not every man's ideal, the salient fact is that without him there can be no play, no play-within-a-play, or even the truncated encompassing play.

Unlike the sudden decision in *A Shrew* to present Sly with a play and to rely solely on the players themselves to bring off the jest, the decision in *The Shrew* involves a good deal of commentary and preparations. In Shakespeare's play, we hear considerable talk about the means by which Sly will be forced to give up his real role as tinker for the fictive role as lord and spectator, the technical business of "working-up" a part and staging a play, and the possible effects of the performance on the spectator.

The Lord, the playwright-director of the Induction, knows that if Sly is to be converted from a laborer to an

aristocratic spectator, he must be made to "forget himself"
(Ind., sc. 1.41): being an unconscious actor in a successful
theatrical illusion is different from being a skilled tinker.
The "same" Sly exists both outside and inside the theater,
yet, paradoxically, he cannot be *exactly* the same inside.
This discarding of his former identity is more than a
matter of simply forgetting himself. Sly must reconsider
his former life as a period of insanity. He must be per-
suaded that "he hath been lunatic" (Ind., sc. 1.63), that his
past life was nothing more than a "dream" (sc. 1.44), and
that his new role as lord is, and always has been, a reality.
The joke played on him stresses the primacy of the spectator. Sly is not simply a man presented with a play but a
man for whom the play is an extension of his own wealth,
privilege, and taste. The play is *for* him, not just performed
before him. This sense of involvement with the stage
action, even if the audience is partially duped, echoes the
oldest tradition of the theater. One thinks of the Greek
audience, their collective mentality represented on stage
by a chorus intervening between them and the figures of
the tragedy. Or we may think of the audience at village
mystery plays seeing their fellow townsmen performing in
the cycle.

If the play elevates the status of its audience of one, the
other side, that degree of attention given the play by the
spectator, is a moot point. Much would depend not only on
the play involved but also on individual scenes within a
play. Might the audience be more engaged by the closet
scene with Gertrude than by Hamlet's light conversation
with Polonius before the playlet? Beyond this, the fact that
the Elizabethan audience was not rendered anonymous by
darkness, as in a modern theater, would influence both the
degree and the span of each spectator's attention. In the
daylight of the Globe the spectator remained conscious of
himself and of others. This situation may have reinforced

the sense of theater being a union of performers and audience, both out in the light, facing each other, both equally visible. This awareness of an audience may partially explain the frequent use of audiences in Elizabethan drama. We think of ourselves watching Hamlet watch Claudius at *The Murder of Gonzago.* At one point in Kyd's *The Spanish Tragedy,* Revenge and the ghost of Don Andrea, watched by us, watch Hieronimo stage a playlet in which his attention is focused on his victims who have taken parts. Earlier in that same play Lorenzo and Balthazar, watched by us, watch a love scene between Horatio and Bel-imperia. And, as discussed later, in the final act of *A Midsummer Night's Dream* we overlook Puck and Oberon watching Theseus and his court in attendance for Bottom's *Pyramus and Thisby.*

The satire in Beaumont's and Fletcher's *The Knight of the Burning Pestle* may be extreme when the Citizen and his Wife become so involved with a fifth-rate romance that they step into the play, cheering on their hero Rafe, demanding first that lines and then the plot itself be changed to their liking. As a private play satirizing the manners of those who frequent public playhouses, the play is suspect in the accuracy of its portrait. Perhaps the Lord's insistence on Sly's total renunciation of his former identity represents a playwright-director's dream of what the spectator might become if he or she were totally malleable in his hands. Actors speak of good and bad audiences. Yet an audience composed solely of well-wishing friends of the performers would provide only a superficial triumph for those performing. And whereas there may be some pleasure in converting a cold or unruly audience to something finer, no actor would be willing to start from zero.

In his Prologue to *If This Be Not a Good Play, the Devil Is in It,* Dekker gives voice to that wished-for situation in which the playwright can "tye" the spectator's

Eare (with golden chaines) to his Melody:
Can draw with *Adamantine Pen,* (even creatures
Forg'de out of th' *Hammer,*) on tiptoe, to Reach-up,
And (from *Rare silence*) clap their *Brawny hands,*
T'Applaud, what their charmd soule scarce understands,
That Man give mee; whose Brest fill'd by the *Muses,*
With Raptures, Into a second, them infuses.

(31–38)[5]

Sly is most likely a man of *"Brawny hands."* Still, it is
doubtful whether Shakespeare is so confident of swaying
Sly *"T'Applaud,* what [his] charmd soule scarce understands." The one real judgment we have from him is that
"Tis a very excellent piece of work, madam lady," to which
he adds "would 'twere done" (1.1.258–59). This is hardly
the enthusiasm imagined by Dekker. The preparations for
Sly may exceed the results, though, excluding his impatient remark about the play ending, we have no way of
knowing the degree to which he responds in kind to this
excellent comedy.

A little attention spent on an audience, however, goes a
long way, as was demonstrated some years ago in a production of Cole Porter's *Kiss Me Kate,* that backstage musical comedy whose cast is involved in the vicissitudes of
staging the very play Sly is about to see. On opening night
the audience sat pleasantly but distantly involved with the
events on stage, until that moment when the two hoods
stumble on stage. Their business is to see to it that the show
goes on so that the leading man (Petruchio) can pay off his
gambling debts. Unaware for a moment that a play is in
progress, they look out at the audience and then suddenly
grasp the situation. In effect, the opening night audience
is called *into* the play, forming that fictive audience that
initially embarrasses the comic villains. Once their fear is
dissipated and the ham-actor emerges in them, the two
hoods break into the lively song "Brush Up Your Shakespeare," whose point is that adroit quotation from The

Bard of Stratford-Upon-Avon will help one succeed with the girls. It was revealing to see the real audience played to so directly and be made to feel that their presence was directly affecting the characters on stage.

-ii-

Whatever the Lord's motives, Sly himself senses that extraordinary changes have come over him. "What, would you make me mad?" (Ind., sc. 2.18), the tinker demands. Yet he accepts the fiction pressed on him when the Lord and his servants maintain that it is precisely this inability to believe that he is a lord, compounded by the strange delusion that he is a tinker, which so distresses his lady, servants, and kindred (Ind., sc. 2.27–30).

Renaissance opponents of the theater, and even some of its supporters, often dismissed plays as mere dreams. Like dreams, plays were deceptive, seeming realities, which, if believed, would lead man away from a concern with what is here and now. Stephen Gosson could condemn the theater in general as a mere "shadow or . . . paper monster."[6] As we see in Chapter 3, Theseus paints a highly unflattering picture of the poet, along with the lover and madman, lost in the night and suspecting a bush to be a bear. Theseus's artist gives vent to "fairy toys," worthless "fantasies" that only expose the "seething brains" behind them (5.1.2–22). In the Duke's harangue dreams, poetry, the theater, night, madness, and nightmarish irrationality constitute a fellowship that is both destructive and pitiful. For such critics "art" and "dream" as derogatory terms were practically interchangeable.

And yet what the Lord and his fellows are here forcing Sly to do is to brand life as a dream and to accept a dream, this new aristocratic role, as a reality. Sly is, therefore, a spectator of a dream staged for his benefit, even as he is caught in a dream mistakenly apprehended as a reality.

The double irony is that from our perspective Sly is merely an actor, a member of a company; and so he is no more Sly the tinker than he is Sly the nobleman. In this way Shakespeare gives a convincing illusion in which the theater in a sense mocks itself. A live, fully conscious actor plays a fictive, fully unconscious actor. In illustrating the seductive powers of theatrical illusion, in "proving" the Puritan's case that the stage could drive men to think of themselves as other than they actually were, *The Shrew* also testifies to the strength of the illusion. The moment we think that the "real" Sly is a tinker, then we ourselves have been partly drawn into that illusion. "He is no less than what we say he is" (Ind., sc. 1.71)—may we not take the line as referring to the playwright-director's control over either his characters or his ideal spectator? Here that character is mesmerized by a stage artifice that is larger than the overt artifice he thinks he views as a nobleman.

Indeed, however cynical this joke of making a man forget his real self, extravagant claims are also made for what the theater can accomplish. Sly has wrongly esteemed himself to be a "poor and loathsome beggar" (Ind., sc. 1.123), but now he is something finer, a lord no less. At court Bottom is literally on the bottom of the social hierarchy that culminates in Theseus; but in the forest where illusion holds sway and reason is of little avail, a weaver has as his paramour Titania, Queen of the Fairies. Bottom is spoken of as having been "translated," the rustic's word for "transformed." And here in *The Shrew* Sly speaks of his own "transmutation" (Ind., sc. 2.21). In "transformed" and "transmuted" we have a sense of conversion to something finer. Whatever a man's occupation in real life, all men are equals once inside the playhouse. A spectator is a spectator is a spectator.

And, appropriately, "transmuted" and "translated" call up the translation of that book epitomizing transmutation, Golding's English version of Ovid's *Metamorphoses*. Ovid's

name echoes throughout the play. That echo is indirect in
the Induction when the Lord and his men refer to pictures
of "Adonis painted by a running brook," Io wooed by
Jupiter in the form of a cloud and changed by him into a
heifer, and Daphne "roaming through a thorny wood, /
Scratching her legs that one shall swear she bleeds" and
later changed into a laurel tree (Ind. sc. 2.52–61). There
are further references to Ovid in the inner play. Taken
together, they suggest not just the presence of *The
Metamorphoses* and the *Ars Amores* on Shakespeare's desk as
he composed the play, but the larger concept of metamorphosis informing both the play and our own experience.
Marshall McLuhan speaks of the pervasiveness of Ovid
when he comments how

> The play within the play of *Hamlet* reminds us that the
> magic of Ovid was omnipresent to the Elizabethans, as it
> was to Dante and Chaucer. The moment of metamor-
> phosis is the moment of frustration, arrest, the hang-up.
> This moment can be realized dramatically in an illusion,
> a parenthesis, an aside, or a sub-plot parallel to the
> larger action. The interface generated in these intervals
> is itself the occasion of metamorphosis and transforma-
> tion of awareness.[7]

Coleridge professed to feeling a bit of Hamlet in himself; if Hamlet's problems were not totally alien to those of
Shakespeare's audience, perhaps one of the reasons why
the Elizabethan preferred seeing princes and kings suffer,
instead of the Willy Lomans of our own stage, was that for
a moment he also felt a touch of the royal Hamlet in
himself.

The least of the extravagant claims made here for the
theater is that it lets one "frame" his mind to "mirth and
merriment, / Which bars a thousand harms and lengthens
life" (Ind., sc. 2.137–38). The most extravagant claim is
that in forgetting ourselves we find our true selves. In
seeing man thus represented as a mere player we touch on
the essence of being human, beyond our shallow status as

tinker or lord. The second Man puts the matter in the optative sense: "O that once more you knew but what you are!" (Ind., sc. 2.80). In *Hamlet,* Ophelia echoes these sentiments when in her perceptive madness she tells the courtiers, "Lord, we know what we are, but know not what we may be" (4.5.42–43).

It has already been suggested that we too may be seduced into the concentric circles of the play's illusory worlds. Shakespeare provides a few realistic details that elicit this feeling that somehow Sly's world is a bit more "real" than Padua. We are given some concrete facts: Sly is the son of old Sly of Burton heath, "by birth a pedlar, by education a card-maker, by transmutation a bear-herd, and now by present profession a tinker." The name of Marion Hacket is invoked; we learn further that Sly owes her fourteen pence for some ale (Ind., sc. 2.20–22). The players also seem to be real players, though we know in fact that they are players impersonating players. Like the actors who come to Elsinore, they have a reputation of which the Lord is aware. He recalls a production, outside the confines of the present play, in which one of the visitors "play'd a farmer's eldest son [and] / 'Twas where you woo'd the gentlewoman so well" (Ind., sc. 1.84–85). The Lord praises the part as "aptly fitted and naturally perform'd" (87), and the player himself supplies the name ("Sotto") of the character in question.[8]

This situation is perhaps similar to that in Peele's *The Old Wives' Tale,* where we also have spectators watching a play narrated by the old woman Madge. When the servants in the outer play refer to the White Horse (probably a local inn) or Albion's Cliffs, or commend Madge's hospitality as a good example for the wives of the town, Peele shows his hand in making the adventures in the old woman's cottage more immediate to the everyday life of his audience than are the adventures in the enchanted forest. And yet if we assume that the spectators watching the supernatural play-within-a-play are more real than the magician, the bewitched Venelia, or the dead man Jack, we give way to that same fallacy in thinking of Sly as a real man. This fallacy is surely something of a testament to our faith in the theater. It may be added that the players themselves are drawn into the general illusion, for unlike their counterparts in *A Shrew* they are not told of Sly's real identity. Rather, they know only that they are to stage a play before a lord of "odd behavior" (Ind., sc. 1.195) who, having never seen a play before, is easily offended. Thus, the actors themselves are caught in a smaller fiction that is intricately involved in that larger fiction perpetrated on Sly. To succeed, therefore, the illusion demands a certain suspension of belief on the part of Sly the spectator, the actors, and the audience itself.

The art of the theater, of the playwright-director, is spoken of here in ways that are repeated in the analyses of the other plays examined in this book. If being an artist was a sacred vocation to the Romantics, with the work itself seen as a potential avenue to issues not understood in the mundane world, in *The Shrew* and elsewhere in Shakespeare the profession and its product are subject to more practical definitions. Shakespeare held many and various notions about his profession, a healthy bag of conflicting ideas rather than a single-minded notion.

The illusion that so captures Sly, as the Lord well knows, will also appear a "flatt'ring dream or worthless fancy," a mere "jest" (Ind., sc. 1.44–45); for the perpetrators it will be a "pastime" or "sport" (91). The Lord is also a practical-minded director, for he knows that the boy impersonating a lady might go to extremes, might overact; hence his own "presence / May well abate the over-merry spleen" (136–37). Like Hamlet, the Lord gives some last-minute "instructions" (130) to the cast. The play must be "husbanded with modesty" (68), and the players already know that the type of acting preferred by their aristocratic host is one "naturally perform'd." The performance should be a mirror for nature but should not be done "naturally" in the sense of the "realistic" mannerisms of our own method actors. To perfect his role the youth impersonating Sly's wife is told to "bear himself with honourable action, / Such as he hath observ'd in noble ladies / Unto their lords, by them accomplished" (110–12). With a minimum of distortion or exaggeration the mirror may appear one with what it reflects, even though the stage world is ultimately the antithesis to what is real. Still, for a time seeming will appear as truth.

Along with these somewhat demeaning comments and practical instructions there is also a qualified celebration of the imminent performance. The Lord tells us he will "practice" (Ind., sc. 1.36) on this drunken man, and we may think ahead to Prospero with his spirits and magic practicing on the drunken trinity of Trinculo, Stephano, and Caliban. Instead of a bare setting for Sly's transformation, props and art of a rather high order will be required. Sly is to be taken to the "fairest chamber" hung with the Lord's own "wanton pictures" and pervaded by music of a "dulcet and heavenly sound" (46–51). The metamorphosis also demands that sweet wood be burned. As undignified as are some of the comments about the illusion to be practiced on Sly, the product itself merits something more than a shoestring budget.

However contradictory both the motives behind the production and the production itself, *it works*. Sly accepts an illusion for a reality, and rejects a reality as an illusion, as a maddening dream that has plagued him for years. Like the lovers emerging from Oberon's forest Sly is unsure of whether he dreams, has dreamed until now, or is still sleeping. As we have observed earlier, Sly is moving in the opposite direction from the aristocrats of Athens. Yet so convincing is the illusion of his being a lord that he confesses himself "loath to fall into [his] dreams again"

(Ind., sc. 2.128–29). This reverses the situation of Caliban who, hearing the island's sweet music in his sleep, cries to dream again (3.2.151–52). In his ignorance, Sly joyfully accepts a dream as a reality.

Cleopatra's situation may suggest an interesting contrast with Sly's. In Act 5 she at first praises the fancy that creates an Antony in her sleep, but soon confesses that the real Antony is "nature's piece 'gainst fancy, / Condemning shadows quite" (5.2.76–100). The real Antony, in Professor Kittredge's explication of these lines, is Nature's "masterpiece that would quite discredit even Imagination's shadowy figures."[9] At first the queen wishes for "another sleep" so that she might dream again of the Antony whose "face was as the heavens," but she admits that the real Antony can only be approximated by a dream, however majestic it may be. A man of flesh and blood is to be preferred to a lifeless illusion. Yet Sly prefers the dream that, in his newfound bliss, he confuses with reality. And if it was part of Shakespeare's design not to have him appear again in the play, if Sly *is* meant to fade into infinity, permanently sealed within the world of *The Shrew*, then his ironic wish not to "fall into" his dream again is fulfilled.

-iii-

If the Induction concerns the role of the playwright-director and the spectator, the Kate-Petruchio story may be said to concern the director and his material. Several recent studies have already suggested thematic relations between the Induction and the play-within-a-play: the use of supposed identities or "supposes" (the change of roles for both Sly and the suitors in the Bianca plot), the ways in which acting in both stories is a way of "moving people toward a desired feeling and role," and the creative power of the imagination as both Sly and Kate become the picture held up to them by the Lord and Petruchio, respectively.[10] In a perceptive article on the play, Richard Hosley also suggests that with some minor changes in the performance the Lord can double as Lucentio or Petruchio; Sly as Grumio; and the Lady as Biandello, Kate, or Bianca. Surely such doublings would underline the unity between the two "worlds."[11]

My concern, however, is not in "proving" the unity of the play but only in showing that the theatrical issues in the Induction are also raised in the main story itself. One note of caution might be appropriate here. Feminists argue that it is Kate who covertly tames Petruchio: like all women she creates the illusion that it is a man's world when actually the tamer himself is tamed. Petruchio mistakenly believes that he has won and fashioned a woman to his "specifications." If this is so, then our response to the tamer can be ironic as well as comic. But if Petruchio is really his own master, then his comic portrait still admits some serious issues about the role of the playwright-director.

Just as the Lord elevates Sly from tinker to a lord himself, Petruchio holds before himself an ideal to which he drags Kate kicking or, from the feminist's perspective, only pretending to kick. What Kate could become always existed in potential: Petruchio's transformation depends on material that is ready for such transformation. By a sort of metaphorical displacement Petruchio eliminates or diminishes aspects of Kate's personality that prove distracting to others:

> Think you a little din can daunt mine ears?
> Have I not in my time heard lions roar?
> Have I not heard the sea, puff'd up with winds,
> Rage like an angry boar chafed with sweat?
> . . . .
> And do you tell me of a woman's tongue,
> That gives not half so great a blow to hear
> As will a chestnut in a farmer's fire?
> Tush, tush! fear boys with bugs.
>
> (1.2.200–211)

Kate's elevation involves what we might call a formal artistic process. There is first of all an invocation to the muse, a sort of incantation on the name "Kate" that is a prerequisite to the work itself:

> You lie, in faith; for you are call'd plain Kate,
> And bonny Kate, and sometimes Kate the curst;
> But Kate, the prettiest Kate in Christendom,
> Kate of Kate Hall, my super-dainty Kate,
> For dainties are all Kates, and therefore, Kate,
> Take this of me, Kate of my consolation;
> Hearing thy mildness praised in every town,
> Thy virtues spoke of, and thy beauty sounded,
> Yet not so deeply as to thee belongs,
> Myself am mov'd to woo thee for my wife.
>
> (2.1.185–95)

We might think here of the pagan sounding out all possible combinations of a god's name lest in the invocation he ignore some aspect of his divinity and risk offending him. We may also think of the Catholic repeating "Hail Mary's" as prelude to a petition. Petruchio here seems to try out all the various roles for Kate, from plain shrew to queen, the paragon of women. He balances her against what she seems to be at present in the world's opinion and against the exalted station to which his "taming" shall raise her. The poet, like Walt Whitman's spider, throws out a coil, attaching it to some conception or vision beyond his or her present reach. Through his art, the spider's web of the playwright here, the poet makes his or her way toward that end. In the Renaissance sense of "invention," the idea already exists, and it is to this preexisting idea that the poet gives form. Kate, in Shakespeare's and in Petruchio's conception, is always in potential what she is at the end. One obviously does not make up a play as one goes along, and whereas, thematically, Petruchio improvises with material, such spontaneity is only an illusion. Even that penultimate play about improvising a play, Pirandello's *Six Characters in*

Search of an Author, is fully predestined from the play-wright's view.

Petruchio's ideal is staked out early in the play:

> Did ever Dian so become a grove
> As Kate this chamber with her princely gait?
> O, be thou Dian, and let her be Kate;
> And then let Kate be chaste, and Dian sportful!
> (2.1.260–63)

No surface actions can efface this ideal. As Kate screws up her face at her wooer, bites her lip, frowns, and does all the things that Petruchio persists in saying she does not, the physical combat of the lovers is juxtaposed against Pe-truchio's recitation of that ideal:

> I find you passing gentle.
> 'Twas told me you were rough and coy and sullen.
> And now I find report a very liar;
> For thou art pleasant, gamesome, passing courteous,
> But slow in speech, yet sweet as spring-time flowers.
> (2.1.245–48)

Lesser men see only what is there, what is immediate. Greater men, like Petruchio, have a vision beyond the immediate; they look into the true reality of the thing. The physical would chain us; the verbal on that Renaissance stage with its plentitude of words serves as liberation. For Petruchio, the possibilities of development for Kate are unlimited: she can be his goods or chattels, his house or household stuff, field or barn, "My horse, my ox, my ass, my any thing!" (3.2.232–34). He will fashion her, or she will let him think he fashions her, into something finer. It is his "hope to end successfully" (4.1.192).

This sense of looking below the surface of Kate pervades the play. In the midst of his wedding-night tortures, Pe-truchio reassures Baptisto that "To me she's married, not unto my clothes," calling up the adage that clothes do not make the man, at least not the real man (3.2.119). Petruchio knows well enough the proper priorities: "For 'tis the mind that makes the body rich; / And as the sun breaks through the darkest clouds, / So honour peereth in the meanest habit" (4.3.174–76). The union with Kate, superficially embodying sex and violence, may be ultimately a deep and spiritual one, a marriage of true minds. This "mad match" means one thing in the eyes of the shallow spectators on stage, such as Lucentio and Grumio. But if "mad" may be aligned with the imagination, as it is unflatteringly so by Theseus in *A Midsummer Night's Dream*, then the seemingly ill-matched couple share a precious gift. The jest, "That, being mad herself, she's madly mated," that "Petruchio is Kated" (3.2.246–48), goes beyond the merry implications of the speaker.

The union of tamer and tamed is ultimately no union, but rather the assertion of a single mind. In Plato's sense, Petruchio and Kate are the original halves of a single being. And when Petruchio speaks of how "she won me to her love," the irony is that whereas he seems to be reversing the true situation for his listeners, he *is* speaking the truth. Beneath their surface violence are the still waters of a single personality being reassembled after an absence: man is rejoined after his division at the hands of the gods. The harmony of Petruchio and Kate is thus far deeper than that of the attendant characters. Bianca, for example, delights in "music, instruments, and poetry" but only in the surface and tangible expression of such musical accord (1.1.93). Kate's essential harmony surpasses this, and it will be Bianca who is exposed as the potential shrew at the end of the play. Kate in Petruchio's vision "sings as sweetly as a nightingale," her singing embodying the cosmic implications of nature in song (2.1.171). But her "music" has gone unheard until Petruchio's entrance.

The word "tame" that echoes throughout the play might be akin to "transform." To effect such transformations,

Petruchio uses all the trappings of the theater: set speeches, costumes (as on his wedding day), contrived entrances and exits, scenes where we sense the presence of his director's hand. Kate speaks correctly when she says that she feels like his "puppet" (4.3.103). Petruchio controls Kate, transforms her with force on the surface but ultimately with words. Kate herself describes Petruchio as "A mad-cap ruffian and a swearing Jack, / That thinks with oaths to face the matter out" (2.1.287–88). Kate also is infected with his celebration of the power residing in words, for she vows that she "will be free / Even to the uttermost, as I please, in words" (4.3.79–80).

The spectator directed in the Induction here becomes the actor directed by a consummate artist. Like Sly, Kate acknowledges the immensity of the change, for we hear in Act 4 that she "sits as one new-risen from a dream" (sc. 1.189). One world has fallen away and she is about to enter a finer "reality."

Surely a high point in this relationship between playwright-director and his actor is act 4, scene 5, where the married couple meets the aged Vincentio on a public road. Petruchio demands that Kate think of the sun as the moon, reverses the ascription, and then demands that she see in the old man a "budding virgin," again reversing the ascription. We are surely meant to enjoy the high comedy as Kate and Petruchio confuse Vincentio. Still, behind the fun may there not be Shakespeare's apostrophe to the mind, to its power in fashioning a world that defies the facts, even if just momentarily? Here is a larger world unconfined by anything so dull and obvious as reality. In point of fact, Kate is not a real person looking at the sun shining above the outdoor theater. If a mixture of fiction (an actor impersonating Kate) and reality (the sun is the sun) suggests an adulteration of some degree, then in the name of purity Petruchio would have a fiction (Kate) matched with a fiction (seeing the moon at midday). What now elevates Kate and her husband above the attendant figures is not that they are better but that the world they choose to view, if only in jest, is bigger, less given to mechanical certainties. They both encourage an illusion and yet mock it. Artists now working in unison, they are above mere craftsmen but happily below the semidivine figures whom later advocates of the theater would have us accept. The play is what we think it is, even if the achievement be as short-lived as a thought itself: "And be it moon, or sun, or what you please. / An if you please to call it a rush-candle, / Henceforth I vow it shall be so for me" (13–15).

(As they move toward what we might call a shared vision, Sly himself moves toward the physical. In the last moments of his "life" as a dialogue character, we find him tiring of vision, wishing that the play " 'twere done." He hopes that there will not be "any more of it" so that he can get down to lovemaking with the Lady at his side [1.1.256–59].)

This artistic collaboration is inseparable from the act of love. Even as the comedy moves toward a celebration of the playwright-director aided by a skillful and willing actor, it also moves toward love and marital union. It is fitting that Lucentio's metaphor for the reunions and unions that brighten the last act of a play otherwise given to tempers and hostilities is that of "jarring notes" now harmonized (5.2.1). Again, Ovid's *Metamorphoses* suggests the pervasiveness of the transformation. It is that other work of Ovid, *The Art of Love*, which suggests the union between change and love. Lucentio tells us that what he reads is what he professes, "The Art of Love" (4.2.8). And Tranio reminds his master, "Let's be no Stoics nor no stocks, I pray, / Or so devote to Aristotle's checks / As Ovid be an outcast quite abjur'd" (1.1.31–33). He wants a movement from Aristotle, logic, mathematics, and metaphysics to Ovid, common talk, music, and poetry. He wants arts that bring men and women together, rather than philosophies which separate and distinguish the fibers of our existence. The miracles in the play, the transformations, are "wrought" by "Love," as Lucentio tells us (5.1.127).

The last scene where Bianca and the Widow fail the test celebrates the deeper union brought about by Petruchio and Kate. Bianca, on the other hand, gives only the appearance of harmony for actually she was the disguised shrew all along. Petruchio's triumph as lover is inseparable from his triumph as a married lover in the closing moments of the play. Again, whether Petruchio is directing this final scene, or whether he only assumes he is in charge, depends on one's viewpoint. If Petruchio is mocked as a playwright-director in a way in which the Lord of the Induction is not, we would also admit, holding Kate against Sly, that clearly the woman tamer is working with far more difficult material.

The Shrew is much less concerned with Sly's actual story than *A Shrew*. In the latter, the tinker has apparently learned a lesson from the performance through which he has for the most part slept, for he vows on his return home to tame his own wife "if she anger" him. Whereas the concern in Shakespeare's play may more often be aesthetic, there is in *A Shrew* at least a touch of the didactic. Similarly, Grimeston's translation of Goulart's *Trésor d'histoires admirables et memorable,* which repeats the legend of the beggar transported to luxury, draws a moral from the metamorphosis:

> The dissolute spend the night, yea the last night in false joyes. O man, this stately usage of the above named Artisan, is like unto a dreame that passeth. And his goodly day, and the years of a wicked life differ nothing but in more and lesse. He slept foure and twenty houres, other wicked men some-times four and twenty

thousands of houres. It is a little or a great dreame: and nothing more.[12]

Although the theme of love, the commentary on marriage, and the splendid example of the reaches of farce are important aspects of the play, its aesthetic statement is no less striking. For *The Shrew* tells us about the power of the playwright-director to make the audience and actors cross the line betwcen this world and the theater and about why we profit from that journey. The play provides a good induction for Shakespeare's plays to follow. Indeed, the next play discussed, *Love's Labour's Lost,* at once continues, reverses, and intensifies the issues raised in *The Shrew.*

2

Love's Labour's Lost:
Language for the Stage

If *The Shrew* contains two illusions that succeed, namely
that perpetrated on Sly and that played by Petruchio and
Kate on Verona, *Love's Labour's Lost* offers two plays that
fail, a masque and an interlude. In its simple way *The Shrew*
celebrates the theater, the illusion-producing abilities of
the playwright-director. *Love's Labour's Lost,* perhaps a
more substantial play, considers the elements leading to
theatrical failure and, in its course, the function of stage
language in producing not merely a successful but a
meaningful illusion. Not just slapstick, and not without
commentary on the pleasure in expanding vision beyond a
commonplace reality, *The Shrew* still depends on action, on
an unsophisticated audience of one, and on townspeople
who are relatively easy foils for the playwright-director—
and his love—in the inner play.

In *The Shrew* love was linked with transformations, with
the playwright's ability to bring together disparate elements, to produce a comic ending, and, in the case of Kate,
to draw to the surface qualities that, although always there,
remain hidden without love's evocative power. *Love's
Labour's Lost* is also about love, but its focus, like that of *A
Midsummer Night's Dream,* is on the relationship between
love and imagination and on meaningful language result-

ing from their combination. In *The Shrew* "performance" was something akin to a pleasant trick; unlike the author of *A Shrew,* Shakespeare does not bring Sly back at the end to point a moral and it is unclear whether the "victims" of Petruchio and Kate learn anything. In *Love's Labour's Lost* "performance" has the added implication of acting responsibly, and lovingly, and sanely in the present world. *The Shrew* is set mostly in the never-never land of the inner play, though that land is not without implications for our reality. But *Love's Labour's Lost,* despite all its artificial elegance, is concerned with performance in the real world.

Whatever the differences, *Love's Labour's Lost,* like *The Shrew,* speaks of what the theater can "do," or, more properly, what it cannot do. In its final act we witness a masque and an interlude. The four courtiers disguise themselves as Russians "to parle, to court, and dance"; their goal is for each to advance "his love-feat" (5.2.122–23). The ladies, however, penetrate the disguise and thereby constitute a cynical audience not seduced by the intended illusion. The interlude offers the portrait of Nine Worthies staged by the characters of the comic subplot; their reception is roughly on a par with that accorded Bottom and his rustic crew in *A Midsummer Night's Dream.*

Again, we have just witnessed both a play that succeeds and a transformation from a shrew to a model wife. But the two pieces of theater in *Love's Labour's Lost* fail; in that failure is a valuable distinction between language and poetry as something natural and as something artificial (in the most pejorative sense of that word). That *Love's Labour's Lost* succeeds as a play illustrating the "wantoning with words," as one commentator has termed it,[1] only celebrates Shakespeare's larger achievement as a playwright. His successful artifice balances the unsuccessful artifices of the plays within the play. The masque and the interlude, which are our ultimate concern here, themselves comment on the playwright, actors, and audience.

Love's Labour's Lost, even more than *The Shrew,* also looks beyond the immediate stage, for the Messenger's report of the King's death places in a diminished perspective the successful artifice of the theater. If two stage presentations fail, reality, not failing or succeeding, intrudes at the end. An illusion itself, the Messenger's sad news seemingly expels less significant fictions.

-i-

The language of the men in *Love's Labour's Lost* is at fault, for theirs is the sort of shallow dialogue one hears in the most transparent comedy of manners. In an excellent essay on the play, James Calderwood has shown how the courtiers' dialogue degenerates to "mere verbal promiscuity."[2] Nothing lies behind the wit, the dazzling puns and conceits; the verbal battles have the shallow ring of what in our age is branded as mere "cocktail-party conversation." The issues at stake, love and death, demand more. But such introspection here is frustrated specifically by the courtiers' monastic vows, and generally by their disregard for the larger ramifications of speech. Subjects such as beauty, the Princess reprimands Boyet, require something more than "the painted flourish of your praise" (2.1.14).

Armado, the extreme example of the verbose courtier, cherishes the "Sweet smoke of rhetoric" (3.1.64), but such a phrase only exposes his own violation of the language. Listening to Armado and Moth speaking provides a microcosm for just what is wrong with the dialogue of the characters:

> *Armado.* How canst thou part sadness and melancholy, my tender juvenal:
> *Moth.* By a familiar demonstration of working, my tough senior.
> *Armado.* Why tough senior? Why tough senior?
> *Moth.* Why tender juvenal? Why tender juvenal?

Armado. I spoke it, tender juvenal, as a congruent epitheton appertaining to thy young days, which we may nominate tender.

Moth. And I, tough senior, as an appertinent title to your old time, which we may name tough.

Armado. Pretty and apt.

Moth. How mean you, sir? I pretty, and my saying apt? or I apt, and my saying pretty?

Armado. Thou pretty, because little.

(1.2.7–23)

One mistake made in productions of this play is for the actors playing Armado and Moth to convey the impression that this is witty speech. Surely, it is parody of witty speech, if we define the function of wit as exposing its object, rather than its speaker.

Indeed, we might set gradations of witty and pseudo-witty speeches in Shakespeare. Hamlet's toying with Osric in the final scene, laying bare the shallow courtier as he forces him to change his mind about the temperature, is of the highest, purest rank. This is rightly so since Hamlet is highly conscious of language and the implications of words. Touchstone bantering with the clown in *As You Like It* exposes both the romantic notions of country life and his own insufficiencies. The courtly life that Touchstone champions is not always pleasant, let alone ideal. And the clown's simple but honest reply to Touchstone reminds us that verbal dexterity is a double-edged sword.

In this instance we observe the lowest rank, the inversion of wit. The dialogue progresses nowhere, since a participant like Armado is bent on making infinite qualifications to every word used by his opponent. Language is used to analyze language, as if one defined a word with the very word in question. As master and servant move from dialogue to this insane analysis of dialogue, the language itself becomes contorted: "congruent epitheton," crabbed enough in itself, stimulates Moth to respond with "appertinent title." When there is a reach for simplicity, "Pretty and apt," it cannot be left at that.

But this burlesque of scholasticism itself mocks that studied approach to life sought by the courtiers in the opening scene. The parody of wit, then, is not confined to the most outwardly comic characters:

> *Rosaline.* Shall I come upon thee with an old saying, that was a man when King Pepin of France was a little boy, as touching the hit it?
> *Boyet.* So I may answer thee with one as old, that was a woman when Queen Guinever of Britain was a little wench, as touching the hit it.
> *Rosaline.* Thou canst not hit it, hit it, hit it, / Thou canst not hit it, my good man.
>   [*Exit Rosaline*]
> *Boyet.* An I cannot, cannot, cannot, / An I cannot, another can.
> *Costard.* By my troth, most pleasant. How both did hit it!
> *Maria.* A mark marvellous well shot, for they both did hit [it].
> *Boyet.* A mark! O, mark but that mark! A mark, says my lady! Let the mark have a prick in't, to mete at, if it may be.
> *Maria.* Wide o' the bow hand! I' faith, your hand is out.
> *Costard.* Indeed, 'a must shoot nearer, or he'll ne'er hit the clout.
>
>   (4.1.121–36)

The pleasure here is a spurious one, centering on the mere sound of words, as "hit" is tossed from Rosaline to Boyet to Costard to Maria. Indeed, this pleasure almost matches that taken in the sexual innuendoes. The thinking moves by an association among words—"hit" to "mark" to "prick" to "hand" to "clout"—rather than by larger segments of logic and thought. The wit is seductive, there is no doubt, but also "too hot," too soon extinguished on its own ashes.

The ladies are perceptive enough to reject the transparent rhetoric of the courtiers. The Princess rightly delivers a verbal negation to Ferdinand's welcome ("Fair Princess, welcome to the court of Navarre") with her " 'Fair' I give you back again, and 'welcome' I have not yet" (2.1.90–92). Their praises are as shallow as their welcomes. Rosaline in judging Biron's love verses finds them "Much in the letters; nothing in the praise." (5.2.40). Verbal proficiency has here sunk to mere penmanship. The insulting images the ladies then use to describe Biron, and by extension the other courtiers, are letters themselves; their verses arc superficially "Fair as a text B in a copy-book" (42).

The dialogue of Holofernes represents the extreme in this abuse of language, for in this man who relishes only "the odiferous flowers of fancy, the jerks of invention" (4.2.128–29), language utters its death groan. Language as "communication" has with Holofernes become mere "ostentation." And as the courtiers renounce their vows of abstinence and struggle for a more proper poetry of love, the absurd Armado is joined on the comic stage by the even more absurd schoolteacher. Holofernes abuses not one but two languages, and his penchant for high-sounding Latin words, such as "Honorificabilitudinatatibus," is more than just comical. As we laugh at his crabbed scholasticism, a parody itself of the courtiers' former scholarly promises, we also witness the final collapse of language. The speech of one of the three golden ages has sunk to pedantry. Listening to Holofernes on stage we can be both amused and yet dismayed by his mad rape of the language:

> He draweth out the thread of his verbosity finer than the staple of his argument. I abhor such fanatical phantasimes, such insociable and point-device companions; such rackers of orthography, as to speak *dout*, fine, when he should say *doubt; det,* when he should pronounce *debt*—*d, e, b, t,* not *d, e, t;* he clepeth a calf, *cauf;* half, *hauf;* neighbour *vocatur nebour;* neigh abbreviated *ne.* This is

abhominable—which he would call abbominable, it in-
sinuateth me of [insanie]; *ne intelligis, domine?* to make
frantic, lunatic.

(5.1.18–28)

Ironically, Holofernes complains here about the dialogue
of another, and yet his own speech, which tests the delivery
of the actor with its stops and starts, verges on the inarticulate. With Holofernes we sink below the merely playful
talk of the comedy of manners.

This is brawling in Latin and English, which serves as a
verbal complement to that "brawling in French" bandied
about by Moth and Armado earlier in the play. When
Armado questions Moth as to the meaning of brawling in
French—he suspects he means dancing a French
dance—Moth's reply is in itself a parody of acting. He
provides instructions not for a good acting style but for
striking the bizarre pose of a lover mouthing only his own
wretched sentiments but thereby thinking to entice a
woman:

No, my complete master; but to jig off a tune at the
tongue's end, canary to it with your feet, humour it with
turning up your eye-lids; sigh a note and sing a note,
sometime through the throat, [as] if you swallowed love
with singing love, sometime through [the] nose, as if you
snuff'd up love by smelling love; with your hat
penthouse-like o'er the shop of your eyes; with your
arms cross'd on your thin-belly doublet like a rabbit on a
spit; or your hands in your pocket like a man after the
old painting; and keep not too long in one tune, but a
snip and away. . . .

(3.1.11–22)

Such instructions for a lover's "performance" read almost
like a parody of the method acting of our own theater. We
have, in effect, a caricature of a good performance, either
as a lover or an actor. Moth, who knows his own master all

too well, is actually directing our attention to Armado himself.

-ii-

Behind this abuse looms the larger fact that in the conversations of the courtiers and the more obvious clowns, such as Armado and Holofernes, words have been divorced from reality. Just as the oaths taken by the courtiers turn out to be mere promises easily and quickly broken, the plan to abstain from the world itself signals this same assault on man's own true nature. If words gain their currency when used by real men in everyday experience, then the King and his friends violate this natural process. Cutting themselves off from love, from the perfection of womanhood as represented by the Princess and her ladies, they threaten to lose themselves in a selfish, single image, in a world symbolically divided between the field outside and the castle within. The women are the object of poetry and the source of it as well. To divorce oneself from the commerce with their society is to divorce oneself from experience as defined in the play. Such divorce promises only Armado and Holofernes as the end product, language of the exotic hothouse or the pages of the scholar's text. Costard's "This maid will serve my turn" (1.1.301) epitomizes the male-chauvinist attitude that threatens language itself.

Breaking the monastic vow itself will not guarantee complete reformation; love and appropriate language are not just the opposite of not loving and primitive speech. Both are things of a holier nature and both are more complicated than these "vow-fellows" (2.1.38) imagine. As in *Julius Caesar*, no vows are needed; that the men formalize their monasticism in language only exposes the shallowness of both the commitment and its object.

Love, not lust or infatuation or a mere change of heart

from celibacy, is here the source of true poetry, of that dialogue of a higher order. In this sense, *Love's Labour's Lost* echoes the concern of the Sonnets where Shakespeare's love for the young man was the sustenance for his poetry, and, conversely, where the poetry elevated the friend above mortality. Both in the Sonnets and in *A Midsummer Night's Dream* the poet is also a lover, giving birth to his fancy even as the lover participates in human procreation. To love well and to speak well are essential to the playwright. Here in *Love's Labour's Lost* that object of love, the source of worthy speech, is actually present, even if it is undervalued. The notion in the Sonnets, that the poet and his poetry are dependent upon even as they enhance the lover's presence, materializes here in the actual appearance of the women. The object is present; the women come to the castle but the language is insufficient. The problem here thereby reverses Shakespeare's frequent concern in the Sonnets with his friend's absence.

For the courtiers to cease abusing language, they themselves must see the women as we the audience do, as the unspoiled essence of womanhood. Their eyes must match ours in perceiving the reality of the situation. Their elevation to the audience at the end of the play is the first substantial step in this direction. Caught in the "world" of *Love's Labour's Lost,* that world of mad language epitomized by Armado and Holofernes, the men can make no progress. Only events from the outside, such as the early arrival of the ladies, the late arrival of the messenger, or a perspective such as the Nine Worthies afford, will help in this renaissance of love and the language of love.

The eye of the mature beholder gives way early in the play to that eye poring over a book, purchasing nothing but pain: "To seek the light of truth; while truth the while / Doth falsely blind the eyesight of his look" (1.1.75–76). Boyet speaks of the King in his infatuation as having "all his senses . . . lock'd in his eye" (2.1.242). When the courtiers break their vows, their sonnets only express this insufficient visual proof. Looking into the eye of his beloved, Longaville finds not a Platonic pathway to the soul but rather only the superficial "Heavenly rhetoric of thine eye" (4.3.60). In his revealing synthesis, language that has earlier corrupted the tongue has now infected the eye as well.

What is needed is a finer eye, the mind's eye serving as an extension of the physical eye. The courtiers must see what we see as we witness the significance behind the physical spectacle. Zukofsky suggests this vital interaction between what we see and hear and the essence perceived through such physical witness when he defines poetry of the first order as combining "sight, sound, and intellection."[3]

(The paradox here is that Shakespeare can offer a meaningful play about an initially trivial world. Our pleasure in the exquisite verbal tricks and the fast-paced dialogue runs counter to, even as it complements, the play's own running commentary about the abuse of language. The "maggot ostentation" (5.2.409) of the speeches is condemned even as it satisfies our craving for the witty talk that is itself the perfect objective correlative for the shallow world exposed here.)

-iii-

Shakespeare condemns not only the dialogue of these "actors" but the very manner of delivery. The organ of speech itself, the tongue or actor's instrument, is here abused. The Princess reminds Boyet that beauty bought by the "judgement of the eye" is not to be "utt'red by the base sale of chapmen's tongues" (2.2.15–16). And Biron's tongue is described as a "tongue, all impatient to speak and not see, / [which] Did stumble with haste in his eyesight to be" (2.1.238–39). Nathaniel reads an embarrassing passage from Biron's poem wherein he speaks both of that tongue as being "Well learned . . . that well can thee commend" and of his own "earthly tongue." Biron's poem is surely too gross for the higher reaches of poetry (4.2.116, 122). After a long play on words Maria denounces the participants as talking "greasily," with "lips [grown] foul" (4.1.139). But it is Boyet who best combines the portraits of a shallow eye and insufficient tongue when he describes Navarre in love: "But to speak that in words which his eye hath disclos'd. / I only have made a mouth of his eye, / By adding a tongue which I know will not lie" (2.1.251–53). Abusers of the tongue, the courtiers ironically impose as a penalty on any woman coming within a mile of the court the "pain of losing her tongue" (1.1.124–25). Rosaline, however, will later find it a "fault" in Biron "to snatch words from [her] tongue" (5.2.382).

Concerned with the larger meaning of language, *Love's Labour's Lost* thus also concentrates on the organs of speech and sight, the physical prerequisites to poetry both devised and delivered. Appropriately, the courtiers' speech can be dismissed as "mouth honor." Moth calls for assistance from his "father's wit" and his "mother's tongue" (1.2.100–101), and he is partly successful, for the poem he delivers, "If she be made of white and red" (104–111), is not without merit. At the very least it strikes a note of simplicity and is a welcomed change from that wretched poetry in which each courtier "spend[s] his prodigal wits in bootless rhymes" (5.2.64). This abuse of the organ of speech is contrasted with Katherine's refusal of Boyet's kiss: "My lips are no common, though several they be" (2.1.223).

Acting coaches themselves come in for ridicule. The herald works against the most careful instructions of the courtiers in their Russian masque, and thus aids in the debacle of their presentation. But it is no less than Holofernes who reprimands Nathaniel for reading the poem: "You find not the apostrophas, and so miss the accent: let me supervise the canzonet" (4.2.123–24). Here is a most unlikely dramatic coach if there ever was one. Armado similarly treats Moth as he would a paid actor, giving him his cues on how to sing when his "spirit grows heavy in love" (1.2.127). There are too many coaches offering advice, coaches who have already set a bad personal example of acting in their ineffective delivery of suspect lines. Actually, there seems to be a correlation here between the amount of discussion about acting and the quality of the performances.

The abilities of an actor are tested since in this play he must impersonate an actor giving a second-rate performance and yet convince the audience that it is the character who is second-rate, and not the actor himself. This was the same problem faced by Sir Laurence Olivier in *The Entertainer,* a film in which he played a has-been comic, ignorant until too late of his own deficiencies as a player.

-iv-

Replete with phony actors, the play also boasts phony artists and playwrights. Armado is described as a man who "hath a mint of phrases in his brain; / One who the music of his own vain tongue / Doth ravish like enchanting harmony" (1.1.166–68). The picture here is of the spurious artist piping to himself, unconscious of, or unconcerned with, the effect or meaning of his or her song on an audience. The portrait is just the opposite of Shakespeare's own in the Sonnets where he worries about exposing and prostituting himself on the stage. Boyet, though more pleasing than Armado, is still too prodigal with words, "spending" his wit in shallow praise of the Princess (2.1.19). Hoarding or wasting—these seem to be the extremes to which the play's several false artists subject language.

The concept of poetry held by these artists is equally wrong. Caught up in his infatuation, Biron dedicates himself to "love, write, sigh, pray, sue, groan," thereby reducing poetry to some sort of psychological release (3.1.206). Armado expresses that same selfish prodigality when, overcome by the "beauties" of Jaquenetta, he promises to "turn sonnet." He would charge into art as into a fortress, with the cry, "Devise, wit! write, pen! for I am for whole volumes in folio" (1.2.189–91). At times even this parody of the true artist degenerates to a mere copyist or plagiarizer. Despite Moth's contention that the lost ballad of the King and the Beggar is inappropriate for his situation, Armado insists that he will have "the subject newly writ o'er, that I may example my digression by some mighty precedent" (1.2.114–22). Love here would turn him into a mere borrower of other men's scraps.

Even lust demands its own poetry, albeit a parody of the real thing. The Spaniard's pathetic love letter to Jaquenetta (4.1.60–89) mocks the courtiers no less than the writer himself, for it takes a hardened soul not to see the banality in the sonnets they themselves bring into the garden two scenes later. The fatuous apostrophe to love ("I do affect the very ground, which is base, where her shoe, which is baser," etc.) with which Armado ends Act 1 illustrates the humorous but also insane depths to which poetry and the delivery of such poetry can sink when the love involved is entangled in artifice and image building. And surely the courtiers' talk in that same act is of little more substance than Armado's silly protestations.

This abuse of language, coupled with failures in the composition and delivery, results in an audience that is either uninformed or unreceptive. What the performer may see as art, as pleading of a lofty and seductive order, is for the audience only "A huge translation of hypocrisy, / Vilely compil'd, profound simplicity" (5.2.51–52). Indeed, the play is marked by a disparity in the judgments of performers and their audience. Very often this failure springs from hostility, in which the attitude of the performer is to "put . . . down" the listener (4.1.143). Such failure in communication, to use the phrase common in our age, is also in evidence when Armado and then Biron give Costard a letter that he cannot read. The result is that each letter is taken to the wrong party; this confusion of audiences is the final blow in the dismantling of the two men overblown in infatuation. Even when the audiences are corrected, and Biron tries to dispose of the evidence of his own bad poetry by tearing up the letter, the pieces are reassembled by Dumain. Biron's one recourse is to confess that he and the others are "pick-purses in love"; his only stipulation is that the "audience" be dismissed and that the secret of the vow breakers be confined to the guilty parties (4.3.209–210). So many of the arguments in the play stem from words being mistaken, from two characters holding to different definitions of the same word, as in the quarrel between Moth and Armado over the word "l'envoy" (3.1.71–119). Indeed, what characterizes this play is argument springing from words, rather than from events or from something equally substantial.

These various contributors to a successful performance (the language itself, the creator, the actor, and the informed audience) are synthesized in Biron's great speech on women's beauty (4.3.290–365). To be sure, this speech still smacks of verbal indulgence, and the courtiers' fraudulent masque, in which Biron also participates, will prove they have not fully learned the lessons of love or of performance. Still, the speech makes several telling points. Biron recognizes that art is inspired not by abstinence but by participation in the world of beauty and love. If his conception of women still seems too physical, perhaps with some readjustments in his thinking women can still be "the ground, the books, the academes" from which true poetry springs, the "Promethean fire" inspiring meaningful dialogue between the sexes. In communicating effectively with others, we come to see ourselves clearly; true language, above the language of self-indulgence and that prodigality so common in the play, is a mirror for our own reality. All other arts are "slow arts" that, being too cerebral, lack the verification of experience and thus "Scarce show a harvest of their heavy toil." But poetry properly inspired and properly delivered is marked by lines that would "ravish savage ears / And plant in tyrants mild humility"—a lofty goal for nondramatic as well as for dramatic arts. It is right that the men will now abandon their oaths to find their true vocation, in the biblical sense losing themselves to "find" themselves (361). Balancing those negative examples strewn elsewhere in the play from which we, if not the characters, have profited, this speech thus begins to define the nature of true "theater," in the most basic sense of communication among poet, actors, and audience.

It is interesting, though, that on the completion of Biron's speech the men jump to the extreme. Agreeing that the earlier academy or retreat was a wrong step, they are now too eager to reverse the trend. Their resolve to woo and win the "girls of France" (371) is too hasty.

But it is significant that the means they pick for the wooing is the theater, "Some entertainment" (373). The courtiers' problem is that they use the theater for the most propagandistic of purposes, as "revels, dances, masks, and merry hours" (379) designed to turn the heads of a supposedly willing audience. Their step toward the theater, in effect, is no less misdirected than their opening step toward the monastery.

Like Theseus who thinks of plays as merely a way of beguiling "The heavy gait of night" (5.1.375), the characters in *Love's Labour's Lost* see the theater for too long as nothing more than "some strange pastime" (4.3.377). Armado, the extreme counterpart of the courtiers, looks forward to little beyond "delightful ostentation, or show, or pageant, or antic, or firework" (5.1.117–19). Violation of language or poetry is one thing, and much of the commentary in this play about language duplicates ideas in the Sonnets that, in all probability, Shakespeare was writing at the same time. But given the medium here, a violation of the theater represents a more direct assault. And it is this violation that occupies the final, long scene of the play.

-v-

As befits royalty, the courtiers' play takes precedence. This time, however, the audience is up to the performance. Boyet sees to it that the ladies understand the circumstances and can see behind the Russian disguises. They are to "Muster [their] wits" (5.2.85), for this time wit will be applied against bad theater rather than against shallow love. Boyet also gives some details about the impending production, particularly about the "pretty knavish page" who is to be the prologue for the play. He has "well by heart . . . conn'd his embassage. / Action and accent did they teach him there" (98–99). (There follows a blow-by-blow description of their training the herald in his part.) With such emphasis on the perfecting of the prologue, we are right in suspecting that the herald will make a shambles out of his brief part and thereby trigger off disaster for the subsequent production. The ladies then learn of the courtiers' theatrical purpose, something on the level of nightclub entertainment: "to parle, to court, and dance." Here, if anything, is a theater whose purpose veers from the aesthetic to the practical. The actors are confident they "know" their audience since each lady has received her own love favor, but here is a prop that can be easily exchanged.

The ladies immediately prepare an antimasque, for they

have properly reasoned that the courtiers bring not entertainment, in the finest sense of that word (*utile et dulce*),
but mere "mocking merriment" (5.2.139). With their own
masque they will "double" the illusion. And if we were not
tipped off ahead of time, as audience we would be
hopelessly lost in concentric circles of illusion: actors
playing courtiers disguised as Russians supposedly playing
to their individual loves but, with the swap of favors and
wearing of masks, playing to actors (actresses in our day)
impersonating characters impersonating each other to
confuse the "Russians." These illusions heaped on illusions, Boyet knows, will "kill" the performance, divorcing
each actor's "memory from his part" (149–50). Such ven-
geance is proper, for the Princess denounces the play to
come as mere "penn'd speech," as dialogue of no account.
We now witness "sport by sport o'erthrown," the theater in
the name of art turning against its worser self.

As we anticipated, Moth butchers his part, with Biron
playing an ineffective prompter for the occasion. The
earlier examples of the tongue's abuse are here realized as
the prologue just barely manages to explain the nature of
the play to follow. If Hamlet worries that the dumb show
promises to tell all, there need be no such worry here.
Ironically, the audience without benefit of the herald
knows all already—and to their advantage. Even the language of the actors, Russian, threatens to get in the way of
comprehension.

What follows is a series of brief "scenes" in which the
courtiers individually fail, each delivering shallow sentiments to the wrong woman whom he imagines to be the
right woman. This very failure justifies the title of the
largest play, *Love's Labour's Lost,* and also shows the futility
of language that is too steeped in desire. The wit of the
superior actors, of those ladies whom the courtiers imagine not to be acting, overwhelms that of the inferior
actors who thought that they brought the advantage to the

encounter. The voice of the courtiers is reduced to the helpless bleat of the victim about to be butchered, whereas the "tongues of mocking wenches" are elevated to the highest level of satire, sharp as "the razor's edge invisible" (255–57). With the courtiers departing in shame, the ladies review their triumph. It is clearly one of language and double illusion over shallow language and fraudulent illusion.

But the play has not ended. The courtiers return in their proper habit, and the ladies continue to mock "Their shallow shows and prologue vilely penn'd" (305). Now the ladies rely on two illusions: their own, dependent on the change of favors and wearing of masks; and the courtiers' transparent one, that they were not the Muscovites who just appeared. It will take, in effect, a revelation on the ladies' part and a confession from the courtiers to restore sanity. This is surely the theater at its illusory best, as well as theater for a practical purpose of destroying conceit.

For this grand purpose Boyet is no longer needed, and when he tries his own verbal tricks in punning on "dismask'd" and "damask" (296), the Princess rightly dismisses him with "Avaunt, perplexity!" The ladies have now come into their own. The would-be victims of male passion are clearly in command, and so language and illusion, the actor's art, are used for the respectable purpose of purgation. Even the courtiers on their return seem to sense the change in mood. Though he is hardly sinless, Biron now clearly sees Boyet as "wit's pedlar" (317), as "honey-tongu'd" but more sweet than substantial. The King appropriately curses him with "A blister on his sweet tongue" (334).

With the ladies' denunciation of the Russians, the world of low artifice perpetrated by the courtiers begins to fall apart. When Biron tries his hand at repentance ("I am a fool, and full of poverty"), Rosaline upbraids him for snatching "words" from her "tongue" (380–82). Sensing a

trick played on them, the courtiers try a bit of improvisation so as to turn their humiliation into a "jest." But we
know that the ladies hold the upper hand since the courtiers remain ignorant of the trick in switching identities
during the masque. Still, the first speech of repentance
does sound a happy note in the play. Biron, spokesman
here and on other occasions, asks for punishment in the
form of a "keen conceit" that can pierce his ignorance.
Then he calls for a simpler speech upholding the sanctity
of words:

> O, never will I trust to speeches penn'd
>   Nor to the motion of a schoolboy's tongue,
> Nor never come in vizard to my friend,
>   Nor woo in rhyme, like a blind harper's song!
> Taffeta phrases, silken terms precise,
>   Three-piled hyperboles, spruce [affectation],
> Figures pedantical; these summer-flies
>   Have blown me full of maggot ostentation.
> I do forswear them, and I here protest,
>   By this white glove,—how white the hand, God
>   knows!—
> Henceforth my wooing mind shall be express'd
>   In russet yeas and honest kersey noes. . . .
>   (402–413)

Biron still overrates the power of his speech, even if
chastened and simplified. Yet we cannot help but admire
this movement toward true speech in a play that is too
often otherwise disposed.

The ladies play their last card now, berating the courtiers for their ignorance of their separate identities. The
men are condemned for having "woo'd but the sign of she"
(469); in the language of our day, they have thought of the
ladies only as sexual objects and have not respected them
as individuals. Appropriately for the focus of this study,
Biron's acknowledgment of the ladies' superiority with
illusion is couched in theatrical terms:

I see the trick on't; here was a consent,
Knowing aforehand of our merriment,
To dash it like a Christmas comedy.
Some carry-tale, some please-man, some slight zany
Some mumble-news, some trencher-knight, some Dick,
That smiles his cheek in years and knows the trick
To make my lady laugh when she's dispos'd,
Told our intents before. . . .

(460–67)

In effect, Biron catches up to us in knowledge, though about four hundred lines later. On the ashes of a disastrous production, the ladies raise their own tribute to a theater that was designed for the purpose of humiliation leading to improvement. These complementary productions are no sooner out of the way than the play itself moves toward its second play-within-a-play. The interlude is to be viewed by an audience harmonized, for the men and ladies are now equals and reconciled. This second, more absurd play will also admit that larger reality that supersedes even the ladies' own brilliant artifice.

-vi-

The play hardly has an auspicious beginning, even in rehearsals. For one thing, Holofernes is in charge, and we have had reason to doubt his handling of the language, let alone such structured language as demanded by the theater. As with Bottom's production, the preparations are centered on potential disasters. The size of the actor playing Hercules presents a problem, but the pedant's solution is that he "shall present Hercules in minority; his enter and exit shall be strangling a snake; and I will have an apology for that purpose" (5.1.140–43). And in case the main production fails, there will be "an antic" to the rescue (154).

The mood of the audience is playful, even critical. The

play itself gets off to a dismal but also curious start. Costard breaks the illusion by openly discussing his part with the aristocrats, thereby violating the theatrical tradition of not mingling with the audience before the show. The King overreacts and orders that the play be stopped. But the Princess, characteristically, is less extreme, and makes a careful distinction between overly serious actors who are too conscious of their responsibility to "Art" and less knowledgeable actors who in butchering the play may produce an effective, albeit unintentional comedy. In some ways she suggests a parallel between the actors and the courtiers who earlier in the play had inadvertently changed high seriousness into a self-mockery. What we will be seeing is "one show worse than the King's and his company"; their failure in the Russian masque will be partially mitigated by what is to follow (514–21).

We now have chastened actors stripped of two false roles, those of would-be celibates and Russians. They now watch actors playing actors who are ill-suited to their parts. Quite rightly, when Costard opens with "I Pompey am," Biron can retort, "You lie, you art not he" (550). Both outside and inside the play the charge rings true. We see not Pompey but a member of Shakespeare's company. Also, Costard murders the part. One illusion succeeds, that Costard is Costard, but the very skills that account for that success are inoperative when Costard takes on an inappropriate role. Ironically, such a failure attests to the skill of the actor playing Pompey: he plays well at playing ill-suited to his part. We have, in essence, a quintessential moment in the theater, the supreme illusion of breaking an illusion. If we believe that the actors are confined to the play, then we grant a temporary reality to the artistocrats. We see them as a real audience when, in truth, they are nothing of the kind. When Costard slips out of his stage role, confessing that he "made a little fault in 'Great' "

(562), we may momentarily think of him as returning to reality. Again, we choose between illusions, preferring the reality of Costard to Pompey. Thus, it is the failure of the play-within-the-play that contributes to the success of the surrounding play. The questionable manners of the aristocrats, as they make side remarks on the performance, are instrumental in sustaining the outer illusion. But this is at the expense of the inner theater, though the Worthies themselves contribute to their failure.

(What happens here parallels the situation in the film version of the play *Marat/Sade*. There the actors of the play-within-a-play are inmates of an insane asylum. Unlikely candidates to sustain an illusion, they only make more plausible the actors impersonating the spectators. Conversely, greater skill is demanded of the "inmates" since they are, in reality, members of the same company playing inmates playing roles in a historical drama.)

The actors themselves in *Love's Labour's Lost* sense their failure when Costard reminds Nathaniel that he was "a little o'erparted" (589) in the part of Alexander. This self-criticism, along with the criticisms and merriments directed by the spectators, now threatens to pull apart the interlude. In addition, the actors playing historical personages are unable to keep out their own reality. Holofernes injects Latinisms into the dialogue of his Judas, and when the courtiers bait him, he abandons the role and openly banters puns with them.

Under such circumstances the play can face nothing but dissolution; the final break occurs when Armado and Costard, playing Hector and Pompey, respectively, revert back to their earlier quarrel over Jaquenetta. The theater can go no further. Either reality overpowers the players' ability to forget themselves in a part, or we see a series of concentric circles of illusion that now strains human comprehension: actors playing characters playing historical militarists, even as they forget their roles and translate their military images into a physical confrontation over a woman. The women who have brought the courtiers to their senses are contrasted here with one who is indirectly responsible for breaking an already faltering illusion. The "incensed Worthies" (703) have carried the theater too far; playing with illusions has matched the earlier unprofitable playing with words.

At such a moment the Messenger rightly intrudes, bringing with him sad news of real events outside the play. He speaks of something substantial, a king's death, in the midst of plays and festivities. This news is able to "dash" (5.2.462) *Love's Labour's Lost* itself, and Biron wisely observes that instead of a shallow, albeit happy ending this "wooing doth not end like an old play; / Jack hath not Jill" (884–85).

Despite two unsuccessful plays, the courtiers still do not make the connection between poetry and love. Biron admits that they have "Play'd foul with our oaths" (766), though he does try to blame the ladies' beauty for "fashioning our humour / Even to the opposed end of our intents" (767–68). But he is overly hasty in his hopes for the purification process: one humiliation in a masque does not a perfect love make. Just as the news of a king's death looks to events outside the play, the ladies rightly look to a maturation of love and language that will take longer than the time allotted in *Love's Labour's Lost.* The courtiers want love granted now, "at the latest minute of the hour" (797). The line itself is spoken even the play draws to a close.

This play shows not the ultimate sophistication of language, but rather language raised from abuse to playfulness to the *promise* of something better. Instead, a twelve-month period is prescribed for the testing of love; the love lasting through such a duration will be love indeed, not lust. And we may speculate that the language of this sequel, this *Love's Labour's Won,* will be of a finer quality. As for Shakespeare himself, the movement toward poetry of a finer order is not an overnight process. For Biron, the testing period will be especially severe: he is to try his language on the "speechless sick" and with them must make his wit "enforce the pained impotent to smile" (861–64). Here will be an audience even more trying than that presented by the semichastened aristocrats. When Biron doubts his ability to "move wild laughter in the throat of death" (865), Rosaline reminds him that this is a task necessary to convert him from his addiction to humor sustained only by that "loose grace / Which shallow laughing hearers give to fools" (869–70). Thus, the play looks beyond its own confines, to a time when language and acting will celebrate art. This will be an art of positive example, rather than the negative examples observed in the masque and the interlude.

Still, we get a glimpse of this future promise in the lovely song "When daisies pied and violets blue," ironically sung by the same "o'erparted" actors who earlier had failed so miserably. At once witty and profound, with their subtle artistry giving the impression of simplicity and spontaneity, the seasonal songs introduce a type of poetry that is far superior to the "Taffeta phrases, silken terms precise, / Three-piled hyperboles, spruce [affectation], Figures pedantical" (5.2.406–08) that Biron has earlier denounced. The specific language of these songs—the intimate picture of Joan keeling the pot or of roasted crabs hissing in the bowl—also admits generalities about seasonal continuity and the semicomic, semitragic juxtaposition of the mocking cuckoo and merry owl. A triumph of poetic synthesis, communication rather than ostentation, these final songs complete a play that otherwise has shown the breakdown of language and meaningful illusion among the majority of its characters. For the two actors assigned the songs, it is a splendid moment, indeed, for the language of the stage. This sense of fullness, where art is more than artifice, where language brings us a more inclusive sense of reality, where the playwright's imagination allows us to move beyond contention or destructive illusion or singleness and narrowness of vision—this sense of fullness receives an even broader statement in *A Midsummer Night's Dream*.

3

The Celebration of Art:
A Midsummer Night's Dream

Not as self-conscious about language as *Love's Labour's Lost*, *A Midsummer Night's Dream* is, nevertheless, a verbal feast. Language here is not simply a way of speaking sanely and lovingly about reality and about love but also a way of penetrating a larger reality. Despite its self-effacing title, the world evoked in *A Midsummer Night's Dream* is one of staggering proportions. We move from the sitting rooms, streets, castles, and camps of the earlier plays to nature in its almost infinite proportions. One critic points out how we continually get "echoes and glimpses of . . . magnificent views and distances": the sweeping panorama in Titania's list of the natural disorders resulting from Oberon's quarrels, Oberon's own picture of Cupid flying between "the cold moon and the earth" (2.1.156), even a mortal's vision of the moon creeping through a hole bored in the earth and emerging on the other side to shine on the Antipodes.[1]

There is a bumbling artist here (Bottom) to match the courtiers and Worthies of *Love's Labour's Lost;* and with its various rehearsal scenes *A Midsummer Night's Dream* is no less detailed in its picture of how plays are mounted. But there are artists here (Puck and Oberon) who dwarf the Lord and Petruchio, even the Ladies of our last play. *A Midsummer Night's Dream* is also not without its failures.

Like the courtiers' masque and the Worthies' interlude, *Pyramus and Thisby* is a flop—but only on the immediate level of performance. For Bottom's play, and the *Romeo and Juliet* that echoes through it, reminds us of what would have happened to the lovers, and reminds us of the cruel, arbitrary, and unimaginative world that would have been theirs had it not been for supernatural intervention. Oberon is an artist moving the world, like Shakespeare in his comedies, toward union, procreation, and meaning. Without slighting their merits, the Lord and Petruchio are mere tricksters in comparison.

Love's Labour's Lost, more than *The Shrew,* is seriously concerned with reality, with how we act in it. This inquiry is taken even further in *A Midsummer Night's Dream* for with its expansive universe, with Oberon's domain that dwarfs but still includes Athens, *A Midsummer Night's Dream* challenges its audience. What limits does a rational approach to reality place on our understanding of what "is"? Can the imagination—the special virtue or vice of the poet, lover, and madman—perceive a larger reality than can unaided reason? *Love's Labour's Lost* is a comforting play: the men's bad sense is balanced and corrected by the good sense of the ladies. And the illusion perpetrated on Sly in *The Shrew* holds little terror for us, since we are made to feel manifestly superior to him. But Theseus is an intellectual; Athens is the hub of civilization. Still, vast stretches of *A Midsummer Night's Dream* are set in the forest, a world incomprehensible to reason, a world not fully defined by the laws of civilization. It is a comedy—let there be no doubt—but humankind is seen as little, as pathetic and narrow in its abilities to cope with anything beyond Athens. There is, in short, a seriousness here, which represents the third level in that progression established by the two plays discussed previously.

Some things remain unchanged. Shakespeare continues to look at the relationship between love and the imagination, the role of the theater for the world offstage, the link between language and vision and meaning, the principles of directing and acting, the portrait of the audience, and the actor's relation to that audience. As in *Love's Labour's Lost,* both positive and negative sides of the theater and of its language are shown. What distinguishes *A Midsummer Night's Dream* from the earlier plays is the breadth of our response. Shakespeare's extraordinary hymn to the imagination must coexist with the wretched *Pyramus and Thisby.* The divided response to art here approaches what we will see in *Hamlet* and in *Antony and Cleopatra.* And, again, the world presented is so large: our focus expands from finite Athens to the infinite dimensions of the natural world encompassing the palace.

Yet all this Theseus would deny. His is the voice raised in dissent against the play's own testament to art. Clearly, Theseus's view is bounded by Athens, by that world synonymous with his reason and available to tangible measurement. This is not to condemn the Duke's approach to life. We may be thankful that he, rather than some irresponsible lover, reigns over Athens. Still, Theseus's reason, the very quality that makes him such an effective ruler, inhibits him from seeing that larger world of which Athens forms merely the small center, only the beginning. Stretching beyond the palace is Oberon's vast domain.

At the heart of this difference between an artist and a rationalist like Theseus is the nature of the world each chooses to see. Theseus establishes a dichotomy between the tangible and intangible, reality and fantasy, life and the theater. But rather than being dualistic, the artist's world is ultimately a single world. By his power of poetic synthesis the artist fuses seeming opposites into a single grand design.

Like Theseus, many critics seems to believe in some sort of dichotomy. For some the issue is reason in conflict with passion, and therefore to "move from the city to the forest

is to choose madness." The clear choice is between
Theseus, the apostle of reason, and those fickle lovers who
can all too easily degenerate to the ass's head, the image
"for carnality and stupidity."[2] Jan Kott would reverse this:
Theseus's kingdom represents the "censorship of day," the
forest "the erotic madness liberated by night."[3] From one
perspective the wild night spent in Oberon's power warns
of the demeaning alternative to anyone who, blinded by
emotions, would flout Theseus's moral code. For by that
code reason holds man's passionate nature in check. Civilization, not supernatural excursions, establishes the
meaning and dignity of human existence. From the other
perspective the return to Athens signals the return of that
surface decorum that is concomitant with society. Still, it
was the night that liberated the Athenians; there, Kott
maintains, they "were their real selves in their dreams."

But rich as its separate halves may be, this dichotomy
obscures the singleness and the inclusive nature of the
poet's own achievement. That achievement is a synthesis,
as Coleridge defines it, allowing for a reconciliation of
opposites, of things which in life or even initially in the
play seem at odds. T. S. Eliot's example from *Burnt Norton*
may be appropriate here. Without art we see only a
meaningless juxtaposition of garlic and sapphires—one
ugly, the other beautiful, one of little value, the other of
immense value. But when we climb above with the poet,
the garlic and sapphires take their place in an artistic
configuration; a synthesis occurs. These otherwise disparate elements form something beyond mere fact, beyond
dualism, even beyond human preference.

Evidence abounds in the play to suggest that Theseus's
dualism obscures the unity and massive dimensions of the
play's single world. If we think of his palace as a safe island
amidst a threatening forest, we must also admit that the
possibility of tragedy clouds that first scene set in Athens.
Helpless lovers are forced to battle implacable odds, the

three horrible alternatives being an unwanted marriage, "death," or confinement in a convent. Hermia has a time limit for her decision that is even less generous than that given Juliet by old Capulet: by the "next moon" she must either resolve to marry Demetrius or "prepare to die." Indeed, her cry that "If then true lovers have been ever cross'd, / It stands as an edict in destiny" (1.1.150–51) echoes the Chorus's opening comment in *Romeo and Juliet* about star-crossed lovers.

Moreover, the forest is benevolent rather than malevolent. Whatever his demonic origins, Puck, in Shakespeare's hands, is more closely aligned with Robin Goodfellow, a less terrifying descendant of the wicked hobgoblin. An Elizabethan audience may have conjectured that anyone with Oberon's powers might like Faustus be in league with the devil; and yet his well-meaning intervention in human affairs would quickly dispel that fear.

The structure of the human drama, in which hate gives way to love, tragedy to comedy, single life to marriage, and barrenness to fertility, is not confined to Athens but informs the supernatural as well. There discord also turns to accord, jealousy to trust, error to the righting of error, and cosmic disorder to cosmic harmony. The lovers' fickleness in changing partners mirrors a larger swapping as Oberon tries to take the changeling from Titania, or as Titania leaves Oberon for Bottom only to return at last the dutiful wife. As the pairs of newly married lovers retire to consummate their marriage on a night made auspicious by the mystical number three (4.1.188), the anticipated joys of pregnancy recall Titania's happy account of that time when the changeling's mother grew "big-bellied" with child. Some basic concerns are common to all the inhabitants, whatever their origins.

It is all one world; the same moon shines on the mortals and the supernatural overseers. Even the vocabulary shared by the "two" worlds suggests that they are not so antithetical. Enumerating the sad aftereffects of her husband's "brawls," Titania speaks of "the green corn [that] / Hath rotted ere his youth attained a beard" (2.1.94–95). Moments before we have heard Flute protest that he cannot "play a woman" because he has "a beard coming" (1.2.48–49). When Theseus pictures his hounds in pursuit of their prey, "With ears that sweep away the morning dew; / Crook-knee'd and dew-lapp'd" (4.1.125–26), we may recall that just seventy lines before Oberon has described for Puck the coronet of flowers that Titania has fashioned for Bottom. In this coronet one finds "that same dew, which sometimes on the buds / Was wont to swell, like round and orient pearls, / [Standing] now within the pretty flowerets' eyes" (56–58). Theseus's word "dew" is part of his glowing account of a personal experience. Oberon's picture is more expansive: the dew falling from the flowers' eyes is at one with the tears of shame shed by Titania, humiliated that she has been enamored of an ass. Still, it is the "same dew," and the lawn on which Oberon berates his queen will shortly be occupied by Theseus and his train. One world will suffice, even though the part comprehended by Theseus and the whole witnessed by the audience are linked by such a fragile substance as dew. Only Theseus would deny the connection.

-ii-

The play poses, then, an existential problem. The vast natural world in which both fairies and Athenians are residents must coexist with a fraudulent reality, the world that the individual wishes to perceive. The irony is that it is the lover, half conscious and lost in a dream world, and not the conscious apostle of reason who perceives this truer, larger reality.

Even here there are complications. Emerging from the forest the four young Athenians become inarticulate when they try to describe the strange events of the night. No wonder Theseus remains unconvinced in the midst of such vague descriptions: what has happened to them now seems "small and undistinguishable, / Like far-off mountains turned into clouds," or like things seen "with parted eye" (4.1.191–93). Attempting to account for the happy pairing off of the lovers, Demetrius can recall only the early moments in the forest with "Helena in fancy following" him. His mind then skips to the present situation in which "all the faith, the virtue of [his] heart, / The object and the pleasure of [his] eye, / Is only Helena" (4.1.167, 173–75). The vast middle part, that extraordinary venture into the unknown, is now beyond recollection.

There in the forest both eyes and ears are rendered somewhat useless. Hermia claims that the ear is more quick of apprehension because of the limitations darkness imposed on the eye. Hence her hearing has led her to Lysander. And yet on seeing him Hermia senses that he is not the Lysander she has known. Enchanted as he is now with Helena, Lysander will prove anything but the lover to Hermia (3.2.177–83).

Within two scenes the lovers, urged on by Theseus, have dismissed their experience in the forest as a dream. They are awake, and there is no question about it—for them. But for us Demetrius's anguished question remains vital: "are you sure / That we are now awake? It seems to me / That yet we sleep, we dream" (196–97). Is what we see the ultimate reality, the final dimensions of the world? Or is it but a fragment of the real thing, a mere point lost in an infinite circle?

The larger reality denied by Theseus is even ambiguous for the lovers, for those most receptive to vision in the play. Although it is the avenue to a larger world, love also admits shifting emotional optics. Hermia confesses that Athens seemed a "paradise" to her until Lysander came: the "graces" in her love for him turned "a heaven unto a hell" (1.1.204–7). Helena acknowledges that although Athens generally thinks here the equal of Hermia, Demetrius has the opposite opinion, and it is this opinion which determines the truth for her. Quite rightly, love "can transpose to form and dignity" things that are otherwise "base and vile, holding no quantity" (1.1.232–33). The opposite is no less true, and it is this absence of love that Helena now experiences. Yet even her present vision of "reality" will be reversed. And if we think that our view of the players marks our superiority to them, Puck in his epilogue taunts us with the possibility that we too have "but slumb'red here." Poe's lines have a special relevance for the play: "Is all that we see or seem / But a dream within a dream?"[4]

We recognize that Bottom is a parody of the lover. A Pyramus he is not, despite his confidence as an actor. Yet Bottom too is allowed to see that larger world denied Theseus. We are, to be sure, oppressed by his pervasive literalism. In the presence of a miracle, where something nonhuman has taken on human form, Bottom greets the live figures of Mustardseed and Peaseblossom as he would old friends, thereby leveling the mysterious with the mundane. Still, on emerging from the forest Bottom knows that what he has seen, even if it be but a "dream," deserves some public attention. If he cannot convey the dream in his own words, he at least has the good sense to turn to Quince, a more accomplished artist, a balladmaker no less. Assuming that Quince would have been up to the task, we never hear the ballad that Bottom proposes singing at the end of the forthcoming *Pyramus and Thisby*. Perhaps it would have been the epilogue that Theseus refuses to hear. If so, we are robbed of an extraordinary experience, of hearing an artist's account of the mysterious, of penetrating a reality that dwarfs smaller concepts as to what is real. But then this is what *A Midsummer Night's Dream* provides; Shakespeare gives us what Theseus, a bourgeois when it comes to art, denies us. Repetition would be useless. Bottom is the artist who fails, though that failure is caused in part by an audience made hostile by the Duke.[5] Still, Bottom shares one thing in common with the play's two other artists: Puck, who manages the human pageant, and Shakespeare. Bottom wants "to make all well" (3.1.17–18), to convert a tragedy into "very tragical mirth" (5.1.57). Similarly, Puck assures us that "all shall be well" (3.2.463), and Shakespeare draws a comedy from what promises to be a *Romeo and Juliet* (Hermia the Juliet, Lysander the Romeo, Demetrius the unwanted suitor Paris, and Egeus the interfering father).

Bottom's power is not unlike that described by Egeus when he argues that a father "should be as a god, / One that composed your beauties; yea, and one / To whom you are but as a form in wax / By him imprinted, and within his power / To leave the figure or disfigure it" (1.1.47–51). Whether controlling a play or caught up in a vision of Shakespeare himself, Bottom at the very most is able "to discourse wonders" (4.2.29); at the very least he can "ease the anguish of a torturing hour" (5.1.37) with his production. Given his heavy responsibility as artist, we can understand Bottom's egoism in wanting to take all the parts in the playlet. A buffoon from one perspective, he is also serious about his art. He wants to know "what the play treats on" (1.2.8–9), the very question we ask here of the larger play. "What is Pyramus? A lover, or a tyrant" (24), and this is a question of substance when we consider the affinity in the larger play between love and tyranny. "What is Thisby?" (47) seems equally valid if we examine the relation between Hermia, Juliet, and Thisby. In a sense Bottom is like us, a representative theatergoer asking questions, looking for significances existing in both the mortal and supernatural realities encompassing the play. It is appropriate that Bottom chooses for his rehearsal area a spot in the "palace wood," where a "green plot shall be

[the] stage," (1.2.103; 3.1.3–4). In effect, he chooses a position midway between the palace (Theseus's territory) and the forest (the domain of Oberon).

Presumably by marrying Theseus, Hippolyta is converted from a huntress to a sober wife; mere sexual passion has thereby been translated into the proprieties of married love. Yet Hippolyta can still take a vicarious pleasure in what other lovers tell her. Despite her husband's disbelief, she is intrigued by their "strange and admirable" story, and after Theseus's cynical equation of lovers and madmen she still gets the last word. Each of the four lovers tells of a fantastic adventure, but taken together their single story, their dream, "grows to something of great constancy" (5.1.26–27). It is here the woman, the object of love, who remains unconvinced by a man's reasoned rebuttal to the larger world we have just experienced.

-iii-

The act of love is prerequisite to this larger vision. In *Love's Labour's Lost* adoration was essential to the proper use of language in the theater or on the world's stage. In *A Midsummer Night's Dream* love is also prerequisite to the fullest response to that creation. Creativity, the issue of the earlier discussions, is replaced here by the issue of receptivity. We have moved, in effect, from artist to spectator; in a way we have gone back to some of the issues raised by the Induction to *The Taming of the Shrew*.

This is not to say that *A Midsummer Night's Dream* represents an unqualified celebration of love as well as of art. We recognize the lovers as fickle and shallow. It is a common observation that, beyond a difference in the heights of the ladies, Shakespeare hardly bothers to give the four youths any separate traits. Lovers are all the same;

in Puck's rather unromantic arithmetic "Two of both kinds makes up four" (3.2.483). Nevertheless, foolish as they may be, they are blessed with a vision, however blurred by their own "mortal grossness" (3.1.163). And it is a vision denied Theseus, superior as he seems to them in his reasoned command over his own world.

As in the Sonnets the poet is also a lover. In making something grow to great constancy, in giving birth to the play that is the child of his imagination, he participates in an aesthetic process that parallels the natural process of birth. Again, birth is here most eloquently described by Titania's recollection of the changeling's mother. The metaphor for pregnancy in her speech (2.1.123–37), the sails that "conceive / And grow big-bellied with the wanton wind," illustrates the poet's art as he transforms two unrelated things (bellies and sails) into something new (the metaphor to which they give "birth"). The metaphor also establishes a relationship in nature between something human and something inanimate, and thus points to the oneness of creation itself. Ships can be pregnant bellies, and a round mother-to-be can "sail upon the land" to fetch trifles for Titania, looking like a ship adventuring for merchandise upon the seas. The word "translated" may be used humorously or inappropriately or pretentiously elsewhere in the play. But here we see an instance in which the poet has "translated" one thing into its antithesis, and in so doing he has momentarily "transported" (4.2.4) those who witness the translation. Art and nature are wedded here; it is the poet's imagination that has captured reality in its universal sense. Polixenes' judgment in *The Winter's Tale* is timely:

> Yet Nature is made better by no mean
> But Nature makes that mean; so, over that art
> Which you say adds to Nature, is an art
> That Nature makes.   (4.4.89–92)

This relation between love and creation is prefigured in that between marriage and the fulfillment of *A Midsummer Night's Dream*. The function of marriage is comic, to "Turn melancholy forth to funerals" (1.1.14). Converted from warrior to lover, Theseus in an aesthetic metaphor speaks of wooing with his sword but wedding Hippolyta "in another key" (16–18). Whether married or familial, love is the "warbling of one song, both in one key" (3.2.206). The first thing that Titania and Oberon do to express their newfound amity is to dance. And it is the absence of love that leads to a time when "No night is . . . with hymn or carol blest" (2.1.102). Without love Hermia will be reduced to a warbler of "faint hymns" sung to "the cold fruitless moon."

Extracting the essence, art thus triumphs over physical mortality. Theseus's own argument for marriage is that "earthlier happy is the rose distill'd / Than that which withering in the virgin thorn / Grows, lives, and dies in single blessedness" (1.1.73–78). This may call up a similar metaphor Shakespeare had used in Sonnet 5:

> Beauty o'ersnow'd and bareness everywhere;
> Then, were not summer's distillation left,
> A liquid prisoner pent in walls of glass,
> Beauty's effect with beauty were bereft,
> Nor it nor no remembrance what it was:
> But flowers distill'd though they with winter meet,
> Leese but their show; their substance still lives sweet.

The argument here is two-fold: the friend perpetuates "himself" through procreation just as the artist perpetuates his friend through his poetry. As Bottom's play moves (or rather stumbles) toward realization, so does Shakespeare's own magnificent play. The latter begins with the promise of marriage and then, after some hostilities and regressions, makes its way toward ceremony and consummation in the final act.

-iv-

Ironically, Theseus is the character who makes this connection between the dreams ("shaping fantasies" in his own words) of the lover and poet. His contemptuous definition of the artist still contains some truth (5.1.2–22). We are perhaps annoyed by his refusal to entertain, even in theory, what the lovers have told him and what we know to have happened. Still, Theseus's remarks have some relevancy, even if it be unintentional. Quite rightly the poet's art is one of shaping fantasies in that like the lunatic and the lover he will not be bound solely by reason. However, whereas the lunatic and the lover abandon their reason unaware, the artist consciously uses reason in conjunction with the imagination. Hermia also makes this association between the lover and poet as she combines references to love's tears with aspects of the imagination in speaking of the "customary cross, / As due to love as thoughts and dreams and sighs, / Wishes and tears, poor Fancy's followers" (1.1.153–55).

In Bacon's words, "reason transmits select and approved notions to the imagination before the decree is executed."[6] Most Renaissance commentators distrust the imagination; they were not Romantics by any means. Burton, among others, could see the imagination as a treacherous force conjuring up "strange, stupend, absurd shapes, as in sick men we commonly observe."[7] Yet properly controlled, imagination could be the servant, and not the master of man. At least this seems to be the argument of the play. Theseus cynically defines the poet as someone giving shape to "airy nothing," but in its self-effacing title the play has anticipated such criticism. Of course, it is all a dream, nothing of great constancy; but if such a dream is properly conveyed and controlled through the language and design of art it may, for the brief two hours' traffic of the stage, *grow* to something of great constancy. Ironically, Theseus's image of the "poet's eye" glancing "from heaven to earth, from earth to heaven" comments on Shakespeare's own achievement in offering us both a sense of universal nature and a specific picture of the nature of things—to borrow the distinction made by Geoffrey Bush.[8] In its vast category of correspondences (the cosmic and the mundane, the macrocosm and the microcosm, Oberon-Bottom, Titania-Hippolyta), the play may well be seen as the artist's own version of the "Elizabethan World Picture."

The artist in this perspective is a man of vast powers. He is aligned with a god, the magician, the restorer of humanity to that peace associated with marriage. Oberon appropriately took on the shape of Corin, the pastoral archetype of the artist, when he stole away from fairy land and "sat all day, / Playing on pipes of corn and versing love / To amorous Phillida" (2.1.65–68). This "king of shadows" (3.2.347) can "overcast the night" (355) or he can take "error from the eye" (368), releasing her "From monster's view, . . . [so that] all things shall be peace" (377). If one chooses to view the forest as the reenactment of Hermia's own mental anguish, or of that anguish collectively experienced by all four love-crossed aristocrats, then it is here the artist who alone has the power to release them from the nightmarish adventures in the forest of their collective minds. If Oberon exercises his power in a somewhat sinister darkness, he still qualifies our fear in reminding Puck that they "are spirits of another sort." He "with the Morning's love have oft made sport," up until the very moment when the sun "all fiery-red, / Opening on Neptune with fair blessed beams / Turns into yellow gold his salt green streams" (3.2.388–93). He works with illusions, but his purpose is for the good. Puck's worst offense is to mislead night wanderers (2.1.39). And although Oberon plans to "streak [Titania's] eyes, / And make her full of hateful fantasies" (2.1.257–58), he is not an Iago. His illusion is meant only to chide.

Nor is Oberon omnipotent. Whatever his godlike status, he still makes the initial mistake of assuming that there is only one couple wandering in the forest. This is reassuring: the artist is not divine and, despite Oberon's supernatural ancestry, he is not inhuman. His is an art whose goal is harmony and love, an art that can with its "dulcet and harmonious breath" make "the rude sea grow civil" (2.1.151–52).

-v-

"How easy is a bush supposed a bear!"—this bit of theatrical criticism applies to the wretched *Pyramus and Thisby* that Theseus sees, not to the larger play we have seen. Shakespeare furnishes opponents of the theater with an example that justifies their complaints and with another that clearly does not. But even Bottom's "bad" play comments on art and the artist and is thus at one with the larger theme of the relationship between artist and lover. There is a world of practical advice in the rehearsals and actual production of *Pyramus and Thisby*.

Accommodations must be made. Snug, who by his own confession is "slow of study," is mercifully given the lion's part. This will involve little work, Quince assures him, since "you may do it extempore, for it is nothing but roaring" (1.2.69–71). Sometimes the advice given borders on the absurd: Flute has to be reminded not to speak all of his lines at once. We may assume that, caught up in his role, Flute momentarily forgets that dialogue, not monologue, is the essence of drama. Bottom speaks at a more practical level: the actors are to avoid onions the day of the performance and see to it that their linen is clean. In a magnificent illusion like *A Midsummer Night's Dream* we may tend to forget the thousands of small details essential for perpetrating that illusion.

But the rustic performers also raise, though unintentionally in most instances, more profound questions about the nature of the theater. The players are stubbornly aware of their own reality, as when Flute tries to protect his incipient beard. The players never seem to be so overwhelmed with their own image making that they forget the audience before them, or their own frustrations or personalities. When they ought to be most unconscious of their real selves, they remain doggedly so.

Conversely, they often lose sight of their own dull reality. Half-man, half-ass, Bottom is not fully conscious of playing a new part since he has somehow forgotten what the real Bottom looked like. He falls out of one role and into another with disarming ease. At one moment too aware that he is an actor, Bottom is at the next moment an actor unawares. In act 3, scene 2 we see Puck consciously playing both "auditor" and "actor" (3.2.81–82) and Bottom taking figuratively rather than literally Snout's observation that he has an ass's head.

Indeed, Bottom walks an especially thin line between reality and illusion. His prologue will inform the ladies that "I Pyramus am not Pyramus, but Bottom the weaver" (3.1.21–22). However, for us it is a hard task, indeed, to untangle the truth here: Bottom is not Pyramus, but then neither is he Bottom but rather the actor playing Bottom. Therefore, he is as much Bottom as Pyramus or, conversely, neither Bottom nor Pyramus. If we share Bottom's concern that he not be confused for Pyramus, then we have celebrated Shakespeare's abilities as an illusionist. But we have also fallen into an ignorance of the reality of the play before us that is as glorious and as blatant as Bottom's own.

Bottom's proposed prologue will break whatever subsequent illusions the actors may establish. It seems a piece of reality, something consciously reminding us of the stage artifice. In point of fact, the truths conveyed by the prologue are as much artifice and lies as anything else in the play. At the very least we seem to see Bottom and his company rehearsing a play. That the rehearsal is successful or a disaster is thematically important but aesthetically of no consequence. Actually, we see actors playing actors rehearsing. Since we are, at base, watching a play, even the events that appear most literal and true in terms of our own experience are themselves wrapped in illusion. When Quince tells his fellow actors to enter "every one according to his cue" (3.1.76–77), the line bursts with antithetical meanings. When the members of Shakespeare's company hear their cue, they will indeed enter or speak. Conversely, we will watch actors actually entering on cue and yet thereby impersonating actors responding to a cue. Here both reality and illusion, actual playing conditions and pretense, are merged.

Thus, when they speak about the theater or even when they are, though unaware, a part of the theater, Bottom and his company comment on the most important aspects of the profession. On waking from his amours with Titania, Bottom cries out, "When my cue comes, call me, and I will answer" (4.1.204–5). He seems to be returning to his own reality, though it was that of a play rehearsal interrupted when Puck had scattered the performers. Yet Bottom makes this tremendous leap between worlds with the same ease with which he initially entered the supernatural. We may want to wring our hands at Bottom's pathetic unconsciousness in the presence of great events. Yet his reaction is also right, though in ways he cannot fathom. His little reality is no more illusory, and no less significant than the larger reality he enjoys for a midsummer's night.

And it is also through art that Titania awakes to the smaller reality presented by Bottom as he stands before her with an ass's head. For her, however, it is a mind-expanding experience. Seeing Bottom unconsciously playing an ass, she makes immediate reference to the two organs, the eye and ear, that are crucial in our own experience as spectators: "Mine ear is much enamour'd of thy note; / So is mine eye enthralled to thy shape" (3.1.141–42). Again, we note that the theatrical allusion here to the ear and eye is coupled with words of love, "enamour'd" and "entralled." The connection between art and love is sustained.

In this highly charged aesthetic world, all things theatrical are both themselves and illusions. The moonlight that Bottom so needs for his production is at once fictive if the play is performed in a public theater during daylight hours, and yet actual if the play is performed at night before a royal assemblage. On that occasion Shakespeare's company, like Bottom's, may have staged *A Midsummer Night's Dream* to help pass the hours between after-supper and bedtime. With the vast cosmic reaches of Oberon's magic kingdom, the play is also one of the most earthly, concerned as it is with a production in the midst of a production.

-vi-

Whatever its other failures, it is that actual production of *Pyramus and Thisby* which brings to a head this commentary on the theater, the playwright, and the imagination. *Pyramus and Thisby* is the theater painfully conscious of itself, a production commenting on "how to do" an illusion even as it is being done. We even observe the process of play selection. Theseus declines three possible entertainments: the battle with the Centaurs sung by an Athenian eunuch to a harp is too asexual for the occasion; the riot of the tipsy Bacchanals has the misfortune to be an old piece; and "The thrice three Muses mourning for the death / Of Learning, late deceas'd in beggary," is too serious and too satirical for a wedding (44–55). He lights on *Pyramus and Thisby,* which is comically described as "very tragical mirth" (57). Yet Theseus cannot make the connection between this *Romeo and Juliet* and what would have become of the star-crossed lovers if it had not been for supernatural intervention. He chooses the play rather "To ease the anguish of a torturing hour" (37), and we may think of audiences in our days who similarly view the theater as some sort of aesthetic "dessert" after a hard day at the office. Philostrate has heard the play before and gives a rather unpromising review: he recalls that it drew tears of laughter for its absurdity rather than tears of passion for the tragic lovers.

We have, then, an audience who in watching the play with preconceptions will translate the would-be tragedy into a comedy. For all that can be said against the aristocrats, they cannot be accused of indifference; their role in the forthcoming production will be one of real, albeit cynical participation. They are even creative in a way that rivals the audience in the most avant-garde theater of today. Indeed, in that contemporary theater audience response is often a factor in the direction of the play. At the Montreal World's Fair of 1967 the Czechoslovakians had the audience decide, by pushing buttons that triggered off movie projectors, among alternatives for possible plot developments in a film.

We ourselves watch both groups, aristocrats and rustics, playing roles both conscious and unconscious. Literally the most mortal of the spectators, we are, paradoxically, closest here to the supernatural creatures observing the "plays" from the wings.

As Prologue, Quince adds to the confusion between the actors as actors and as mortals playing actors. The dumb show for which he serves as presentor tells all, indeed, tells too much. It is not enough that we accept the stage convention of a character impersonating a wall; we must be told that a man impersonates a character impersonating a wall. The chance for a successful illusion is thus weakened, and is then further weakened by the critical side comments of the audience. Here is theater that is too self-conscious; Quince announces what need not be announced: "The actors are at hand, and by their show / You shall know all that you are like to know" (116–17). This almost seems a parody in anticipation of Keats's closing lines to "Grecian Urn." Snout cannot restrain himself. We are not left to figure that a real man impersonates a wall; Snout tells us that "I, one Snout by name, present a wall," and no ordinary wall but one "as I would have you think, / That had in it a crannied hole or chink" (156–58).

The next step is inevitable; the characters break out of the play-within-a-play and address the audience directly. Responding to the aristocrats' criticisms, Bottom challenges them to "Think what thou wilt" (198). Who are the actors, and where is the audience? But these are questions we might ask from another perspective, as we view everybody on stage, both aristocrats and rustics, as either actors or mortals like us. When Theseus protests that the wall should have more lines and curse again, Bottom informs the audience of the exact moment when Thisby's cue comes and what he will do: "You shall see it will fall pat as I told you" (183–89). And thus by its immediate example this wretched playlet before us raises the very questions about reality and illusion informing the larger play.

The same imagination that Theseus so distrusts he is willing to use here to improve a theatrical production: "The best in this kind are but shadows; and the worst are no worse, if imagination amend them." Hippolyta reminds him that it will be his imagination doing the amending, and not the actors since they are singularly literal about the play at hand. Theseus continues this discussion of the imagination as he makes the case for aristocratic charity to the poor: "If we imagine no worse of them than they of themselves, they must pass for excellent men" (213–21). Where he could have made an imaginative leap into the larger play, as Hippolyta does at the start of the present act, Theseus does not. Conversely, here he expends his imagination to elevate a fifth-rate production. In a sense, Theseus is not so much the rationalist that we imagine; as a lover, he is capable of an imaginative act, even if it be nothing beyond courtesy to an underdog.

Gradually, however, reality intrudes as the playlet moves toward Thisby's death. We ourselves move from farcical tragedy to the comic resolution of the larger play, and to the consummation of the three marriages. Hippolyta first marks this final stage when she confesses that she is "aweary of this moon" (255), wearied both by the poorly played character Moonshine and by that time, measured by the moon, before consummation. It is Theseus who reminds her of the necessary courtesy that must be shown the players. As the self-conscious theater is "in the wane," the return of real life is promised. The moment here is roughly like that in the theater generally, when we "know" by some sixth sense that the play is drawing to a close. We feel its resolution imminent, even if by no more profound measurement than looking at our watch. We wish the play to end, and its end we know will satisfy the wishes built up in the course of the evening.

An epilogue is proposed that one likes to believe Quince had composed on the evidence of Bottom's dream. Theseus refuses it—a loss, as we have observed earlier, for him but not for us. Then, in a moment of personal irony, Shakespeare lets Theseus talk about Shakespeare:

No epilogue, I pray you; for your play needs no excuse. Never excuse, for when the players are all dead, there need none to be blamed. Marry, if he that writ it had played Pyramus and hang'd himself in Thisby's garter, it

would have been a fine tragedy; and so it is, truly; and
very notably discharged.

(362–68)

The author must ultimately be Shakespeare himself; he
has written a bad play. Whatever candidates in his canon
might be nominated for the weakest of the lot—one of the
Henry VI plays? or *Merry Wives of Windsor?* or *Timon of
Athens?*—they are caviar compared with what we have just
seen. Paradoxically, Shakespeare triumphs here with the
successful illusion of failure. Even Theseus's comments
about the actors spill over the bounds of his little reality:
Shakespeare's actors, including those playing the aristocrats, will soon be "dead," no longer actors but their real
selves.

The supreme irony is that Theseus still gets the epilogue
he refuses, or rather, we will get one from Puck. Theseus
leaves the stage imagining that he goes to bed with a
voluptuous Hippolyta. But it is no such thing, and he too
will die, and cease to be Theseus. The longed-for marriage
chamber decked with flowers will be nothing more than
actors disrobing in the tiring room. If Bottom is a shadow,
an actor of no substance, Theseus is also. In Peter Brook's
production of the play, the same actor doubled the parts of
Theseus and Oberon, and as I have suggested elsewhere,
the parts of Titania and Hippolyta can also be doubled.[9] If
this doubling does not represent distasteful "tampering"
with the play, then we may observe that Theseus dies only
to be reborn minutes later as Oberon. His reincarnation is
in the form of the very creature for whom he has no
imaginative sympathies. At best, Oberon can become only
the stuff of which Theseus's dreams are made.

The play almost ends with Bottom's production. But
there is a larger play that is no more for Theseus, safe as
he is in love and dreams. And this larger play ends with an
orgy of song and dance, a supernatural spectacle that

dwarfs the recent wretched court entertainment. As in *The Shrew*, if we have identified ourselves with Theseus as fellow members of an audience, it is now we alone who constitute that audience. Our intermediary has vanished to the bedchamber.

Puck's epilogue raises the final questions about the relation between a successful illusion and life. He invites us, if displeased with the play, to think of it as a dream and of ourselves as dreamers. Are we too a part of this play given over to dreams and the dreamers of dreams? "Think but this, and all is mended, / That you have but slumb'red here / While these visions did appear. / And this weak and idle theme, / No more yielding but a dream" (431–35).

-vii-

Theseus opens the play as an impatient lover, anxious that the time before the nuptials pass quickly, but for most of *A Midsummer Night's Dream* he is more restrained. And this lack of passion is both his virtue and his vice. For him the theater remains only a means to beguile "The heavy gait of night" (5.1.374–75), and thus he joins the ranks of those among us for whom art is mere bedside reading to induce sleep. In point of fact, it is through our vicarious experience as spectators that we can remain conscious when what constitutes reality expands beyond the confines of Athens toward the cosmos. The characters themselves drift into unconsciousness the moment the stature of Theseus's kingdom is diminished.

As the forest world recedes and Theseus takes over Oberon's role as arbiter of reality, the certainty, or at least Theseus's certainty, of "what is" and "what is not" becomes more substantial. However, Theseus cannot totally convert Hippolyta to his reasoned view of things. And then just as daylight comes it is gone: the final scene is set somewhere between eleven o'clock and midnight. Like it or not, dreaming will take over from waking. Yet rather than merely challenging what passes as consciousness and reality, this fellowship between sleep and the imaginative visions issuing from the sleeper's dreams calls instead for a more catholic definition of reality. The visions of the poet or the lover may be no less valid than the deductions of a logician; indeed, the imagination perceives a dimension of the true reality beyond reason. Breaking down the barriers, blurring the distinction between what seems to be represented by Athens and Oberon's forest, leads to confusion, to be sure, but also to a reward of sorts, a reward similar to the profit and pleasure gained by an audience when it gives a momentary credence to what is otherwise a mere stage illusion. A rejection of dreams and the imagination is both foolish and unwarranted. Theseus is no less a creature of the poet's imagination than Oberon; his barb that the actors are "but shadows" has a double edge since he too is a mere shadow, an actor's part. His "real" world exists only when we choose to abandon the world outside the theater for the fictive world within.

It has been through "moonlight revels" and the "opportunity of the night" (2.1.141,217) that this larger world has existed. Through the "night's accidents" (4.1.71) we have partaken of a larger vision. Sleep is here a good thing, and we have here seen Shakespeare's "exposition of sleep" (4.1.41). At worst, the artist's creation has been but "the fierce vexation of a dream" (4.1.72). At best, illusion is a reformative force, changing in the course of the play opponents into lovers, and tragedy into comedy. We too have been changed from a mass of people without a common identity into an audience seeing visions beyond daily experience.

Like all of Shakespeare's early comedies, *A Midsummer Night's Dream* is very much concerned with love and with its excesses and contradictions. We have observed how the courtiers in *Love's Labour's Lost* are comic in proportion to their vows to abstain from love. In *As You Like It* Touchstone and Phebe are absurd because they represent the extremes of unromantic and hyperromantic love. Foolish and inevitable, unreasonable and yet beyond reason, "to love" remains a good thing—to this Rosalind and Orlando will soon testify. However, in *A Midsummer Night's Dream* love, besides being a good thing, is associated with the imagination. Liberated by a dream voyage, this imagination is the agent for penetrating that larger reality that reason alone cannot scale.

If we jump chronology in moving next to *Othello,* it is because, as mentioned in the Preface, Iago challenges all the expansive, restorative powers of the artist and of the imagination that are so celebrated here. The world that Iago creates is small and nasty, a world of disharmony as strong as the harmony established in *A Midsummer Night's Dream.* And yet this artist of negation is not without a certain fascination. With *Othello* we also enter the second general "stage" of this book, namely, Shakespeare's portrait of what I have called "controlling" figures.

4

Othello: Art Perverted

In the previously discussed plays, love and the imagination were linked; the artist, a lover, was one who produced a wholesome, unified, and unifying vision. In *Othello,* Iago threatens this ideal for, as the negation of love, he envisions a world where husband is separated from wife, and friend is separated from friend. Art in this sense becomes more like an "indoctrination" to the personal and morbid "vision" of its creator. The antithesis to the creators we have observed so far, Iago is also drawn in greater detail. His character in the play is on an equal footing with the tragic hero and the heroine. And as several commentators have pointed out, Iago represents the culmination of a figure with which Shakespeare had experimented earlier in Richard III and Don John. Unlike the other plays we have considered, *Othello* does not so much question the line separating reality—something that "is" and should not be doubted—as show the manner in which a wholesome reality can be supplanted by an obscene illusion. In a way, *Othello* offers a tragic counterpart to the forgivable trick foisted on Sly when he was made to give up his humble reality for an aristocratic illusion. Nor have we yet encountered a character as skilled in the use of language as Iago.

If *A Midsummer Night's Dream* is a "serious" play in its challenge to our conception of reality, *Othello* is also serious because it illustrates a terrible threat to whatever reality we

104

have. Theseus is narrow-minded, but he is not a villain, and he is a lover. But the love of Desdemona for Othello represents a higher concept of union than anything we have observed so far. And the lovely creation she promises is opposed by Iago's self-creation in passing himself off as "honest" Iago. "Theater" here is closer to the theater of the absurd or theater of cruelty. *Othello* thus looks back at the three earlier plays by way of contrast, and, with its controlling figure, looks forward to our discussion of the controlling figures in *As You Like It* and *Measure for Measure*. In our own divided response to its chief artist, our revulsion and fascination for Iago, we anticipate the divided response that will be a major concern in *Hamlet, Antony and Cleopatra,* and *The Tempest.*

-i-

At one point in *Othello* (act 4, sc. 1) Iago arranges things so that Othello can overhear a conversation between Cassio and himself. It is a stage recreation of our own experience in the theater. Othello is told where to sit, or rather where to "encave" himself (82) so that he can "mark the fleers, the gibes, and notable scorns / That dwell in every region of his face." This is a bit of audience preconditioning for the "tale" that is about to be told "anew" on the makeshift stage. But Othello is too far backstage to hear the start of that conversation; he sees only the animated, suggestive movements of the speakers. In effect, he witnesses only a dumb show rather than a full-blown play. Iago's role is that of the "presenter," Othello's untrustworthy guide to the action. Our experience is less limited since both our eyes and ears are functioning. Otherwise a master of words, Iago here relies on silence.

This is also a theater of improvisation, for it represents a spectacular capitalizing on chance events. Though not part of Iago's initial scenario, Bianca, like Cassio before her, is unawares made part of the performance. Her mention of the handkerchief is perfect but unconscious timing. When Othello moves close enough and can use his ears as well as his eyes, he can only take the insulting remarks as slurs against the wrong woman. The consequences, as we know, are disastrous.

This situation has as its basic metaphor the simple trinity of audience (Othello), actors (Iago aware, Cassio and Bianca unaware), and the playwright-director (here that obscene portrait of the artist, Iago). With its "audience" of one not fully aware of the truth of the performance, Shakespeare graphically suggests the dimensions of that deception practiced by Iago and the corresponding helplessness of his Everyman, Othello, in the face of such fathomless evil.

This theatrical instance may have reminded some of Shakespeare's audience, who would connect Burbage as Othello with Burbage as Hamlet, of a somewhat analogous situation in *Hamlet* (act 3, sc. 3), in which the prince passes backstage while Claudius is at his confessional. Hamlet sees his stepfather's motions of penance. But if Hamlet could hear as well, he would know that by Claudius's own acknowledgment he cannot be absolved of his sin since he is unable to give up Gertrude. As in the case of Othello, only Hamlet's eyes, not his ears, are operating; when he should act, to stab Claudius, he does not. The next scene in Gertrude's chamber reverses this. Hearing someone cry out behind the arras, Hamlet assumes the figure to be Claudius and acts, stabbing not Claudius but his namesake Polonius. In each instance a failure of the spectator to respond with both ears and eyes stands as the playwright's metaphor for the character's existential dilemma: Othello pitted against the Iago mentality, and Hamlet against a world of "accidental judgements, casual slaughters" and "purposes mistook" (5.2. 393–95).

Iago can manipulate both with a paucity of words and

with an excess. In act 1, scene 3 Roderigo unintentionally
sets up Iago with the naive observation that "It is silliness
to live when to live is torment" (309). Deprived of Desdemona through her marriage to the Moor, Roderigo will
take the alternative prescription of death for his misery.
The next sixty-five lines find Roderigo reduced almost to
speechlessness as Iago overwhelms him with a torrent of
words. Iago begins rationally, observing that experience
confirms that nothing in this world is of sufficient import
to make us abandon self-love. But when Roderigo drops
the word "virtue"—"I confest it is my shame to be so fond,
but it is not in my virtue to amend it" (319–21)—Iago
launches into a less impartial speech. As Roderigo protests
"It cannot be" in the face of his companion's cold reduction
of love to sensuality, Iago delivers a prose harangue that
employs some of the most complex language yet heard in
the play: "violent commencement," "answerable seques-
tration," "super-subtle Venetian." Iago's own neurotic
motto ("Put money in thy purse") is here interspersed with
graphic pictures of lovemaking. For us the speech reveals
all of his thinly suppressed desires; his is the hysteria of
that perverse individual whose "truth" is obviated, or is
threatened to be obviated by the example of Desdemona.
This miniscene has its own sense of orchestration, as Iago
moves from surprise at Roderigo's resolution, to the
"light" logic of his opening rebuttal, to that long prose
harangue, and then, with Roderigo's "Wilt thou be fast to
my hopes, if I depend on the issue" (369–70), to a quieting
of passion. That neurotic motto itself dies out to a "provide
thy money" from the earlier "Put money in thy purse."

Iago functions as a manipulator in two senses. Here he
reacts and improvises, stirred up as he is by Roderigo's
foolishness in using a word like "virtue" (besides its moral
overtones, the word has the older meaning of "power"). At
other times Iago sets up a scene, as he does with Othello in
that conversation with Cassio. In Act 2, for example, Iago

alerts Roderigo to the "evidence" of Cassio's flirtation with Desdemona: "Didst thou not see her paddle with the palm of his hand? Didst not mark that?" (2.1.259–60). Such sexual coloring of Cassio's action will effectively blunt Roderigo's ability to distinguish between innocent friendship and lechery. And it is appropriate that Iago seizes on a metaphor from the theater in describing that "inevitable" behavior that Roderigo will witness unless he takes steps against Cassio: "Lechery, by this hand; an index and obscure prologue to the history of lust and foul thoughts" (262–63).

Indeed, Iago can work both with imaginary evidence, such as this Platonic handholding between friends, and with fact, albeit exaggerated. There is a certain truth as to the races in his metaphor of the lovemaking as involving a black ram and a white ewe, although the word "tupping" (1.1.89) is hardly a neutral verb for the act. It *is* a "fact" that Desdemona did not tell Brabantio of her marriage to Othello, and Iago cites this as the first major evidence in his argument for her being deceptive, or overly subtle. Some evidence is more dubious. Did Cassio really have that erotic dream when lying beside Iago? Whatever its source, all this evidence is the basis for Iago's artistic vision that is ironically encased in Shakespeare's own.

Working with men both as unconscious actors and audience, Iago employs a variety of methods to create the right state for the beholders of his "truth." Like Sly in *The Shrew*, Cassio is manipulated on a base level with wine; Othello, the deceived man of the major plot, is assaulted in a more imaginative manner. Cassio's weakness with drink becomes Othello's inclination to doubt what should not be doubted. Once seduced into seeing Iago as the one honest man in an often dishonest, uncertain world, Cassio becomes an actor as well. His unruly behavior while intoxicated forms part of Iago's "play" for Othello, for it is this very behavior that establishes the general case against

Cassio both as potential lieutenant and as loyal friend. Likewise, in pursuing Cassio Roderigo believes he works for his own end, that of winning Desdemona. In point of fact, Roderigo "acts" in Iago's "play" as assailant, just as Cassio unwittingly plays the role of the military and moral failure.

-ii-

If we may be properly called the ultimate audience, we might have two responses. Morally, we find what Iago does repulsive. In a play in which truth and beauty already reside in Desdemona and in Othello when he loves her purely, Iago's artistic "truth" is squalid indeed. What Desdemona truly represents is threatened by theatrical slights of hand, prearranged situations, and by language that, far from being rational, approaches the level of irrational incantation.

Still, Iago's artifice is extraordinary, be it planned or improvised. He is aesthetically pleasing, and at the same time terrifying. One is reminded here of Richard III and the similarly divided response his black artistry invokes.

Once we thus define our response to Iago's powers and his techniques of illusion, we must also realize that he is not totally successful. Act 1 might be classified as an abortive attempt on Iago's part. Here he is less the consummate artist setting up audiences and staging convincing illusions, and more the crass villain working with minimal artistry. Here his art degenerates to the level of slander. It is a lucky coincidence that his "complaint" to Desdemona's father matches the disturbed dreams Brabantio himself has had. To be sure, Iago is miles beyond Claudius, pouring words rather than literal poison in his victim's ear. Still, the words are not very subtle—shouts in the street, with Iago showing no more finesse than that of a soapbox orator.

Moreover, Iago's canvas is too large and too diffused. He depends too much on Brabantio's intervention; the more subtle way, albeit the more difficult, is to have Othello himself, rather than the father, destroy the marriage. "Accidents" happen, such as the enemy threat that places the state's need of Othello over Brabantio's individual case against him. In the play's second half there will be lucky breaks, as when Bianca appears at the right moment during the Iago-Cassio conversation overheard by Othello. These earlier events, however, disturb Iago's work or are too large for him to bend to his own plans. Also, he is too distant from his material, not enough involved. Othello's vital position in the state and Desdemona's own eloquent testimony as to how her heart was won by Othello are more than equal to Iago's charge as awkwardly voiced by an enraged father.

In a word, Iago's initial attempt at being the manipulator is too crude. Like Hitler, he is a failure at first, too much the street agitator, too unsophisticated in his attack, and too open in his motives. Like Hitler after his abortive Beer Hall uprising, Iago recoils from his setback, and adopts more subtle, indirect, and yet more personal methods in his campaign. It is a revealing coincidence that besides learning from a mistake, Iago like Hitler is a master of words, an orator of the first order. The exterior street on which he shouts his filthy charge against Othello will give way in the play to a more interior dimension. Iago will work through words on the minds of those who are most intimately involved with Desdemona.

By the second act Iago's new plan, his Phase II, is already in operation with Othello's victorious return from the war. Cassio's own effusive greeting to Desdemona will later be "used" by Iago. Presumably, in the gap between acts 1 and 2 Iago has reassessed his position. Indeed, he seems to speak from experience as he counsels Roderigo not to be taken back by an initial setback:

How poor are they that have not patience!
What wound did even heal but by degrees?
Thou know'st we work by wit, and not by witchcraft;
And wit depends on dilatory time.

(2.3.376–79)

By Act 3 both Iago and Roderigo are renewed. The master can now begin the longer and more difficult assault on Desdemona, and on Othello through his discrediting of her.

As Cassio exits in act 3, scene 3, Iago plants the first seed of deception in Othello. He opens with a matter-of-fact remark, one of no seeming consequence above its literal question. To Othello's "Was not that Cassio parted from my wife?," Iago gives a more suggestive reply than the Moor has anticipated: "Cassio, my lord! No, sure, I cannot think it, / That he would steal away so guilty-like, / Seeing your coming" (38–40). Desdemona's intervention momentarily silences Iago, however. When she talks, Iago is mostly silent, as if her truth, beyond her conscious realization, drives away his illusion and seductive words. He always seems to work best in her absence. But with Desdemona's parting at line 90 to Othello's ironic farewell, "Excellent wretch! Perdition catch my soul / But I do love thee! and when I love thee not, / Chaos is come again," Iago's most sustained performance as actor, playwright, and director begins. It will be a verbal artistry preceding the visual artistry of the dumb-show scene mentioned earlier (in act 4, sc. 3).

Iago opens with a question that would seemingly admit an answer too obvious to be of real consequence: "Did Michael Cassio, when [you] woo'd my lady, / Know of your love?" (94–95). Either he did or he did not; in any case, the question presupposes only the remembrance of a literal fact. It is a stupid question and invites the retort that a stupid question deserves a stupid answer. Othello answers politely, however: "He did, from first to last." If Othello had stopped here, having fulfilled the literal demand of Iago's question, the play itself might stop as well. For Iago never forces himself on a victim. Like the devil of the moralities, he cannot enter a heart unless there is already an inclination, however faint, to reject or to doubt what should not be rejected or doubted. No insuperable force, Iago can enter only after a way has been in part prepared by the victim himself.

Othello cannot leave be with his answer but, turning to Iago and thus giving him an extended life, replies, "Why dost thou ask?" With that invitation, Iago can now introduce two words which beg further inquiry, "*satisfaction* of my thought" and "No *further* harm" (italics mine). Othello plays into Iago's hands, asking for a definition of "thought." Iago's reply seems literal: "I did not think he had been acquainted with her." And yet perhaps "acquainted" has a slight sexual connotation, for when Othello replies that Cassio went "between" them often, Iago's "indeed," said with a sense of shock, perhaps of outrage, forces Othello to wonder what is so strange about Cassio's work as a go-between. Iago has moved Othello away from that initially literal and stupid question, toward these several suggestive or at the very least ambiguous words. Now, with the introduction of "honest" (both loyalty and sexual decorum), Othello is dragged into that world in which Iago, not himself, is the stronger. This is the world of the demonic playwright, one brimming over with allusive words and double entendres. This is literally a seduction by words. Othello, who confesses earlier to being little versed in the art of rhetoric, soon begins to echo Iago as they bandy about words like "honest" and "think:" "[By heaven, he echoes] me / As if there were some monster in [his] thought / Too hideous to be shown."

The street agitator has become a voyager into the mind, his weapon being language itself, or rather the obscene manipulation of language. The abuse of language observed in *Love's Labour's Lost* is here the tyranny of language. "Men should be what they seem" (126), Iago can say with confidence, knowing that Othello will apply the truism only to Cassio, and not to the speaker. The truth that Cassio is as innocent as he seems is now falsehood. Once language has been so employed, as a destroyer rather than as a conveyor of truth, Iago can move toward a seeming physical verification of his world of words. Once again he sets up Othello: "Note if your lady strain his entertainment / With any strong or vehement importunity" (250–51). To guarantee that the situation will indeed occur, Iago will promise Desdemona to aid her in pushing Cassio's suit to be once again in Othello's favor. Thus, words will assume form; verbal artistry will be transposed to visual artistry. Othello himself demands ocular proof (360); the movement from words to objects is not alone of Iago's making. Arousing Othello's expectations with words, Iago will satisfy when words, which are only words, take on concrete form: "How satisfied, my lord" (394), he inquires. We have here the entire process of creation for the stage: conception in the brain of a demented playwright, the preparation of the script, that initial stage of the play as literature, and then its translation into form, with sets and props complementing the words spoken by actors.

This insane case against Desdemona thus shows how Iago's dream-vision is transformed to words, to action and verification, to that ultimate physical action of the play, the murder of Desdemona. His dream of desire, frustrated by the lady's own purity, is twisted into death. Sexual death turns into physical death, and all this is done by Othello for Iago. When Othello raises possible methods of murdering Desdemona, it is Iago who suggests smothering her in the marriage bed. A playwright working within the frame provided by Shakespeare himself, Iago has substituted his own illusion. In this sense *Othello* is about the replacement, by tragedy, of the original play, a comedy in which old January and young May, contrary to tradition, should live happily ever after.

Act 3 ends with Othello almost totally committed to Iago's vision, and now demanding only ocular proof. The healthy love of Othello and Desdemona that had aborted Iago's initial assault in the first act has been supplanted in the closing lines by the perverted union of the two men. In a parody of a marriage service they kneel together, vowing fidelity, exchanging vows of love: "I greet thy love, / Not with vain thanks but with acceptance bounteous." Initially failing to win the position as Othello's ancient, Iago here succeeds to that office in the war against Desdemona. The battle turns inward, a foreign enemy being replaced by a "domestic" foe. Breathless in adoration, Iago ends the scene with the lover's line, "I am your own for ever."

The full realization of this dream vision will be, of course, the murder of Desdemona. Iago can launch Othello toward this, but he cannot be there for the final scene. The voyeur stops short of the bedroom door. Waiting in the wings, Iago exhibits all the nervousness of a playwright on opening night: "This is the night / That either makes me or fordoes me quite" (5.1.128–29). Curiously, as he had relied on Brabantio in Act 1 to do his work, Iago here relies on Othello. Unlike his stance during the middle of the play, this removal from the source is both an exhilarating test of Iago's artistry and a flaw.

-iii-

Both in our modern sense and in the context of Renaissance theology, Iago makes something out of nothing, and thus revives all the fears of those hostile critics in the Renaissance who saw the artist as a charlatan, as someone rivaling God with a fraudulent creation. God alone could make something out of nothing. When measured against

Jonson's ideal, Iago is clearly an artist who makes things *unlike,* rather than "like the Truth."[1] Artist as dissembler, Iago is also the actor as dissembler. The term "actor" is here used literally; Iago thinks of himself as someone foisting on the stage audience a fictive personality. Since by his own admission Iago is not what he appears (1.1.65), his denial that he can "play the villain" (2.3.342) may actually imply that he is a fully self-conscious villain or Vice parading as Virtue, fooling Othello with his "heavenly shows" (358).

When Iago comments on the serious and most malign aspects of his role as artist of the perverse, and as an actor giving form to that vision, the self-portrait is inseparable from his own warped view of the sexes. He thereby parodies the link between the artist-creator and lover-creator established in both the Sonnets and in *A Midsummer Night's Dream.* In making a fiction appear true, for example, Iago sees himself as bringing some "monstrous birth to the world's light" (1.3.410). Emilia indirectly supports this notion of Iago's art being some unnatural creation when she describes jealousy as "a monster / Begot upon itself, born of itself" (3.4.161–62). Othello's union with Iago, solemnized as they kneel together at the end of that long seduction scene and exchange vows of love (3.3.460–79), thus signals his divorce from that healthy, heterosexual union with Desdemona. There is even a latent sexual metaphor ("deliver'd") in Iago's seemingly modest account of his powers of the imagination:

> but indeed my invention
> Comes from my pate as birdlime does from frieze;
> It plucks out brains and all. But my Muse labours,
> And thus she is deliver'd.
> (2.1.126–29)

If Desdemona is a character in whom there is no conflict between art and nature, Iago, in contrast, represents a spurious artist. His art lacks any spiritual dimensions and thereby offends nature. Emilia herself speaks accurately, though unintentionally, about Iago's art as a false "conception" and "jealous toy" (3.4.156); in Desdemona's terms, it is some "horrible" fancy (4.2.26). On the other hand, Othello rightly, albeit ironically, defines his wife as the "cunning'st pattern of excelling nature" (5.2.11). Iago sees himself as a creature of natural "wit" rather than unnatural "witchcraft" (2.3.378), but in truth his wit is of a gross order. If there are demonic aspects to Iago's character, his invention borders on witchcraft and all the unsavory things connected with that word. Alexander speaks glowingly of the "Birth of [the poet's] Brains;"[2] perhaps, then, Iago may be thought of as a parody of this idealized conception.

Far from the principle of *utile et dulce,* the end of Iago's art is at once destructive and potentially demonic. Observing the newlyweds kissing, he vows to "set down the pegs that make this music" between the "well tun'd" couple (2.1.202–3). Desdemona later speaks of the change in her marriage when she finds her "advocation" (her ability to intercede in Cassio's behalf) being "not now in tune" (3.4.123). Against Iago's plans to destroy the marriage harmony we place Puttenham's description of poetic speech as something "tunable and melodious, as a kind of Musicke."[3] For Puttenham, the poet was a musician whose poetic harmony mirrors that of nature. If we recall again the age's theories about the artist's semidivine, but also semidemonic nature, perhaps Iago may be aligned more closely with the latter.[4] Brabantio's unjust accusation of Othello as a "practiser / Of arts inhibited and out of warrant" (1.2.78–79) might be more appropriately applied to Iago, despite his claim that he did not use witchcraft.

These demonic and perverse notions of the artist begin to attach themselves to the other characters as well, particularly to Othello. Brabantio speaks of Othello as having "practiced" on his daughter, and we may recall old Egeus in *A Midsummer Night's Dream* making a similar charge against Lysander. Othello is thus accused of the very theatrical deception that Iago is about to practice. The first Senator asks Othello directly if he by "indirect and forced courses" did "Subdue and poison this young maid's affections" (1.3.111–12). In truth, Othello is not a man of letters; as he himself confesses, he is one "Rude" in his "speech" and "little bless'd with the soft phrase of peace" (1.3.81–82). His services to the state, rather than an ornate rhetoric, will "out-tongue" Brabantio's complaints (1.2.19). Only when Othello abandons Desdemona and moves into her enemy's camp does he become capable of Iago's deceptive artifice. Then he demonstrates that ability to divorce words from feeling and to speak with ironies unknown to the listener.

-iv-

The ultimate illusion created by Iago is, of course, himself. At a successful performance of *Othello*, Iago is at once an actor impersonating a dishonest character impersonating an actor seen as an honest character by everyone else on stage. Even Roderigo, who knows that Iago's public pose before Othello and Desdemona is at variance with his true self, cannot fully penetrate the deception.

As she struggles for some reason to account for her husband's suspecting her of relations with Othello, Emilia charges that Iago has had his "wit" turned "the seamy side without" (4.2.146–47). Her denunciation of the villain who ought be lashed "naked through the world / Even from the east to th' west" only celebrates Iago's accomplishment in seeming the victim while, all the time, being the very perpetrator standing before Emilia.

The implications of such dissembling are vast, for if Iago is the "demi-devil" that Othello claims him to be (5.2.301), he is then a supernatural creature parading as a mortal. If, as has been argued, there is something of the Vice figure at the bottom of Iago, then we must remember that it was the morality Vice "who first invested the 'play the part' idiom with specifically theatrical connotations." The Vices similarly fashioned themselves as "actors, artists in deceit," creating by their conscious theatricalization counterfeit worlds challenging the truth.[5] As actor, Iago raises for us the question: What is he? Is there a reality behind the role playing? He tells us early in the play, "Were I the Moor, I would not be Iago" (1.1.57). Professor Kittredge's note on this is interesting: "This amounts to an assertion that Iago is always himself—always devoted to his own interests."[6] Perhaps the line has implications for the theater as well. Might it suggest the relation of an actor to his part? An actor could not play both Othello and Iago at the same time. In addition, his goal is to transform a reality, where Othello in love with Desdemona is unlike Iago, into an illusion where "In following him [Othello]" Iago follows but himself (58). He makes Othello into his own image. This is his "peculiar end" (60): to project his real self onto others and thereby to transform a healthy world into a diseased one.

If we believe Iago to be sincere in his statement that the world is only seeming, that the only reality is a physical one, and that love is only sex, then he is something of a perverse savior. He reestablishes reality and truth, rescuing Othello from a belief in the illusion of Desdemona's goodness. To create an illusion Iago needs working material, an Othello, something to transform from "what seems" to "what is." Quite rightly he is "nothing if not critical" (2.1.120). As god of an antiworld, Iago has no substance; he exists only by challenging the substantiality of his opposite in Desdemona. His is the triumph of seeming; Iago succeeds by what Robert Heilman has called "his skill at simulating the creditable emotions" by his "theatricalization of merit."[7] In a strange way Iago justifies Webbe's definition of the skilled artist as one who can so "hyde [his] cunning, that nothing should seeme to bee laborsome or exquisite," as a man possessing the "special gyft" to seem artless when actually "evey part is pollished with care and studie."[8] For a time Iago perverts Othello's view of Desdemona. Whether Othello ever fully recovers, whether in his last speech he regains some of his nobility or merely tries to hoodwink the audience and "cheer himself up,"[9] is not so clear. It remains a matter of considerable debate among the critics.

Iago's illusory world is ultimately just that. With the sacrifice of Desdemona his obscene creation is exposed and then vanishes. In terms of the play's commentary on the theater and the actor, one great irony in Act 5 is that Iago, who has been the master of words, ends the play with a sullen lapse into silence. His last lines are the peevish "Demand me nothing; what you know, you know. / From this time forth I never will speak word" (5.2.303–4). And he keeps *this* promise. The talented man of words ends by refusing to speak further.

Iago dissolves, lapses into silence, just as the world of the theater dissolves when the spectator, who for some two hours has given momentary credence to a stage illusion, emerges from the playhouse and returns home. Whether beautiful or ugly, the play is woven from some baseless fabric; a dream world, joyous as in *A Midsummer Night's Dream* or nightmarish as in *Othello,* at last melts into thin air. Iago has hoped earlier that "consequence do but approve [his] dream" (2.3.64). And, indeed, the illusory "consequence" of a stage fiction has given apparent form to his vision. But that vision dies with the creator, or when the actors return to their own reality. The actor impersonating Iago dies as a character only to live again as a real man. And this is a reality that is never totally absent, though it is submerged for the period of the stage illusion.

Iago *is* terrifying. A loner, he seeks to make other men loners, and thus this dangerous artist mocks the Renaissance ideal of the man who with his poetry can make his audience "gather together and keepe company . . . and keep fellowship together."[10] Art as a useful instrument in society here becomes society's enemy. Iago practices on Cassio as well as on Othello, and thus in Cassio's desire once more to "Exist, and be a member of [Othello] love" (3.4.112) we see the fruits of Iago's efforts. A mutual society has been splintered, its members divorced from that reassuring center once located in Othello.

We are right today in seeing the Puritan denunciation of the playwright, as a man who seduced people into vices by representing Vice on stage, as much more wrong than right. Yet in a strange way Iago's artistry gives a momentary truth to Gosson's charge that theatrical productions were nothing more than "straunge consorts of melodie to tickle the eare, . . . and wanton speache to whette desire to inordinate lust."[11] From this perspective Iago is terrifying—and profound.

Yet the very theater that makes Iago seem so also reminds us that he too is an illusion, that he is like our reality but not equivalent to it. Our pleasure in his artistry, his thespian skills, and in those of the actor impersonating Iago does not mean approval. Nor is it like the perverse pleasure that one might take in the evil of the real world. Iago's "evaporation" in Act 5 grants us immunity. But our response to him is not voyeurism, for he is a mirror, as truthful and yet as illusory as a mirror can be, of our own reality. It is in the persons of Rosalind and Duke Vincentio that Shakespeare will remind us of the pleasure and the profit to be found in those controlling figures who do not share Iago's perverse vision of reality and of love.

5

The Art of the Controlling Figures:
As You Like It and *Measure for Measure*

Though the vast middle portion of *As You Like It* is set in a forest of pastoral and poetic license, and though *Measure for Measure* hinges on the Duke's disguise, both of these plays, like *Othello,* are about reality, about the mundane world. But "what is" is here affirmed, not supplanted with a fiction. They are both serious or "dark" comedies, and are to be distinguished from *The Shrew, Love's Labour's Lost,* and *A Midsummer Night's Dream.* They, however, are still comedies and their concern is about making sense of this world, about getting along in it. This concern is vested in the controlling figures, an aristocratic, beautiful young lady and a Duke who is most effective when he is not officially the Duke. There are villains, but Duke Frederick and Angelo are minor figures compared with Iago, and Jaques himself is more morbid than villainous. The two late comedies are joyous, but not so much because they present an expansive universe or celebrate the powers of the imagination or the pleasures of love and language. Rather, they celebrate a "practical" imagination, the use of role playing, the good sense and that desire for order on the part of their controlling figures. The Duke and Rosalind understand their worlds with a clarity that matches Hamlet's; they are not foolishly optimistic. But they stop short of renouncing reality because it is sometimes, or even most often, corrupt or cruel. And, unlike Iago, they are able to divorce personal motivation from that common good as sought by those about them. Not tricksters like the Lord or—in a more profound way—like Kate and Petruchio, and no less wise than the ladies in *Love's Labour's Lost,* not Oberon or Titania, and most certainly not Iago, they champion, through their tricks, disguises, scene arranging, control of language, and art, the "art" of living.

-i-

At the court in *As You Like It* the controlling figure is purely political; there Frederick, not Rosalind, is in command. Frederick's court is, correspondingly, a stultifying world where control leads to suppression rather than to expression and growth. Although Orlando complains that in court he experiences only "growth" (1.1.15), his word implies a meaningless aging process that is quite unlike the character development that will take place in the forest.

At the court art either suffers or is parodied and perverted. An actor at court giving voice to eloquent poetry degenerates to the speaker "With his mouth full of news" (1.2.98), or someone "news-cramm'd" (101). In the forest, music has a significant function, especially with the supernatural appearance of Hymen and her wedding song. At court it is only "this broken music in his sides" (1.2.149–50), the metaphor for the damage Charles promises to inflict on Orlando. If she is witty and lively in Arden, at court Rosalind is bored, and confesses that she shows "more mirth" (1.2.3) than she feels. She acts and feigns emotions to no end other than that of comforting Celia.

Indeed, at court Rosalind can only "kill" time in tedious wordplay, in a wantoning of words that lacks the high spirits of the courtiers' dialogue in *Love's Labour's Lost.*

Celia, with relief, acknowledges Touchstone's entrance as a merciful act of fortune "to cut off the argument" (1.2.49–50). Imagination at court, then, is sterile. Celia's indictment of fools serves as a self-indictment as well: "the little foolery that wise men have makes a great show" (1.2.95–96).

Turning closer to the theater, we see that here the concept of a performance itself is something purely physical. The wrestling match, which Charles hastens "to perform" (1.2.155), is mere entertainment, not "theater" in the grander sense of that word. "Tricks" and "devices" are the truer descriptions for what acting means at court. It is, ironically, Oliver, a trickster if there ever was one, who accuses Orlando of plotting "some treacherous device" against him (1.1.157).

In this restrictive atmosphere, where force is elevated over wit, time rules supreme, catching man in its sway. It is a destructive time, hostile to poetic license and to that larger theatrical view of the world that characterizes Rosalind's actions once she is free from court. Fortune not art, chance and not human design, dominates the court. Mere chance has placed Oliver in the position of controlling the estate of Sir Rowland de Boys, and thereby his younger son Orlando. Events for which she is not fully responsible make Rosalind the despised guest of Duke Frederick and yet the confidante of his daughter Celia. Rosalind realizes that "Fortune reigns in the gifts of the world" (1.2.44) and accurately labels herself as one "out of suits with Fortune" (1.2.258). The old proverb, which the melancholic quotes from Touchstone, adequately describes life outside Arden: " 'Call me not fool till heaven hath sent me fortune' " (2.7.19). That is, when we are most fortunate, then we are most foolish, the fools of fortune.

Even in the country the characters are obsessed with the idea of fortune's power. One of the Duke's first requests is that Orlando recount the "residue of [his] fortune"

(2.7.196) so that he can his "fortunes understand" (1.200). Corin upon meeting Rosalind wishes that his "fortunes" were more able to relieve her misfortunes (2.4.77). Even "Ganymede" promises Orlando that despite the "straits of fortune" in which his Rosalind is "driven" he shall be able to marry her (5.2.70–71). Driven by fortunes merited or unmerited, men at court "ripe and ripe" and "rot and rot" (2.7.26–27) as life is devoured by a cruel, amoral time. And clearly time is linked with fortune. Rosalind observes that in the real world "Time travels in diverse pace with diverse persons" and then illustrates the influence of time on a young maid anxious for her betrothed or on the thief treading the path to the gallows (3.2.326–51). Birth, love, marriage, death—all possible happiness and sorrow in the real world are under time's dominion.

The movement to the forest, then, has the sense of an act of liberation. The forest seems a place where fancy, not fate, the imagination rather than raw power, is prized. Here Rosalind's benevolent control supplants the malevolence of both the Duke and the unreformed Oliver. At least this is one's initial impression. There is "no clock in the forest" (3.2.319); it seems that Arden is somewhat out of that time scheme peculiar to the court. There *is* "time" in the forest to celebrate the ideal of romantic love, even time to mock it with impunity. There one has time to cherish something that is also fleeting and very foolish. In a word, the time operating in the forest seems particularly hospitable to the artist, to those given to imagination and to the pleasure in illusions as opposed to those relishing political power.

But the signal question remains: To what degree *is* the country a mirror image of reality? Is Rosalind, who so flourishes there, really a controlling figure dealing with situations analogous to that reality for which the theater serves as a mirror? And how absolute, how unqualified is her character? To what degree is she unique, to what degree like the other mortals wandering about the forest? The extreme alternatives seem to be that she is an absolute controlling figure operating either in a world of pure fantasy or in a world mirroring reality. Knowing Shakespeare, one suspects the third alternative, a complex compromise between the two others.

The world of the forest demands our first consideration. It has the surface appearance of a purely pastoral world, one where poetic license reigns supreme. Here in Arden, the antithesis to Frederick's devouring society, the exiled Duke and his men happily spend their time in a golden world, scorning "painted pomp" (2.1.3), finding "tongues in trees, books in running brooks, / Sermons in stones" (2.1.16–17). Yet this last line has a strange ring since the banished Duke habitually thinks of the forest in terms of the things of the court (tongues, books, sermons). Is there perhaps a dimension of the court in the forest?

Nor can we ignore Jaques's presence. If cruelty seems stifled in the forest, it is Jaques who nevertheless brands the Duke and his men as murderers of wild life and as counterparts to Frederick: "usurpers, tyrants," who "fright the animals and . . . kill them up / In their assign'd and native dwelling-place" (2.1.61–63). And it is a fact that at the end of the play everyone leaves Arden for the court. Jaques alone, the arch critic of those with forest pretensions, stays behind.

Pastoralism does not seem to go unqualified, and Helen Gardner reminds us of some unattractive features of Arden: Corin's churlish master, the weather that is not always sunny, the doltish and insipid characters among the inhabitants.[1] Rosalind and Celia enter the forest "weary" (2.4.1); in fact, Celia pleads that she can go "no further" (9–10). Touchstone's rejoinder that "travellers must be content" (18) is more sober than comic. The retreat to the country fails to absolve the exiles of physical discomfort;

old Adam is dying "for food" (2.6.2) and Orlando soon
notes that the forest is "uncouth" (6) to visitors. Though
we are spared the sight of physical violence, Oliver does
bring Rosaline a "bloody napkin" (4.3.94), the tangible
proof of Orlando's wound where the "lioness had torn
some flesh away" (148). Gardner points out how Amiens's
melancholy song about the "wintry wind" is terribly echoed
by Lear's outburst to the elements, whereas Corin's natural
philosophy, that the "property of rain is to wet," parallels
the deposed king's recognition that the thunder will not
peace at his bidding.

Like Juliet with her "unnamed naming,"[2] Shakespeare
here seems to want Arden both ways, as a mirror for
reality and as its reverse image. Appropriately, the controlling figure Rosalind is powerful and yet operates in a
world pervaded more by art than by reality. The forest is
both closer than we think, and yet artistically remote. Since
evil in its darkest manifestations cannot gain prominence
there, we respond to the play as a comedy. Yet it is a
comedy of importance, relevant to our own situation.
What happens there is applicable, with some conversion,
to events happening outside the forest. At the same time,
Arden is an insular and pleasurable world of art, where
Rosalind never needs to deal with evil such as that which
has infected the Duke.

-ii-

If in terms of reality and escapism the forest world
occupies some sort of middle position, it is equally true
that Arden provides fertile ground for the arts, for both
language and acting. Even here there are clear gradations
among the characters.

At court, Touchstone is only a fool, not a wise fool but
simply foolish and the butt for the ladies' wit.[3] In Arden,
however, he blossoms, receiving from Jaques that rarest of

all praise, albeit mixed with a touch of irony. Recognizing himself as a fool, Touchstone sets minimum standards for mankind as a thinker and lover. He himself is not without faults, and Corin correctly, though innocently, chides him for his wit's being "too courtly." Yet we welcome Touchstone's bawdy counterpoint to the inflated or naive concepts of love scattered about the forest—literally, scattered in the verses the lovesick Orlando has carved on trees. Touchstone's wit is corrective wit, at worst cruelly neutral, like that of the Fool in *King Lear.* In that later play the wit is even harsher, just as the setting itself may be thought of as a nightmarish variation on Arden. Touchstone cannot lead the way, and is no controller or reformer of others. But he can retard false movement; he can tell us where *not* to go.

Consequently, Touchstone's notion of art matches his own comic stance. For him the truest poetry "is the most feigning, and lovers are given to poetry, and what they swear in poetry may be said as lovers they do feign" (3.3.19–22). A rather narrow definition of feigning, but, granted Touchstone's obsession with the variety of lies to which courtiers are given (5.4.99–101), we can hope for nothing higher. His obsession with truth and his correspondingly low estimation of art together define but also limit the nature of that truth he can follow.

Complementing Touchstone is Jaques, in whom practical, albeit limited, wisdom is supplanted by a more profound but melancholic truth. Still, it is a truth colored by the gloomy preoccupations of its spokesman.[4] In a way Jaques's dark "philosophy" is not fully integrated into the play, and so often what he says seems more appropriate for a world like that in *Hamlet.* The "Seven Ages of Man" speech (2.1.139–66) is a case in point. In itself it is impressive, very much a set piece triggered off by the Duke's optimistic observation that the world at large "Presents more woeful pageant than the scene / Wherein we play in"

(138–39). But the speech itself forces man into a series of inflexible caricatures, and this runs counter to a play that stresses change brought about by time and by Rosalind's controlling presence. If "The Seven Ages of Man" rings true enough in general terms, it also fails in specific cases. Rosalind, Celia, Orlando (with a little more common sense), and Oliver (upon his conversion) are too good for the mold. Jaques's is a voice that, as has been suggested, expresses ideas otherwise left unsaid or unexplored in the play.[5] For this very reason his is very much a voice out of tune, particularly in a comedy working toward love, order, a happier future.

Appropriately, it is an aesthetic metaphor that suggests how far Jaques himself is from the comic spirit and philosophy controlling the play. The Duke observes that if Jaques who is "compact of jars, grow[s] musical, / We shall have shortly discord in the spheres" (2.7.5–6). No such thing happens: Jaques remains bitter while the world, if not making its way to some seventh sphere of perfection, does improve. If Jaques's denunciation of the forest world is a corrective, it also fails to recognize the fluidity, the sense of play, in human existence that characterizes an alternate world such as Arden. Jaques provides the most direct satire, and we realize that he "must have liberty / Withal, as large a character as the wind, / To blow on whom" he pleases (2.7.47–49). He has the satirist's need and that of the playwright uncensored "To speak [his] mind" (59). But Jaques's satire is academic, verbal, and therefore theoretical. Beyond Jaques, Rosalind can both satirize and, as a controlling figure, move men toward reform. Loving asks that one participate rather than talk. To paraphrase the Clown in *Hamlet,* love and life are acts with three branches: to act, to do, and to perform.

Jaques's promise of cleansing the foul "body of th' infected world" (60) with his medicine also smacks of Brutus's fatal scheme to cleanse Rome by the assassination of Julius Caesar. We might raise the question: Do such men provide any alternative world as they disembowel what we have at present and what, however unlovely, is also certain? The Duke underscores the darker qualifications of Jaques as a satirist: his ideal of purging the world may stem not from a positive philosophy but from a pathological need to "disgorge into the general world" all "th' embossed sores and headed evils / That [he] with license of free foot hast caught" (2.7.67–69).

What seems called for, then, is a reformer who includes himself in the reform, who *acts* as part of a community rather than acting against what he sees as an unsightly multitude. If Touchstone suggests the impressive but often shallow verbal ingenuity of the courtiers in *Love's Labour's Lost,* or of Lyly's courtly comedies, then perhaps Jaques is closest to Marston. Jaques's anger at injustice and foppery sometimes becomes so excessive that in casting doubt on others the satirist, in his disgust at perversions, calls himself no less into doubt.

Balancing Touchstone and Jaques are Orlando and Phebe; here practical and satirical wit finds its opposite in optimistic, artificial "romanticism," both about one's self and love generally. Orlando hangs his inflated, conventional verses on trees; appropriately he attaches something aesthetically dead to something alive and green: the "trees shall be [his] books" (3.2.5). Orlando learns not from nature but by superimposing courtly love on what is otherwise natural and unaffected. If he complains of experiencing nothing but growth in court, it is clear from the evidence of his sophomoric poetry that he will need growth of another sort in the forest. Rosalind will serve for this purpose. Orlando's paradox of love's being the "unexpressive she" (3.2.10) gives him away. Love is something about which one *can* talk; inarticulateness and courtly overarticulation are the extremes to be avoided. The play mocks an overly literal attitude toward love. Rosalind is ultimately stronger than Touchstone and his gross views on the subject. Excessive romanticism, steeping itself in paradoxes such as the "unexpressive she," is also beyond reasonable bounds.

Orlando's Petrarchan poetry gets an appropriately stern and unfavorable reading in act 3, scene 2, where Rosalind provides the text:

> *Rosalind.* From the east to western Ind,
>   No jewel is like Rosalind.
>   Her worth, being mounted on the wind,
>   Through all the world bears Rosalind.
>   All the pictures fairest lin'd
>   Are but black to Rosalind.
>   Let no face be kept in mind
>   But the fair of Rosalind.
> *Touchstone.* I'll rhyme you so eight years together, din-
>   ners and suppers, and sleeping-hours excepted. It is
>   the right butter-women's rank to market.
> *Rosalind.* Out, fool!
> *Touchstone.* For a taste:—
>   If a hart do lack a hind,
>   Let him seek out Rosalind.
>   If the cat will after kind,
>   So be sure will Rosalind.
>   Wint'red garments must be lin'd,
>   So must slender Rosalind.
>   They that reap must sheaf and bind,
>   Then to cart with Rosalind.
>   Sweetest nut hath sourest rind,
>   Such a nut is Rosalind.
>   He that sweetest rose will find,
>   Must find love's prick and Rosalind.
>   This is the very false gallop of verses. Why do you
>   infect yourself with them?
>
> (93–120)

Touchstone's version is appropriately bawdy. It parodies Orlando's own effusiveness, and yet would in itself reduce poetry to doggerel.

Surely, at moments such as this tremendous demands are being made on the audience; we must note the double function of the parody, as both a commentary on the present situation and a celebration of that finer poetry found in Rosalind. Rosalind, albeit playfully, sees beyond Touchstone's poetry when she comments that, like his poetry, he will "be rotten ere [he] be half ripe, and that's the right virtue of the medlar" (126–27). When she criticizes a second poem brought to her by Celia, as a "tedious homily of love," we can then respond both to the criticism itself, that its "feet were lame" (178), and yet trust the sobriety of the critic.

Jaques correctly identifies Orlando as Signior Love and thus complements Orlando's identification of him as Monsieur Melancholy. Orlando will need to break from this caricature, and when he does, language will itself be re-formed. But Orlando has the desire for such reformation when he tells Ganymede that "I would I could make thee believe I love" (3.2.404–5).

Rosalind's second pupil and the other major object of her manipulation is Phebe, the coy, disdainful mistress of innumerable pastorals. Phebe's problem is not so much articulation as a misuse of acting, as in act 3, scene 5 when she pretends not to be in love with Ganymede. This is surely an unnatural state in a play celebrating the natural passions of mankind:

> Think not I love him, though I ask for him;
> 'Tis but a peevish boy; yet he talks well.
> But what care I for words? Yet words do well
> When he that speaks them pleases those that hear.
> It is a pretty youth; not very pretty;
> But, sure, he's proud, and yet his pride becomes him.
> He'll make a proper man. The best thing in him
> Is his complexion; and faster than his tongue
> Did make offence his eye did heal it up.
> He is not very tall; yet for his years he's tall.

His leg is but so so; and yet 'tis well.
. . . .
There be some women, Silvius, had they mark'd him
In parcels as I did, would have gone near
To fall in love with him; but for my part,
I love him not nor hate him not; and yet
I have more cause to hate him than to love him,
For what had he to do to chide at me?

(109–29)

Unlike Orlando, Phebe would deny love, saving herself for
what we know is an impossible relationship. The simple,
physical fact is that beauty is but a flower; not to love, when
a reasonable love is offered, is a restraint that dries up the
human spirit.

-iii-

As the play swings between the extremes of cynical
literalism and fatal artifice, between Touchstone-Jaques
and Orlando-Phebe, it generates its own need for
Rosalind. Like Madame Pace in Pirandello's *Six Characters
in Search of an Author,* she seems to be born of the scene. In
her there is a perfect marriage between action and language, and this is why Rosalind is the most catholic and
advanced "character" on stage. If she is little more than
words in the battle of wits at court, she elevates language in
the forest, knowing and using words well, striking the
proper balance between the extremes of language that are
so rife in the play. Denounced unjustly as Frederick's
enemy at court and there forced into a role, Rosalind
blossoms in several roles in the forest. Being "falser than
vows made in wine" (3.3.73) is for her a virtue since by her
tricks she brings others to their senses.

On Shakespeare's stage we see a boy actor playing
Rosalind playing Ganymede playing Rosalind when Orlando requires some practice in wooing. If the forest is not

so antithetical to the court, it surely is freer on a theatrical level. For here illusions are not the indictment of a shallow world as in *Hamlet,* or a way of perverting a wholesome reality as in *Othello.* An arch illusionist, Rosalind remains true to love. She counterfeits only to avoid a bad fortune, to realign personalities that have fallen to extremes, to move others toward wholesome love. She may be said to possess the poet's license, using artifice as a way of molding a world. A prophet, she practically sets up conditions so that her vision may be fulfilled.

Rosalind is nonetheless aware of the theatricalism that invests every human action. She thinks, for example, of the forthcoming scene between Phebe and Silvius as a "play" in which she can "prove a busy actor" (3.4.62). Jaques's reductive metaphor for the ages of man is here a constructive vision of reality, where "play" both mocks the human condition and suggest the very spirit in which one approaches it sensibly. Still, Rosalind does not confuse playing with reality, for at the very height of her illusionist's powers, she can still wish that she were "at home" (4.3.162). In this sense she is like the human embodiment of Genet's theater: conscious of her own fakery, she holds the precious truth about man's condition in a world marked by unconscious fakery.[6] To Rosalind, reality is not pretending to love, but loving; if she shares the theatrical consciousness with Jaques and Touchstone, she can still take that larger, and more profound pleasure in reality that is denied them. If to dissemble at court, to use the Lie-Direct (5.4.86), is a crime, to dissemble for love in a forest that supports the artist and his illusions is no crime but a public service. Indeed, Rosalind's natural role as lover overwhelms that of actor-dissembler. The former role gives a purpose to the latter, making it something beyond mere trickery or impersonation.

Moreover, this natural role invests the artifice with some pain, for her masculine impersonation is in conflict with her reality as a woman. As a woman Rosalind would at one point cry, but she finds such a response inappropriate for a "man." Her "Woman's gentle brain" clashes with her outward appearance in doublet and breeches, especially when Orlando is present. But such a conflict can dissolve, and Rosalind too can thereby participate in the comic movement in and out of the forest.

Her impersonation of "Rosalind" for Orlando works both ways: educating her lover in the ways of a more mature love, and allowing her to experience a love made impossible by conditions outside of Arden. Rosalind can always avoid a direct commitment to love, buried as she is under four layers of illusion (Rosalind, Ganymede, "Rosalind" performed by an actor). Giving pleasure as a dissembler, she also receives pleasure.

Rosalind may stand for all actors, giving and receiving the pleasure and profit of a role for both the witnesses and the participant. This is a gift enhanced by each other's presence. The correlative here is between the actor's pride in his performance and the realization of a fictive character for the audience. And though an actor in Arden, Rosalind must return to the reality of the court, just as the actor himself returns to reality when the stage world closes. We also so return; it would be abnormal to remain in our seats, as if life could be bypassed forever for the sake of the theatrical experience. As defined by the actor impersonating Rosalind and by Rosalind impersonating Ganymede-Rosalind, the theater is ultimately an excursion from reality so that one may return. As audience we cannot be the same after the play since a part of our experience in life now includes the play. Moreover, seeing the play a second time we could not recapture that original experience.

No actor would give up his real identity for a stage character, no matter how superior that character may be in intellect or position. The character is pure but insubstantial, alive only by the momentary "collusion" of actors and audience. Rosalind as the controller has a higher level of consciousness than the other characters, and it is through her that we experience a theatrical "omniscience" to which we cannot pretend in our own world. But literally outside the play and thematically in the play Rosalind is also "One of their kind," as Prospero himself admits (5.1.23)—just another human being.

Rosalind's part as controller and observer, then, expands both our perspective and her own. As one critic terms it, she can draw a line between "permitted romance and prohibited reality,"[7] and this is a virtue applicable both in and out of the forest. It is her "more inclusive consciousness"[8] which makes her both superior and also more human, more in tune with the human condition. And it is this equipoise that she carries into the two scenes, act 4, scene 1 and act 5, scene 1, to which we now turn.

-iv-

The opening of Act 4 is a moment of obvious theatrics, one promised by Rosalind in which she ("he" rather) will impersonate Rosalind to aid Orlando in his wooing. It is an artificial encounter from Orlando's false perspective as he constitutes an audience of one on stage. The female part is also realistic: Rosalind is being herself, rather than impersonating a man. We ourselves know that illusion here is used to suggest an illusion: an actress impersonates an impersonator. Without the Renaissance prohibition against women on stage, in our own theater we would have a woman being herself, thus bypassing the sexual change required by the earlier impersonation of Ganymede. Rosalind grasps this higher truth with "And I am your Rosalind" (65), translating what is pretense for Orlando into something literal. Celia also testifies to the power of illusion when she acknowledges that "It pleases him [Orlando] to call you so" (66), that is, to call Ganymede Rosalind.

The scene is ironically a celebration of reality in the guise of an artifice, for the lines Orlando takes as feigned passion, "Come, woo me, woo me; for now I am in a holiday humor and like enough to consent" (68–69), we now and Orlando himself later will see as real. Rosalind's love, we know, exists under the mask and will materialize for Orlando after this holiday humor has passed. A superior figure, she is only that much more secure in the center of a play that harbors lovers not feigners, true emotions not artifice. Here in act 4, scene 1 Rosalind balances artifice and reality in a way that Hamlet cannot and Cleopatra can, though only after converting reality into her own erotic vision.

Even though inspired by love, Rosalind also knows that lovers often kiss when they lack things to say. Even Orlando, Signior Love, is not fully genuine in his emotions, for his threat of suicide is a denial of love. The suicide, quite simply, cannot love. No man, Rosalind correctly observes, ever died by or for love—except sexually. The death wish is hostile to the emotion of love, and thus *As You Like It* challenges the tragic affinity of love and death in *Romeo and Juliet.* Rosalind can still love, and can call in Celia to play the priest and marry them. Yet she is concerned with being too serious about such a thing as love. It may in reality be only acting, and so she is properly suspicious of lovers' vows to be faithful "For ever and a day" (145). Indeed, it will take her twelve lines to make the necessary qualifications to such idealism (146–57). Still, unlike those of Hamlet or Iago, Rosalind's qualifications do not lead to the negation or the reversal of ideals. The wit she uses digs deep and yet also masks the romanticism and idealism that in her character exist happily with a superior knowledge, even a skepticism. She can be a sexist against her own sex, condemning a woman and her tongue, and yet also the supreme example of a liberated woman. Surely, she is the comic Hamlet of the play.

For Rosalind the scene ends not in more feigned but in real passion as she and Orlando part for two hours. This will be an eternity for Rosalind, and would be equally so for Orlando if he were not so much a believer here in the illusion that Ganymede is Rosalind. But Rosalind's knowledge extends beyond this scene, for she knows that with time, that supreme healer and restorative of comedy, all will be well. "Time is the old justice that examines all such offenders" (190–91), such as those who come too late for a love meeting because they err in thinking that the impersonation (Ganymede) of their lover (Rosalind) is not sufficiently important. Orlando would dismiss the theatrical "mirror" as inferior to the real thing. But in the thematic world of *As You Like It,* the mirror *is* the reality, and the impersonation *is* the impersonator.

With the departure of Orlando, truth surfaces completely. Rosalind breaks down and confesses how many fathoms deep in love she is (210–11), so many fathoms deep that the love so buried cannot be sounded. The scene closes with a perfect expression of love. And this occurs in a play where, with characters such as Orlando and Phebe, that expression too often has been imperfect, suffering from immaturity or affectation.

In the final scene Rosalind's plotting comes to a head, and it is here that reality also triumphs. We learn of conversions and of a loss of power that are not depicted on stage. These events cannot properly be said to occur by means of artifice or theatrics. *As You Like It* itself may avoid the darker issues of tragedy, and thus the bloody scarf seems that much more gruesome because of the pervasive unreality of the previous four acts of the play. What was hyperbolic, the heart of man wounded by a woman's cruel eye, has now become literal. Yet here in the final scene this "reality" must also share the stage with more artifice than we have yet seen in this play so given over to the poet's fancy.

The rest of Act 5 serves as preparation for this achievement. In act 5, scene 2 Rosalind conjures up as her tutor a religious uncle, a "magician, most profound in his art and yet not damnable" (66–67). Since no such uncle exists in the *dramatis personae,* the uncle here may be Rosalind herself. The "character" thus suggests the fuller aesthetic dimensions of her power: she is a Prospero, rather than a Faustus. This second scene then ends with a listing of what Rosalind proposes to accomplish, as in formal fashion she turns to each participant (Silvius, Phebe, Orlando) and promises resolution of what they currently think is a dilemma.

There follows a short scene (act 5, sc. 3) between Touchstone and Audrey, a last look at Touchstone whose practical wit is now something less than appropriate. If he blossomed initially in the forest, it is Rosalind who has now surpassed him. We are moving toward marriages, and thus the song "It was a lover and his lass" (17–34) signals the enjoyment of what, through art and the work of a benevolent controller, *is* possible in this world. As such, Touchstone's reply that there is "no great matter in the ditty" (36) seems vacuous; unlike us, he cannot understand its full context. Acting, impersonation, is about to bear fruit, and Touchstone's opinion, like that of Theseus in the final scene of his play, is not all we know or need to know of truth. The First Page, who has no personal motives to make us qualify what he says, corrects Touchstone by observing that "We kept time, we lost not our time" (38–39). And this is so; the properly ordered artifice of the song is at one with the comic resolution brought about, or about to be brought about, by Rosalind. Time is kept in art, the lyric, and the play. Abandoning the unreliable time of a forest in which there are no clocks, Shakespeare or Rosalind keeps time by returning the

characters *to* time. The play itself has kept time as it
hastens toward its own ending. Touchstone therefore runs
counter to art and the theater.

With act 5, scene 4 Rosalind has her vision. Like the
Duke whom we shall shortly observe and like Prospero
who is far distant, once Rosalind completes her role she
can return to human shape, to her own reality. Rosalind's
very words convey the artist's desire to make all well: she
has "promis'd to make all this matter even" (18). The play
itself supplies the alloy as we watch the working out of the
plot in which Rosalind has proved a "busy actor."

Touchstone has one more moment for his frivolity as he
categorizes the devices of quarreling, reducing life to a
bookish parody of art where one can "quarrel in print, by
the book, as you have books for good manners" (94–95).
But with Rosalind's entrance such abuses of language and
such low-level deception are abandoned. The plan of this
controlling figure is perfected: the removing of a disguise
aborts Phebe's design on Ganymede, gives her to Silvius,
and fulfills Orlando's quest. The language itself moves to a
higher order, the play itself taking on a supernatural
dimension as Hymen appears to sanctify the marriages.

If reality is intruding now, then it is also true that here in
the waning moments of *As You Like It* Hymen offers a
vision, such as we have seen in *A Midsummer Night's Dream,*
of a world beyond our own, or of a world for which reality
as we imperfectly perceive it is only the beginning. In the
simple language of Hymen's song we have moved to the
effortlessness, grace, and symmetry of true poetry. As it is
at the end of *Love's Labour's Lost,* poetry is purified. Similarly, the world itself has been purified by Rosalind of the
unpromising events in the opening scene.

Combining elements of the satirist, the romantic lyricist,
the actor, and the playwright, Rosalind goes beyond a
cynic like Jaques, a literalist like Touchstone, or even a
conventional lyricist like Orlando. Appropriately, the end-

ing is both symbolic, comic, realistic, and unrealistic. Indeed, Rosalind's inclusiveness is so great that, denying tradition, she herself appears as Epilogue. She literally escapes her play, speaking for or as the author. Until the end, she preserves her illusion as Rosalind, but she also destroys it by removing herself from the "world" both of the court and of the forest.

-v-

In the later comedy, *Measure for Measure,* there is no forest retreat. The world at times may seem closer to that we associate with tragedy.[9] Duke Vincentio alone "retreats" but only for a scene or two before he returns in disguise. Role playing here broadens to include unconscious feigning, not knowing one's true self, and feigning for selfish, potentially destructive ends. Such acting for one's own pleasure is soundly castigated. Its chief practitioner Angelo is all the more heinous since he has been "dress'd" with the Duke's love (1.1.20). He follows his own will all the while giving the pretense of being one "that can [the Duke's] part in him advertise" (1.1.42). Isabella will later see Angelo as the tyrant "Dress'd in a little brief authority" (2.2.118) who, believing that he is elevated beyond his normal self, "Plays such fantastic tricks before high heaven" (121). Actually, Angelo's twin roles as an angelic character and the Duke's substitute may be too great for him; like Macbeth, he breaks under the strain of office, even as he is willing to violate his principles for that office. By his own confession, the Duke himself has failed as the kingdom's supreme ethical authority, though that failure has sprung from incompetence or excessive permissiveness, rather than from lechery.

Angelo complicates his life by continuing to fabricate what he knows is a mere pose, that of the man not given to the flesh. If we may call this self-imposed state a dilemma, his problem is that of any ruler but only more extreme since his private self perverts his exercise of power. "Role" can therefore mean everything from a hypocritical pose to a position in society that is antithetical to reality as defined by one's true self. In this play "to know one's self," to cease being an actor either to one's self or to others, or both, is a desired end. And it is this end toward which Angelo and others are moved by the Duke. As a spectator, the Duke may also learn about himself. Perhaps Angelo's "education" may be a vicarious learning experience for Vincentio.

We fault Angelo because he is a hypocrite administering justice and also because he deceives Isabella when he promises her brother's life in return for a sexual favor. The irony is that he fails at being a good administrator and a truthful man, even if being truthful involves fidelity to an extralegal agreement. To reform Angelo will take the additional pretense of the bed trick, not to mention the several disguises and staged revelations by the Duke.

That hierarchy of viewpoints and spokesmen in *As You Like It* is here a hierarchy of dissemblers ranging from the cursed to the blessed. The blessed dissemblers may be distinguished from the cursed in that the former are directed to an object beyond immediate gratification. The bed trick staged for the benefit of Mariana and Claudio also draws Angelo out of himself. "Selfish" theatrics are replaced by "human" theatrics, as at the end the actor playing Angelo can become a happy member of the majority. He escapes the soul-destroying circle of illusion that once separated him from others.

The Duke, then, is a feigner for the good. Rightly, he professes a distaste for cheap theatrics designed for one's personal image. Vincentio does "not like to stage [himself] to the eyes" of the public (1.1.69), nor does he relish "Their loud applause and Aves vehement" (71). Again, the indictment seems to be against spectacle such as royal processions, and not against theater as constructively

employed by the Duke in the play's second half. He
prefers the subtlety of disguise, rather than exhibitionism.
In the theatrical sense, the Duke is an actor who can
successfully impersonate a character for another's benefit,
rather than the second-rate actor or "star" (in a pejorative
sense) who can play only himself.

Indeed, when the Duke does condone feigning of a
lower order he is unsuccessful. If one of his motives in
leaving the kingdom is to have Angelo enforce unpopular
laws, then this permitting a substitute to impersonate the
Duke figuratively and to do what the Duke himself could
not do fails miserably. From what we know, the Duke has
not been successful as a public person. Curiously, when he
works in disguise as a private person, he is successful. The
success, though, rests not in enforcing a law but in testing
and educating Angelo and Isabella, saving Claudio, and
bringing happiness to Mariana. If politics is an art, a
complex game of role playing and language, then the
Duke is both politician and actor in his friar's disguise. Far
from staging himself before the audience of his people,
the Duke uses his audience unawares. Having "strew'd it in
the common ear" (1.3.15) that he has relinquished power,
he acts *on* them rather than directly *before* them. Yet it will
be before the common ear of Shakespeare's audience that
the aesthetics of power are fully employed by the Duke
and by the playwright acting through him.

Low art is arrayed against high art; the coarse language
of Lucio's rumors and exhibitionism such as Angelo's are
balanced by the exquisite language of repentance and by
impersonation that literally denies one's self for the sake of
others. There is present a purity of speech and of acting
that validates artifice; it rescues the word itself from abuse
and from selfish manipulation. In the youthful beauty of
Isabella, for example, there is "a prone and speechless
dialect, / Such as move men" (1.2.187–88). Modest yet
powerful, the Duke is willing to "play" for others. He will

even take instruction from others as when he asks the Friar to "instruct" him so that he "may formally in person bear" the gravity of a religious man (1.3.46–48). The Duke literally puts himself in another's place, courting danger by deposing himself to become a friar. He can also figuratively put himself in the place of others. This type of empathy is violated by Angelo when he speculates on changing places with Claudio: "If he had been as you and you as he, / You would have slipt like him; but he, like you, / Would not have been so stern" (2.2.64–66). Angelo can imagine being a prisoner instead of a judge, but such imagination does not lead to Claudio's release. And Angelo is offended when Isabella tries to "put . . . sayings upon" him (2.2.133). She threatens to invade his circumscribed world.

In Angelo, then, there is pride, and in the Duke there is selflessness. Yet in both characters acting is the root metaphor. For the audience this theatrical metaphor is especially timely, for just as the Duke plays before a respectable audience at the Globe, Angelo plays unawares before the Duke. In a theological sense both actors go through their "tricks before high heaven" (2.2.121). For the goal of reformation or revelation the theater will use any means. Even death itself is thought of as a "great disguiser," a sort of makeup artist working backstage (4.2.186). Its human occupant dead, the body of Ragozine still plays an appropriate part since the role demanded by the Duke's plot is that of a dead man. By that curious alchemy of the stage, Ragozine's head can save a life by impersonating Claudio.

-vi-

If theatrics are used to bring about a comic ending, the art itself is nonetheless "used." It remains a means and not an end. In this sense the return to reality, as it is in *As You*

Like It, is a step up. The ending here reverses that in *A Midsummer Night's Dream,* where Theseus's real world is a step down imaginatively from the expansive forest. The tricks in this play seem to many observers forced, smacking of overly clever mechanics. But as in the pleasing but ultimately fragile world of *As You Like It,* we witness an art that must be subordinated to reality; it is only a tool to order and reform mankind. In both plays a court is restored to health.

The feigning here, the tricks and disguises, are all in response to the natural act of pregnancy. Although a minor character, Juliet herself is beyond feigning, willing to bear her shame overtly and patiently. She is what she is, though this fact initially has led to the feigning, for good and for bad, among the other characters. What she knows of the virtue of repentance has come from love, from experience in the world. Art thus becomes a way of jolting people back into participation, for both Angelo and Isabella would leave life for an abstraction, either Angelo's inhuman sanctity or Isabella's nunnery. As in *Love's Labour's Lost,* one exists not for himself but only in terms of others; our virtues and what we are both "should go forth of us" (1.1.34–35).

Like Prospero, the Duke is too removed and bookish to be an effective leader. He must also participate in experience, even if it be at the lofty but covert position of a controlling figure. Through his art he deals with the most seamy side of life, and like Rosalind he uses art to return himself and others to reality.

This insistence on the truth of experience comes from the common people themselves, the closest representatives in the play's world to Shakespeare's audience crowding the Globe. Pompey, the lowest of the low here, cries, "I am a poor fellow that would live" (2.1.234–35). He refuses to change life for an illusion and clings instead to physical existence, however sordid it may be. Barnadine prefers life to the loss of life and will not play a role in the Duke's scheme. He refuses to let his head impersonate Claudio. Lucio's slur on the Duke is also, in the larger context of the play, a compliment for he contrasts the Duke, who had "feeling of the sport" (3.2.126–27), with the "congeal'd ice" (118) of Angelo. Too much of that Shavian Life Force, as in the case of Claudio and Juliet, still seems preferable to a deficiency as in Angelo. The excess can be modified; the deficiency, a divorce from what is natural, takes a whole play to correct. Juliet comes to her cure in a single scene outside the major action of the play.

Even morality itself, that "outward order" (1.2.153) that Claudio and Juliet have violated, may not be fully squared with life. The first half of *Measure for Measure* is flooded with moral issues. Is evenhanded justice possible? Should the judge himself be pure? Is fornication a crime in any absolute sense? What rights does the individual have to exempt himself from those laws governing others? And is it possible to "Condemn the fault, and not the actor of it?" (2.2.37)? But such questions are abandoned in the second half of the play, in which debate gives way to action, and ethics give way to some practical tricks for making people more human, if not more ethical. The title of the play itself seems to lose relevance as the play progresses from the intense moral tone of the first half to the human stratagems inaugurated by the Duke in the second half. And it is in this second half that the Duke comes into his own.

-vii-

The characterization of the Duke in *Measure for Measure* presents some problems. Why he leaves the kingdom in charge of Angelo probably admits no single reason. Will he thereby test Angelo? Or will Angelo enforce laws that he himself did not or could not enforce? Is the Duke a human being who can rediscover his own humanity only when he abandons public position? Or does he verge on the divine, the god-controller directing the microcosmic stage? Or are we permitted several responses to his character? Is our own uncertainty a sign of Shakespeare's failure adequately to characterize the Duke? Or perhaps in the Duke, Shakespeare is interested in something beyond psychological characterization.

Clearly, the Duke's scheming is more pervasive and has deeper implications than that of Rosalind. Both *Measure for Measure* and *As You Like It* are comedies separated in time by only a few years. Yet the world in which the Duke acts is still potentially more sinister than that of Arden. Again, it is his kingdom, and yet he decides not to act in his own person. Might we not sense behind this the dual position of the playwright, of Shakespeare himself? He is an individual working by indirection, by art rather than by naked political power. He does so in a world that is his own creation and yet that also reflects his own personality.

The comforting fact is that the Duke is behind the scenes almost from the start of the play. Angelo begins early his posing and his sinister plans for Isabella. In the opening scenes the Duke seems preoccupied with his entrance into holy orders, learning the methods of impersonating a cleric. Still, he is there, only waiting to be fully activated when Angelo's proposition creates a moral dilemma for brother and sister. If the Duke is not active at first, he has not been inattentive; he has "overheard" (3.1.161) what has happened between Isabella and Claudio.

At this point in the play we do not yet know of Angelo's double dealing. However, his character has been called into question, and so any contract with him may be suspect. But as Claudio leaves, fearing the worst now that he has been rejected by his sister, the Duke is activated. He abandons preparation and theory for participation.

His control now has two objectives: comforting Isabella by extricating her from a dilemma, and saving Claudio. The Duke himself straddles both worlds, those of the artist and the human. He is not omnipotent; it is fortune, he tells Isabella, which has brought her problem to his attention. But having looked on humanity from a moral viewpoint, and having witnessed the dilemma posed by imperfect man trying to live by an absolute morality, the Duke will take another approach. Problems will be solved by artifice and improvisation rather than by judgment according to some preconceived ethics. The play seems to argue for a minimal ethic (thou shalt not kill) and a humane use of virtuous rather than villainous tricks. To "heal" (3.1.24) rather than to judge is the concern. Isabella herself, who has been a judge of her brother and of Angelo, now seems to relish the role of participant: "The image of it [the Duke's proposed bed trick] gives me content already; and I trust it will grow to a most prosperous perfection" (3.1.270–72).

Angelo as controller will soon have to share the stage with a more indirect and powerful controller. Again, the Duke's superior control serves not lust but love; he himself can marry rather than rape one of his clients. Act 3 ends with the Duke vowing to match Angelo's "vice" with his own "Craft" (291). In effect, two acts have been given to Angelo, with the third act serving as transition; we can now anticipate the final two acts given to the Duke.

Act 4 of *Measure for Measure* widens this distinction between creative and destructive dissembling, between actions in the name of others and actions that will at length double back on the destroyer himself. In this second half this finer theater comes clearly to the fore. An improviser, the Duke now finds the stage literally full of props. Again, if one head is unavailable, that of Ragozine will be supplied by good fortune, through its owner's own bad fortune. Death itself functions in the name of the theater, supplying the basic material while the humans shave the head and tie the beard. In a way, Shakespeare, the god of *Measure for Measure,* provides for all so that all will be well.

Like Prospero, the Duke in *Measure for Measure* is confident in his powers, but is also cognizant of his reliance on fate: again, Ragozine's death is "an accident that Heaven provides" (4.3.81). Like Hamlet's, the Duke's return to the court has grown in significance. Conversely, the "other side" begins reacting and acting. Angelo is suspicious of the "uneven and distracted manner" of his letters, and finds himself made "unpregnant" (4.4.3, 23) with news of the Duke's arrival. Just before the actual return, some preparations are made: the Duke leaves the "purpose and our plot" with the provost (4.5.2), and warns Isabella that "if peradventure / He speak against me on the adverse side, [She] should not think it strange; for 'tis a physic / That's bitter to the sweet end" (4.6.5–8).

-viii-

Act 5 is properly the Duke's act, this long, complicated act with its revelations and reversals galore. Rosalind manages things so as to control romantic excess; the Duke returns the world from a hypermorality and its perversions to forgiveness. Indeed, the Duke's "trial" at the end mocks the play's title as he moves the characters beyond judgment. Isabella provides the motto for the act: "To make the truth appear where it seems hid, / And hide the false seems true" (5.1.66–67). To this end she would "conjure" (48) the Duke to perform his miracles; the Duke is here appealed to as a discloser and chronicler working "with rip'ned time [to] / Unfold the evil which is here wrapt up" (116–17). The process is both direct and indirect, with the Duke first pretending to disbelieve Isabella and then, with Mariana's coming to center stage, allowing her to speak in her riddles: "I am no maid. / I have known my husband; yet my husband / Knows not that ever he knew me" (185–87). Angelo falls deeper and deeper into ignorance, not knowing that he has had relations with Mariana, while believing he has had them with Isabella. Our own awareness of the Duke's pose in rejecting the women's story separates us in our full knowledge of the truth from the participants. In terms of omniscience, Angelo who was once the first is now tumbling to the last. As the Duke's control becomes more subtle and profound, the deputy himself makes an ironic comment on that power: "These poor informal women are no more / But instruments of some more mightier member / That sets them on" (236–38). That "mightier member" surely defines both the Duke and the playwright as the god of this creation.

The ultimate complication occurs when the Duke himself appears as the Friar, joining the women in the ranks of the suspected. Rightly, it is with his uncovering by Lucio that the complications are finally resolved. Lucio's physical action is both theatrical, as it unmasks the impersonator, and philosophic, a deposing of one's outer self to reveal a true man underneath. Angelo is instantly struck with remorse. Some critics deplore Shakespeare's own apparent swiftness here and agree in a way with Doctor Johnson when he accuses the playwright of being too hurried in the last acts.[10] The conversion, it must be admitted, is not psychologically convincing. But surely the principle of the play justifies Angelo's action. What we are witnessing are situations sustained by the playwright's artifice in a work also celebrating that artifice as a way of bringing about the good. The play offers a correlative for conversions in reality but a correlative only, not an exact copy. Our own movement as audience has been from early concern with Angelo's ascendancy, to anticipation generated by the moral dilemmas of the first half, and now to pleasure as situations are resolved through the Duke's art and Shakespeare's.

With Angelo's conversion, the Duke can concentrate on that of Isabella. Still believing her brother dead, she makes an eloquent plea for Angelo's life and is then followed in that plea by Mariana. The women's former anger is justified only by ignorance: Claudio is not dead and Angelo has unknowingly performed the sexual function of a husband. Potential tragedy—but "literally" only potential—becomes comedy. The concept of seeming as Angelo would practice it has become that beneficial tool of the Duke and the playwright. The extensive acting, the role playing, and the frantic use of masks and disguises here seem to anticipate *The Winter's Tale*, where those separated by tricks or ignorance are reunited by Paulina's art. Claudio's unveiling appropriately follows that of the Duke and serves as the final comic triumph.

The Duke is playwright, director, and character, just as Shakespeare serves both as playwright, actor, and shareholder for his company. In the course of the play the Duke plays all roles, from the public controller to underground power, from the man suspected of sexual transgressions in his youth to the saintly cleric, from the suspect to the victor, from a bachelor to a husband. Knowing Shakespeare's views of the comic end of marriage, he probably becomes a father. With this last "role," however, we commit the cardinal sin of stepping outside of the play proper; one pregnancy seems to have been enough for the time being in *Measure for Measure*.

Like Prospero, the Duke and Rosalind are ultimately "One of their kind," part of the people they so beautifully manipulate. *As You Like It* combines with *A Midsummer Night's Dream* in its comic view of controllers and their world. Perhaps *Measure for Measure* is at one with *Hamlet* in being a play in which the controller tries to move others toward a more thorough or profound purification. In this the Duke is a bit more effective than Hamlet, for no one perishes in *Measure for Measure*.

Truth is established, all is disclosed, and yet with this truth we move beyond judgment. Jaques alone "perishes" with his judgments in *As You Like It.* And the one judgment applied in *Measure for Measure* is against Lucio as one who violates the Duke's role as truth bringer and restorer to harmony. With his rumor Lucio would separate man from man. His punishment, appropriately, unites the issues of sexual violation and the abuse of language: this spurious controller with words is given the choice of physical death or sexual death with his whore.

Stage illusions have been the means of promoting marriage, moving the spectator from grim possibilities to a happy ending. Yet the sense of theater for Rosalind and the Duke never hardens, as it does for Hamlet, into a philosophy that views life as a mere stage, as something to be endured and from which one is liberated by the felicity of death. The means of control here ultimately are abandoned. The Duke goes back to being a Duke, now a controller politically but no longer aesthetically since he has literally run out of tricks and a play. Similarly, Rosalind becomes the bride of Orlando once she has literally run out of the forest. Whatever their profound differences, both plays reveal the artist as controller *and* participant. In saying this we look back to Petruchio and Oberon and thereby restore the name of the artist so sullied by Iago or comically sullied by the courtiers of *Love's Labour's Lost.* We can now look to *Hamlet* and *Antony and Cleopatra,* whose central figures have that sense of life's theatricality. But Hamlet's theatrical metaphor for life produces a fatal split in his very being; unlike the Duke and Rosalind he cannot go on with what he knows. Cleopatra goes on, even until the final moment, but that going on produces a divided response both to her morals and to her aesthetics.

6

Hamlet: The Double Edge
of Aesthetics

In many ways *Hamlet* pushes the general aesthetic
metaphors considered so far to their limit. Hamlet's consciousness of the theater, of life as a play, rivals that of
Petruchio, Iago, or Rosalind; like the Lord of *The Shrew*
and like Duke Vincentio in *Measure for Measure* Hamlet is a
controlling figure. But Hamlet's consciousness, his use of
the theater doubles back on him, diminishing his vital
spirit, his pleasure, and his ability to act positively in this
life. The play's insistent aesthetic metaphors and Hamlet's
own grasp of the playlike quality of Denmark only show
the limitations, and indeed the danger of such a theatrical
perspective on reality. *The Murder of Gonzago,* even in its
silence, celebrates the theater in a way that matches the
celebration in *A Midsummer Night's Dream.* But the play is
just that, a play; and, however appealing he may be in
other ways, the play's director, the prince, cannot survive
its revelations. A brilliant dabbler in the theater, an individual properly concerned with language as a bringer of
truth in a world where language as truth bringer is otherwise abused, a visionary who sees to the core of his kingdom and in his well-intentioned way tries to right things
and to restore decency and sanity, Hamlet also perishes.
And his death is proper, inevitable, "right" in the way that
the deaths of all tragic heroes are inevitable and right.

If *A Midsummer Night's Dream* and *Othello,* when combined, suggest both the virtues and vices of the artist, both the celebration and the condemnation of the theater when it is perverted, *Hamlet* itself spans the same gamut—and more. The prince's hyperconsciousness about life's theatricality at once identifies him with Rosalind and with the Duke in *Measure for Measure,* and yet prevents him from serving as a comic agent for order. For if Hamlet brings order it is as much by his own death as by his murder of Claudius.

Concerned with language, with fitting the right word to the deed, *Hamlet* underscores the concern in *Love's Labour's Lost* that language and action, the conceptual and the physical, be in harmony. Yet Hamlet's wordiness, his "abstracting ability," is at once his most endearing trait and the sign of a sickness in him, a removal from that life that most of us manage to survive either on a comic or—at worst—melodramatic level.

The play is difficult, I believe, not so much because Hamlet's character is, at length, unfathomable but rather because its boundaries are so wide, because for every aesthetic metaphor on the side of light there is a corresponding one on the side of darkness. That Cleopatra has the same dimensions to her character, that *Antony and Cleopatra* allows the same divided response toward the theater, is the reason for discussing that play after *Hamlet.* The extraordinary difference between these two plays is that, until the very end, literally until her final line, Cleopatra continues to assert her sexuality, her addiction to this world. Her playfulness, her sense of life as an art, never hardens into a philosophy of negation; her energies, both sexual and imaginative, are at opposite ends from Hamlet's weariness and the imagination that would trace Alexander stopping a bunghole. Even as *Hamlet* pushes to the ultimate limits the concerns we have examined in earlier chapters—the function of the theater, the relation between the worlds off stage and on, the playwright as visionary and healer and controlling figure, the divided response toward his craft, the relation between language and truth—it anticipates not only *Antony and Cleopatra* but also Shakespeare's most catholic and serene statement of his art, *The Tempest*.

This chapter examines the following topics: Hamlet's fascination with the theater, a fascination bordering on an obsession; the play's own sensitivity to the theater and, particularly, to its audience; the possibility that Hamlet suspects he is in a play; the converse fact that the theater is also a metaphor for the corruption and duplicity of the Claudius faction; their own abuse of language which contrasts with Hamlet's celebration of words; the enervating effect that Hamlet's theatrical consciousness has on him; and the tremendous split in the play between Hamlet's theatricality and reality, between the conceptual and the physical, ultimately, between the demands of the stage and the inexorable demands of life itself.[1]

-i-

Clearly, Hamlet has an obsession with the theater, an extraordinary sensitivity to the theatrical metaphor that underlies whatever passes for reality in Denmark. His first extended speech, "Seems, madam? Nay it is" (1.2.76–86) provides a veritable list of the mannerisms and costuming for an actor playing the role of a grieving son: an inky cloak, a black suit, heavy and disturbed breathing, tears, a downcast expression, "Together with all forms, moods, shapes of grief" (82). Lest we fail to identify the theatrical metaphor, Hamlet provides the apostrophe himself: "For they are actions that a man might play." The principle upheld here is that his true emotions are beyond theatrical expression; no objective correlatives provided by the actor, director, or costumer can portray real grief. Claudius believes that his brother *has* indeed died, and if we also accept this, his call for more rational behavior on Hamlet's part is reasonable. Hamlet's inability to show grief, though, has a double cause: the depth of his passion and his sense that all things in Denmark are illusory.

As Hamlet hastens toward his revenge such theatrical metaphors increase. The coming of the players (act 2, sc. 2) is a happy accident, a means for Hamlet to determine for once and for all whether Claudius is guilty of his brother's death. But the arrival of the players is also the culmination of Hamlet's obsession with the theater, with playacting both as an indictment of Claudius's court and as a means, the antic pose, by which a sensitive young man can steer his way through the labyrinth of double-talk, posings, false smiles, fraud, and those staged sincerities unleashed by his uncle. With the players Hamlet meets consummate actors, members of Shakespeare's company playing members of a company. Here, then, are men who are what they seem to be, certain entities in a world filled with hypocrites, imposters, or, in Gertrude's case, individuals wavering in their loyalties. It is little wonder that Hamlet, who cannot delight in real men and women, delights exceedingly in the actors. Clearly he is at his happiest, his gayest, with the players; still wearing his customary suit of solemn black, he seems like a different person in their presence. If he cannot welcome into his heart a Claudius who only impersonates the King, then "He that plays the king shall be welcome; his majesty shall have tribute of me" (32–33). This player king *is* a conscious play king, and thus at least as much of a king as what currently passes for kingship in Denmark. Given to contemplation, despising men who act boldly as if this world were a fit stage for such assertion, Hamlet can still admire the "adventurous knight [who] shall use his foil and target." Incapable of love, Hamlet can delight in the stage lover who "shall not sigh gratis." If the buffoon Polonius dies miserably, the humorous man in the play "shall end his part in peace." The dead Yorick, an image of man's dreadful mortality, does not die on stage but "shall make those laugh whose lungs are tickle o' the sere." The lady "shall say her mind freely, or the blank verse shall halt for't" (2.2.332–40). The remark extends to all conscious players. Poor in the world, their company feeling too much competition from a troupe of boy actors, the actors are rich in Hamlet's estimation. In short, Hamlet identifies himself with the actors. This sympathy is all the more understandable when we think of Burbage meeting on stage men whose occupations are identical with his own. They match his own reality, one that goes deeper than the complicated "show" in his impersonation of Hamlet. The actor playing the poisoner may only "seem" to console the Queen, yet his seeming means literally that: he truthfully gives the illusion of feigning sympathy. In Claudius's court, "seems" refers, instead, to the hypocrisy that infuriates Hamlet. Little wonder that Hamlet so prefers the "truth" exposed by the actors that he would like to "get . . . a fellowship in a cry of players" (3.3.290–91).

This is the power of the players; they talk truthfully about a reality that Claudius's world either contradicts or purposely obscures. By definition, the player himself must place a certain faith in illusion or else be forced to look anew at what passes for reality. It is this illusion, never pretending to be real, that offers Hamlet a purpose and a certainty that are denied by the world in which Claudius and Gertrude confide. If *The Murder of Gonzago* is the focal point for Hamlet's detective work (a thoughtful counterpart to Claudius's own crude "play," that swordfight in the final scene), then this encounter with the actors is the happy prelude. An outsider in Denmark, a man who, by his own confession, finds no delight in men or women, Hamlet pours what human sympathies, what ties he feels to our race, into the acting company. It disturbs him that the company has fallen on hard times. The successful child actors, he speculates, might turn from acting once their voices change (2.2.361–68). They now mock the adult actors. But when they themselves turn adult, will they be embarrassed at having formerly exclaimed "against their own succession?" What the actors do *is* of value; and it is therefore important in Hamlet's eyes that they play their roles well. And so he cautions them to speak their speeches "trippingly on the tongue" (3.2.2), to steer some middle course between excess (ham acting in our sense) and deficiency.

How one speaks, no less than what one says, is the issue; the injunction serves for life as well as for the theater. With the witty Clown, Hamlet knows one "must speak by the card, or equivocation" will undo one (5.1.148–49). This concern for acting extends even to the physical, to how one conducts oneself or suits the "action to the word, the word to the action" (3.2.19–20). Not separable from life, acting and that theater it establishes become "the mirror up to nature" (3.2.24–25). Hamlet's advice works for both the actors of Shakespeare's company and for us all. Doing one's part well in the play (both in *Hamlet* and *The Murder of Gonzago*) becomes indistinguishable from Hamlet's philosophic concern for truthful acting. He champions the proper use of words in a hypocritical world. There the theater is mere entertainment; *The Murder of Gonzago* is only a pageant to entertain a drowsy king before bedtime.

Hamlet can even admire dead performers such as Yorick. His first observation about the skull is that it "had a tongue in it, and could sing once" (5.1.83–84). Hamlet then reflects on those lips that he used to kiss and which formerly were the source of gibes, gambols, songs, and flashes of merriment. As Hamlet, a skull with yet a layer of flesh, holds before him Yorick's skull cleansed by time, we see Hamlet looking at himself, holding up a mirror of his own nature. Here the live antic confronts the dead. Yorick has been fortunately removed from the devouring world of sex and politics, from that physicality and statesman's practical "art" which so threatens Hamlet. An illusion of the illusion of Yorick necessary if Yorick were "alive" in the play, a dead jester here provides Hamlet's own mirror, his moment when, in Virginia Woolf's words, he has his "vision."[2]

-ii-

Hamlet's "obsession" radiates beyond his own person to the play itself. In some ways he *is* the play, and the title may refer as much to a state of mind, a unique and yet fatal way of viewing reality, as it does to the specific character. Ultimately, of course, Hamlet is not the play; all is not within his perspective, let alone within his control. When he perishes life goes on, however inferior in some respects young Fortinbras may seem to Hamlet. Still, Hamlet's obsession and the play's own pervasive theatricality give a special emphasis to the Renaissance commonplace: all the world's a stage and the stage is a little world. We know this from the start, that the "world" of *Hamlet,* whatever its thematic significance, is nothing if not theatrical. The characters move in a seemingly substantial world that, in reality, is nothing more than the momentary "collusion" of actors and audience. Our knowledge that we are attending a play thus feeds into this sense of theatricality.

It is surely the dumb show, more than any collection of aesthetic metaphors, that enforces our sense of play. Instead of coming near the end—as is the practice with such inner plays when used in revenge tragedies as a means of flushing out and punishing the guilty—Hamlet's is at the very center. The dumb show is a present action, one so graphic that once words are added with *The Murder of*

Gonzago it will rouse the hitherto unassailable consciousness of a king. And it gives physical form to an event not yet materialized on stage, the death of Claudius, the second king.[3] For a moment, by means of the theater, we escape the restrictive, narrowing revenge world and float free in time. We go with a godlike perspective from present to past and then to future. The simple dumb show, then, complements *Hamlet,* theater at its most complex and profound.

It may also be a direct address to the audience, familiarizing us with the story so that when the play with words follows, all of our attention will focus on Claudius. Claudius's lack of reaction to the dumb show has puzzled some audiences. Perhaps, like Hamlet's opening aside, it does not exist for the characters on stage. Not part of the time scheme of their world, it is designed solely for the spectator. Hamlet may speak derogatorily about "inexplicable dumb show" (3.2.13), but the truth is that the timeless dumb show serves as the perfect correlative for Hamlet's sense of the everpresence of past and future.

Our own role as audience is stressed during the dialogue-play that follows, for we watch both Hamlet, a conscious actor and here a controller (he has picked the play, given directions to the actors, even substituted some lines of his own making), and Claudius, an actor both aware (eager to preserve a commanding and guiltless public image) and unaware (duped into believing that the playlet is mere entertainment). Here is theater talking about the significance of theater; Hamlet reminds us all of this: "Give him heedful note; / For I mine eyes will rivet to his face, / And after we will both our judgements join / To censure of his seeming" (3.2.89–92). This self-conscious theater, designed to make some of its viewers equally self-conscious, will be employed later in Gertrude's chamber where the Queen is forced by her son to hold up her mirror and there to see her self, or at least the adulterous and incestuous self that Hamlet would have her see.

More generally, the play abounds with audiences: Hamlet and his friends waiting for the ghost's appearance; Polonius's two stations behind the arras; Claudius and Hamlet watching each other; the audience for Ophelia in her madness. Claudius and Polonius, for example, will "So bestow [themselves] that, seeing unseen, / [They] may of their encounter frankly judge" (3.1.33–34). The irony is that although Hamlet may not be aware of their presence, we surely are; these spies will not go unseen.

The play's self-consciousness, its wealth of audiences, only reminds us of our own significant role. Hamlet is most appealing, and we tend to see Denmark through his eyes. But he is not the only spokesman, nor should his theatrical perspective blind us from its darker side. The actor, properly coached and given a good play, can be a powerful instrument. Hamlet himself knows that if he could perform his part well by summoning up real emotions equal to those fictive ones portrayed by the actor impersonating Priam, then he could "Confound the ignorant, and amaze indeed / The very faculties of eyes and ears" (2.2.591–92). Our responsibility, then, is to recognize his power but also to put in the proper perspective the "plays" he stages, consciously or unconsciously, for our benefit.

Hamlet is our chief repository for aesthetic metaphors, but not the exclusive owner. As noted in the Preface, if Cassius and Brutus could retain their theatrical perspective, when they speak of the assassination as "acted over / In states unborn and accents yet unknown" (3.1.111–16), they could escape their assigned parts, escape the world of *Julius Caesar,* which, like all revenge worlds, relentlessly closes in on them. Hamlet, also, can only push his theatrical perspective so far; it cannot substitute for life itself and it cannot exonerate him from an onrush of action in the final scene. In this sense the play *Hamlet* is larger than the character, no matter how much he dominates its nutshell world. The play's own theatrical perspective supersedes that of the prince.

On Hamlet's death, Horatio takes over his theatrical function, one similar to Hamlet's earlier role with the traveling players. Horatio becomes Hamlet's voice, promising to tell Fortinbras and the "audience" he will assemble the story or play we have just witnessed.

In our time, we are the seven o'clock audience leaving the theater, satisfied, knowing who did it and how it all came out. And as we make our way through the doors, we are met by Fortinbras, the nine o'clock audience. He is in the dark as to what the play portends, just as we were ourselves two hours earlier. Horatio remains to stage a play, something involving "carnal, bloody, and unnatural acts . . . accidental judgments, casual slaughters . . . deaths put on by cunning and forc'd cause, / And, in this upshot, purposes mistook / Fall'n on th' inventors' heads" (5.2.392–96). He provides a veritable plot summary of the play we have attended. During the run of *Hamlet,* in Shakespeare's time and our own, Horatio anticipates tomorrow's performance. Tomorrow the play will start again, with that confused exchange of greetings between Bernardo and Francisco. All that Hamlet sees, or thinks he sees, all he accomplishes philosophically by means of his obsession with life as a play—all is dismantled, as brusquely as stagehands strike a set.

Hamlet is conscious of the theater until the end. Appropriately, once apologies and explanations are made to Laertes, Hamlet refers to the "audience" (251). He addresses here both the audience on stage, and those surrounding the stage. But it is Horatio whom Hamlet must beg to report his story to "the unsatisfied" (5.2.351). And

Fortinbras, for whom we have no evidence of any great interest *or* disinterest in the theater, will be the one to assemble an audience for Horatio's tale (398).

In a way we might want to think of Horatio as our own representative on stage. He is there almost from the beginning, and he promises to be there after the present play is over, telling Hamlet's story to the new king. In a way Horatio seems to be a "Hamlet" who has already gone through the play, and who has already experienced tragedy, for the one fact about his previous life we learn is that he is "one, in suffering all, that suffers nothing" (3.2.71). This friend of Hamlet, this stoic, this character whose dialogue flourishes only when the prince is off stage, may represent a perspective, duller yet more useful, that survives Hamlet's. Although not adverse to seeing life as a play, Horatio himself steers clear of the fatal frontiers of theatrical obsession and self-consciousness.

-iii-

Before turning to the darker side of the play's aesthetic metaphor, one more dimension of Hamlet's theatricality should be suggested, albeit in a *very* tentative fashion. At various times Hamlet suspects that he is in a play. He identifies with us, with the audience, suspecting what we know to be a truth, that he himself is merely an actor's impersonation.

Hamlet's opening line, the punning aside "A little more than kin, and less than kind," is not part of that world experienced by Claudius and Gertrude. The line goes unheard by Claudius. In effect, the second or so it takes to deliver that line is missing in the time scheme of Claudius's world. Hamlet speaks here only to us, the spectators; from all that Claudius knows his first lines to Hamlet are the composite "But now, my cousin Hamlet, and my son,—. . . How is it that the clouds still hang on you" (1.2.64, 66). It seems best that the actor playing Claudius freeze while Hamlet delivers his opening line, rather than having Claudius, as he is sometimes portrayed, show impatience when Hamlet does not respond directly to his attempt to call him "son."

Or consider that conversation with Polonius where Hamlet calls the old man a "fishmonger" (2.2.174). Hamlet seems to anticipate Polonius's future role of fishmonger, "panderer" in a broad sense, in pushing his daughter on the prince in order to pry loose the cause of his discontent. Though initially shocked by the allegation, Polonius, within some thirty-seven lines, will do just that, contriving "the means of meeting" between Hamlet and Ophelia.

There are other instances in the play where, beyond using the aesthetic metaphor to gain some perspective on Denmark, Hamlet *seems* to give some indication of knowing that he is in a play. Consider, for example, his remark to Ophelia that follows some bantering about the lady's lap. Hamlet's claim that his father died "within's two hours" (3.2.135) confuses Ophelia; from her thematic time scheme the death occurred four months earlier. But we will recall the Chorus's remark in the Prologue to *Romeo and Juliet* about "the two hours' traffic of our stage" (12). Two hours is right as we know it: the death of the king is a fictive event, prior to our own two hours' experience with the present play.

Finally, there is that fascinating interchange between Hamlet and Polonius, just before the dumb show begins. To Hamlet's enigmatic "I eat the air, promised-cramm'd," Claudius replies, "These words are not mine." That is, these are not the sort of words I would say (3.2.99–103). Properly, the words are not Claudius's but Hamlet's since the lines are assigned to Burbage rather than to the actor playing the king. Hamlet seems to pick up this implication when he says, "No, nor mine now." This may mean once the line is said it goes into the consciousness of the audience, becoming part of their own experience with one play. Moreover, the words Hamlet speaks are not his own, since he is not a real man but only a character manipulated by Shakespeare and by the actor playing the part. How fitting that on this note Hamlet turns to Polonius with "My Lord, you play'd once i' th' university, you say," as if to keep alive this discussion about the theater.

Polonius sees an easy distinction between life and the stage. Just before *The Murder of Gonzago* he confesses that he played the part of Julius Caesar in a university production (Shakespeare's own play on that subject was performed toward the end of 1599). To Polonius's revelation Hamlet seems to react cynically, perhaps even angrily: "It was a brute part of him to kill so capital a calf there" (3.2.110–11). We know that Polonius is only an actor's impersonation, but from his own perspective he is now Polonius and only once impersonated Caesar. But the irony of the roles is staggering. Polonius believes that what one really "is" is separable from what one is on the "stage." From Hamlet's view there seems to be no such simple distinction between "roles." Polonius is an impossible Caesar; more properly, he should have played a comic Cassius to Claudius's Brutus, with the elder Hamlet being the betrayed and assassinated monarch Caesar. And yet there is also a certain rightness in Polonius's college role, since he like Caesar will soon be stabbed unawares. The arras itself can serve as a monstrous parody of Caesar's own cloak through which the conspirators passed their bloody swords.

The idea of Hamlet's knowing that he is in a play is just a tentative one because it is only a "suggestion" surrounded by the larger argument about the double-edged nature of Hamlet's theatrical consciousness and—as we will soon see—the play's own divided attitude toward both the theater and its hero so given to aesthetic metaphors. But the idea is also tentative because of a revealing and not altogether successful experiment with the thesis. When I was teaching at the University of Illinois I directed a production of *Hamlet* built upon this very thesis, that the prince knows that he is in a play. With what I think were good intentions I instructed the actor playing Hamlet to use every resource at his command to impress upon the audience the fact that he, Hamlet, knew that it was just a play. Accordingly, the actor would leave the stage at times, mingling with the audience and saying his lines from there. He would, while he was on stage, alternately play to the other characters and then, as if dismissing them as pathetically unconscious actors or as characters unaware of the "reality" behind their impersonations, he would play directly to the audience. I even asked that he deliver his lines in conversational tones, with no sense of projection and with none of the artifice we associate with the stage. In short, I instructed this actor *not* to act, or to act as if he were not acting. The audience, I must admit, hated the production, perhaps because my thesis did not hold water. Perhaps it was an extension of the play's own theatricality that went too far. I suspect another contributing factor: no matter what conception one has of a character, the rules of good acting remain constant. On stage one "acts" to the world of the play, no matter how the character sees that world. And this applies, I now sadly realize, to characters as far-ranging as the theatrically conscious Father in Pirandello's *Six Characters in Search of an Author* and as psychologically intense as, say, the suffering heroes of an O'Neill play.

-iv-

We must be careful, then, not to confuse Hamlet's fascination with the theater with the play's own statement about theater. The fact is that, on the other side of the coin, aesthetic metaphors are often identified with the corrupt world of Denmark. The Puritan complaint about the theater is at one with our own revulsion with Claudius and his court. (And even saying this is not to condemn that court absolutely, for, as shown in the next section, the reality trusted in by Claudius has a claim no less strong than the unreality, the theater, championed by Hamlet.)

The mockery of the theater here is intense and pervasive. In *A Midsummer Night's Dream* we have seen how Theseus holds the stage in low regard. This attitude dwarfs his vision but also makes him practical and rational, the very qualities necessary for an efficient leader. But in the tragedy those who mock the theater, who trust too much in their own reality, are morally corrupt rather than fortuitously shortsighted.

For Claudius, particularly, the theater seems to be little more than entertainment; for him *The Murder of Gonzago* and a duel between Laertes and Hamlet as participants are all one. Polonius would use acting as a trap, advising Ophelia to "Read on this book, / That show of such an exercise may colour / Your loneliness" (3.1.44–46). Here are instructions to an actress, although they are designed to pry a secret out of Hamlet rather than to penetrate the heart of life. Polonius will soon fail with such sophomoric "productions." For the Claudius faction, then, the theater is entertainment in its basest form, a place where one acted years ago, a way to beguile the heavy gait of night, and something to be avoided when the mirror it holds scorches the soul. Appropriately, at the end of the aborted *Murder of Gonzago,* Claudius is absent, fleeing what threatens to intrude too much on his sordid reality.

The unsavory meanings of "theater" run throughout the play. Polonius is cautioned by Hamlet to "play the fool [nowhere] but in's own house" (3.1.136). And Ophelia's playful remark that Hamlet is "as good as a chorus"

(3.2.255) prompts him to think of human beings generally as "puppets dallying" (257), observed and interpreted by Hamlet, the choral figure.

Even the prince's celebration of language generates an antithetical abuse of words so rampant that it serves as metaphor for Hamlet's dilemma: how to share words. In a larger sense, how can one be a part of a world that violates words and hence cannot grasp any vision beyond the immediate? At best, the other characters conceive of words only as public utterance. We observe this in many forms: Laertes's assertion that Hamlet acts toward others no "further / Than the main voice of Denmark goes withal" (1.3.27–28); Claudius's commendation of Hamlet's shallow promise to obey his mother as "a fair reply" (1.2.121); or his earlier image of that "common theme" that "still hath cried, / From the first corse till he that died to-day, / 'This must be so' " (1.2.103–6). Claudius would elevate "deed" over words (4.7.126–27). Laertes's vow "To cut his throat i' th' church" (127) is an appropriate humiliation for a man of words such as Hamlet but also a denial of that physical "instrument" through which words can take us to the farthest reaches of abstraction. For these individuals words are a way not of grasping what exists beyond matter but of getting along in the present world. Hamlet links "words" with matter, with a state of alienation "Between" men. But for Polonius "matter" refers to subject matter, something almost solid and surely of this world (2.2.193–97).

Ironically, the others are concerned about Hamlet's abuse of words. Their fear is that what he says will not result in something positive, that his vows of love will not be translated into fact, the marriage contract. To Polonius, Hamlet's soul is "prodigal" in lending "the tongue vows" (1.3.116–17), and Ophelia is enjoined not "to give words or talk with the Lord Hamlet" (134). The assumption here seems to be that words that fail to result in *some thing* are words wasted.

Words can be chained to this world as mere tools, or words of repentance anticipating something beyond the present can be invalidated because they are spoken hypocritically: "My words fly up, my thoughts remain below. / Words without thoughts never to heaven go" (3.3.97–98). The language of the other characters is sometimes profound as in Claudius's prayer scene, his only moment of genuine introspection, in which he uses words properly to define his violation of prayer. Sometimes the language is shallow, as when Polonius acknowledges his own "poor phrase" when he puns on "tender:" "Tender yourself more dearly, / . . . Or . . . you'll tender me a fool" (1.3.108–9). That Polonius in the extreme, Osric, spends words the way one spends gold: "His purse is empty already. All's golden words are spent" (5.2.136–37). In speaking the way he does Osric touches on the periphery of issues, and is a mere footnoter edifying one only with the "margent," with notes peripheral to the text.

Against the theatrical perspective so championed by Hamlet, the Claudius court clings to its reality. That this reality is a sordid one is one issue, but it is real for them. Having succeeded as lover and as king, Claudius has no doubts as to the substantiality of his world. He and Fortinbras, who emerges briefly at the end, epitomize the successful ruler, and if it were not for Hamlet's presence we could sympathize with them more.

Uneasy about Hamlet's obsession, we can be no less uneasy about the implicit trust in Denmark that distinguishes those opposed to Hamlet. That they do not see the world as Hamlet does is both their strength and weakness. Even Gertrude is correct, in one sense, when she sees "nothing" (3.4.133) in her chamber. It is all nothing; we know from *A Midsummer Night's Dream* and from Prospero's final speeches in *The Tempest* that the stage world, including that of *Hamlet,* is all built on a baseless fabric. At the same time Gertrude consciously divorces herself from the play metaphor, and from us. However welcomed here, any maternal love cannot lead to a shared sense of vision.

In that unique and well-known judgment, T. S. Eliot complains that *Hamlet* lacks an "objective correlative," that the prince's grief is in excess of the facts. In effect, the play's world is an inadequate vehicle for those larger mysteries of Hamlet's character that Shakespeare struggles to convey.[4] From this Eliot concludes that the play is something of an artistic failure. One way of responding to this charge is to suggest that it is in aesthetic metaphors that Hamlet finds his proper objective correlative, for the theater, that seemingly reality which is at bottom an illusion, serves as the perfect metaphor for a man who doubts the substantiality of Denmark. But this means of "realizing" his character is also at the heart of his problem, and Hamlet accordingly deprives himself of any meaningful relationship between life and art. Like Hamlet, Bottom also dabbles in the theater, but acting never becomes for the clown a metaphor for existence. Bottom is as gloriously unconscious of his "transformation" as Hamlet is conscious of his own.

Hamlet goes too far. As he rejects the "seeming" reality of the Claudius faction, confessing that he knows not their "seems" (1.2.76), he dismisses this world as a "dream" or "shadows" (2.2.271). He expands Rosencrantz's simpleminded point, that the goal of the ambitious often turns out to be a dream, to the larger, more terrifying notion that all of human existence, that hierarchy from beggar to king, may be insubstantial. In a sense he is right and only confirms what we know, that it is all a play. But we can and we must step out of the theater, and for the audience that two-hours' traffic of the stage is thus finite, a play time. But Denmark is all that Hamlet can know or should know. Seeing one's world for what it is still cannot obscure the fact that one must also deal with it, live in it—for what it is.

Hamlet, in this sense, is a victim of his own imagination. Indeed, after the interview with his father he is said to wax "desperate with imagination" (1.4.87). Though caught in a physical revenge that is the antithesis to visionary experience, Hamlet finds that this imagination threatens to overwhelm him. To Ophelia he confesses that he has "more offenses at my beck than I have thoughts to put them in, imagination to give them shape, or time to act them in" (3.1.126–29). Conversely, if his vision is not ratified, if the ghost is a delusion rather than a meaningful vision, then Hamlet is prepared to admit that his "imaginations are as foul / As Vulcan's stithy" (3.2.88–89). For Gertrude such imagination is only the "coinage of . . . the brain." How fitting that her metaphor is economic. For her vision of a ghost is nothing more than "bodiless creation ecstasy / Is very cunning in" (3.4.137–39).

In the best sense of the word, Hamlet is a "dreamer," one who with words and art goes beyond what is only temporal. It is right that he is a creature of the night in everything from costume to preference for the evening. Claudius in contrast "cannot dream of" what "thus hath put him [Hamlet] / So much from th' understanding of himself" (2.2.8–10). Polonius uses his "brain" only to hunt "the trial of policy" (2.2.46–47); his is a mundane employment and a dangerous one. And the Clown would choke off larger speculations, advising "Other" to "Cudgel thy brains no more about it" (5.1.63). For Hamlet, however, imagination is not to be restrained but to be employed. For him "Why may not imagination trace the noble dust of Alexander, till he find it stopping a bunghole" (5.1.224–26)? When Horatio tries to moderate that desire to get a fellowship in the company of players by arguing for the more conservative "Half a share," Hamlet insists, "A whole one, I" (3.2.290–91).

It is not so much a question of whether or not Hamlet hesitates, or delays. He is not that delicate, passive individual romantic critics often saw, nor is the play simply a debate between those who think and those who act. Rather, in Hamlet dazzling and fatal qualities are impossibly mixed. Even that language which Hamlet uses so well works gainst him. For along with a theatrical obsession he has, as W. R. Robinson has brilliantly argued, an addiction to unpacking his heart with words and, in the process, to abstracting and ultimately nullifying existence.[5] Accordingly, the prince reduces the miraculous physical presence of his father to a "commandment" in the "book and volume" of his brain (1.5.102–4), the schoolboy triumphing over the adventurer. Hamlet must interpose words even on the dumb show, thereby using the theater as a mere tool. He simply cannot resist this inclination to "interpret" (3.2.246), and if interpretation, in or out of the play, gives us order, we all know that it is order at a price.

Hamlet's rationalization, his use of redundancy to explain everything away, is a form of paralysis. Increasingly, the play becomes less a mirror for nature generally and more a small pocket mirror, revealing the hero's own egocentric quest for identity and certitude. In the process, Hamlet simply passes down the line the accumulation of past miseries from his father's day. He himself senses this restriction, this feeling of being controlled: his will is not his own (1.3.17). Hamlet would, in effect, reduce the world in the same way that a literary analysis in forgetting that the play is a piece of theater would do. By this verbalizing abstraction, Hamlet works against life, is himself "unpregnant" (2.2.568), and even that word he sullies by linking it to his "cause." Like his progenitor Oedipus, he blinds himself, but Hamlet's blindness is, in a way, deeper because, unlike the Greek hero, he cannot go on after passing judgment. That task rests with Fortinbras, and he is a man of vision—both in his approach to life (he will stage Hamlet's funeral as a military spectacle) and in his concern with planning.

I do not mean to suggest a Hamlet who is unheroic, or a dupe of his own virtues. He is wide as a character, much wider than the Hamlet we too often get in stage productions. For those productions and, perhaps, some of the scholarship on *Hamlet* have often given us an unqualified hero, manifestly superior to the Claudius world and irresistibly attractive in his lust for negation and nothingness, or a pathetic neurotic, driven mad by his own sensitivity as well as by the philistine mentality of his Nixon-like opponents.

Hamlet is larger than these two views, and, for that matter, more than their sum. For me, personally, it has taken some involvement with another medium, that of the movies, to realize this wide, albeit contradictory dimension of Hamlet's character. The film medium itself must be concerned with things that "are": one cannot film an abstraction. And the visuality of film puts action on at least an equal footing with contemplation. Surely the theater has this same profitable tension between its own physicality (real people, at the present time, speaking and moving before real people) and its abstraction (its words that can move beyond the immediate reality). I am thinking here of the film versions of *Hamlet* by Olivier and by the Russian director Kozintsev.[6]

Instead of portraying Hamlet as a sensitive deer or as that unqualified intellectual, Olivier sees him, in his own words, as a "nearly great man," as one who cannot "make up his mind."[7] Olivier blames Hamlet, stressing his faults to the degree that Claudius himself is more sympathetic than the lecherous, shallow fool we are often accustomed to seeing on stage. Like Hamlet, Olivier's camera strains to escape the claustrophobic castle set. But that escape is also balanced by the use of the camera to reveal shifting viewpoints—in the same way that a fuller production of *Hamlet* does. Instead of the monolithic perspective of stilted, speechifying stage productions, that Denmark as

seen through Hamlet's eyes, we see the action through
Ophelia, Claudius, Gertrude, and the other characters.
The stage sets, the framing devices, Olivier's tendency to
confine the action within rather than between scenes—all
may give the movie a "theatrical look." But his "meta-
cinema" also underlines the fact that the restrictive stage
metaphors are of the characters' own making. It has been
frequently observed that Olivier's film talents were more
suitable for Henry V, an action character. Still, what "happens" in his *Hamlet* and Olivier's criticism of the hero are
partially attributable to the aesthetic demands of the
cinema. Significantly, the film concludes with a reaffirma-
tion of physical life, taking us outside Hamlet's own mind
now that Horatio is in charge of the kingdom.

This attempted balance between stage and life—and it is
not at all certain if Olivier has achieved that balance—is
clearer in Kozintsev's film. Here the external world is
prominent. The crowded castle sits in the middle of skies,
seas, and stones. The peasants, the silent spokespersons of
this world, turn the wheels for the castle door, walk the
roads to its walls, listen to Claudius's stagey proclamations,
are pushed back at Ophelia's funeral, and look on in
silence at the end. While Hamlet sits on the wagon listening to Hecuba's speech, chickens scratch in the yard and in
the background a man silently leads a horse past the
camera. Kozintsev's Hamlet rebels against the artificial
society of the court. His very room embodies the tension
between the natural and artificial. Whereas books galore
attest to his interest in arts and language, there are also
maps, a sextant, and a ship's model. Hamlet, in this Russian film, is caught between his disgust at life's theatricality
and the life outside the stagelike castle. The sea pounds at
its walls in mockery, and there is an energy in the prince's
attempts to free himself. And if we bring our stage con-
ceptions to this film, if we take pleasure in Hamlet's brutal
questioning of existence through aesthetic metaphors and

the traveling players, the film uses that response as *one* part of a creative tension generated, on the other side, by the concrete existence embodied in the peasants. At the end the opening images return: the sea, the fortress, fire, and rocks. Hamlet and all that he represents are washed away. But Hamlet is also a part of the life that endures beyond man, even the contemplative man.

-vi-

Hamlet, both play and lead character, thus embodies all the energies of a conflicting attitude toward the theater. Even the genre of the revenge tragedy itself embodies that conflict, for, as Geoffrey Bush has observed, revenge is symbolic of all the contradictions inherent on this earth. It is at once "a descent into barbarism," since it forces one to encounter the physical world at its most detestable, and a potential "leap into sanctity."[8]

The play is thus about Hamlet the young revenger and about "Hamlet" as a state of mind, a way of approaching existence. At the end, Hamlet's theatrical consciousness culminates. The murder of Claudius, which would be the revenger's ultimate and most glorious act, has now the importance born of necessity. Hamlet fulfills his duty to his father, but his achievement as a tragic overseer of life's theatricality is the greater. The action in the final scene is compelling as four principal characters die within minutes of each other. The claim that Hamlet serve as revenger has been paid, and for a moment the frantic stage business catches the amoral brilliance of energy itself. The conventional revenge tragedy is coming to a necessary and striking end; our own aesthetic demands are satisfied. But Hamlet's awareness of life's theatricality follows him to the grave. He is acutely aware of the audience, the mutes or audience to this act (5.2.346). His last bequest is his dying voice to Fortinbras. Thematically, Fortinbras gets Hamlet's political endorsement; aesthetically, the actor playing Fortinbras now takes the center stage with Burbage's "death."

But when all is said and done, the actor is just a voice, the theater (as a thing in itself or as a metaphor for reality) only an illusion. Hamlet's political endorsement that will help in ensuring the succession is alone powerful. Horatio comments that now words can come "Not from his mouth, / Had it th' ability of life to thank you" (5.2.383–84). With Hamlet now silenced, Horatio, as Antony did for Caesar, becomes his voice. Hamlet's last word, appropriately, is "silence"—"The rest is silence" (5.2.369). That simple word explodes in meaning: after life there is only silence; the greatest pleasure is the silent rest after the absurdity of this world; once out of this world, character and playwright lapse into silence; at a certain stage all philosophies, all art, must stop as we dissolve happily into silence.

Life goes on; the kingdom will be in good hands, we may assume. Fortinbras's first act will be to call together an audience for Horatio's narration of Hamlet's story. But then more pressing, more practical, more concrete matters will take center stage.

Words in this play are like "daggers" (3.3.414), and it is Hamlet himself who links the essence of physicality in the play, the murder instrument of the revenger, with the basic word for language, "word" itself. Gertrude picks up the metaphor when she calls Hamlet's words "daggers" in her ears (3.4.95). The aesthetic metaphor, as employed by Hamlet and his play, is just such a double-edged instrument. It destroys its chief practitioner, robbing the prince of pleasure, let alone concrete achievement in this world, however tawdry that world may be. But it is also the means by which he exposes a corrupt court and in his way—by murder and by his own death—helps restore order and a new government. It is terrible that this should be so, that Hamlet's theatricality should be both productive and destructive. But surely we could not wish it otherwise.

This divided response, the double-edged aesthetic perspective, informs Cleopatra and her play; and yet she is not Hamlet. Working with a similarly diverse aesthetic metaphor, Shakespeare produces a considerably different reaction to her. What that reaction is and how it is produced is the issue of the next chapter.

7

Love and the Imagination in *Antony and Cleopatra*

*H*amlet and *Antony and Cleopatra* are similar in many ways: the central characters' sense of role playing, their use of aesthetic metaphors, their uniqueness in a world where others trust in the "reality" of politics and power, their delight in the theater (albeit a bit more loosely defined in Cleopatra's case), and our own divided response to them. But unlike Hamlet, who takes no delight in the flesh, Cleopatra revels in the physical world, her Egypt of soft beds and sexual pleasures. Perhaps this is why her death is not "tragic" in the sense that Hamlet's is. Hamlet goes to the duel in the throne room with serenity, yet his thoughts are not fully of this earth. But Cleopatra, even in her final minutes, is busy transforming even the death instrument itself, the asp, into an object of sexual pleasure. In a sense, her theatrical obsessions make her almost a comic figure, celebrating until the end her pleasure in this world, in the flesh.

Plays of tremendously wide dimensions, both in the pervasiveness of the aesthetic metaphor (and the lead character's grasp of that metaphor) and the divided response toward art and the artist, they are, at length, vastly different plays. For these reasons *Antony and Cleopatra,* as a tragedy, forms a link with *Hamlet* and, as a comedy, with *The Tempest,* the subject of the final chapter. All three plays constitute the third stage in this book, Shakespeare's mature examination of the boundaries of art and the artist. We first examine the divided attitude of the play *Antony and Cleopatra* toward that art and then talk about the character of Cleopatra.

-i-

In *Antony and Cleopatra* the theater is often spoken of with contempt. Cleopatra abhors the possibility that the lovers' story will be brought to the stage:

> The quick comedians
> Extemporally will stage us, and present
> Our Alexandrian revels; Antony
> Shall be brought drunken forth, and I shall see
> Some squeaking Cleopatra boy my greatness
> I' th' posture of a whore.
>
> (5.2.216–21)

The audience she fears would consist of nothing but slaves wearing greasy aprons, smothering the actors with their thick breaths (209–13). Caesar's garish victory parade is branded as an "imperious show" (4.15.23), and Enobarbus similarly describes Antony's own desperate plan to duel with Octavius as a mere "show" (3.13.30). Ridiculing Antony's vows of fidelity, Cleopatra chides him to "play one scene / Of excellent dissembling, and let it look / Like perfect honour" (1.3.78–80).

But the most thorough questioning of the power to give a momentary credence to an illusion comes when Cleopatra, while at first praising the fancy that creates "strange forms" beyond nature's, finds in the real Antony "nature's piece 'gainst fancy, / Condemning shadows quite" (5.2.97–100). Later, when Antony denounces himself, he does so by equating "black Vesper's pageants" with his own shameful wavering between the demands of empire and his personal indulgence in Egypt (4.14.1–14). "Pageant" can be a general word referring to everything from the floats of mystery plays to court masques. Here it is used to describe both clouds whose own shows "mock our eyes with air" and the once-famous soldier who now "cannot hold [his] visible shape," torn as he is between love and politics.

This censure of mere theatricality and of the imagination as fickle or uncontrollable is at one with the complaints we may bring against Cleopatra's own seductive arts. Indeed, in Antony's speech just quoted it is the woman's sexual power that has robbed a soldier of his "visible shape." The word "play" in the sense of sexual play is frequently interchangeable with "play" as it refers to the illusion produced by an actor. Perhaps the most intricate use of this double meaning occurs when Cleopatra comments that in Antony's absence her eunuch Mardian is no worse than a woman as a sexual partner. She then distinguishes between the poor actor who can at least "plead pardon" from his audience for a bad performance and the sexually incapable man who has no such recourse when he is found "too short" (2.5.4–9).

This association of sex and art culminates in the queen's own character. It is a common observation that Cleopatra is a skillful actress, conjuring up moods to lure or deceive Antony and the other men in the play. She is a creature, in Barbara Everett's words, who lives entirely in a "world of 'play.' "[1] The gay, world-weary aristocrat or the martyred lover "sudden sick" (2.3.3–5)—her repertoire is no less varied than our responses to her. Able to switch roles at a moment's notice, to "be Cleopatra" (3.13.187) whenever the occasion demands, she is at once actress and playwright. Granville-Barker in listing her several charms stresses her extraordinary "imagination,"[2] whereas Derek Traversi speaks of her ability to "impose upon her surroundings a vitality which is not the less astonishing for retaining to the last its connection with the environment it transcends."[3] By her so potent art Cleopatra is able to imagine fish as "every one an Antony" (2.5.14) or the horse on which he rides as herself.

Cleopatra herself is conscious of these abilities. By her own admission she knows she will "seem the fool" that she is not if she believes in Antony's constancy (1.1.42). Her emotions, which she finds distress Antony, are spoken of as her "becomings" (1.3.96), as if all that she is comes from practice and artifice. A more direct acknowledgment of her essentially theatrical approach to others is found in her resolve that "since my lord / Is Antony again, I will be Cleopatra (3.13.186–87). Even emotions are rehearsed by this woman "[whose] every passion fully strives / To make itself . . . fair and admir'd" (1.1.50–51). Such artifice accounts for the speed of her emotional changes, for her being capable of appearing "sudden sick" when the occasion demands (1.3.5). Her dialogue itself is consciously planned, as when she instructs Charmian to report to her lover that at her counterfeit death the last word she spoke was "Antony" (4.13.8). The circles of illusion widen here as we have on the Elizabethan stage a boy actor impersonating Cleopatra devising dialogue for Charmian that all the time has been supplied by the playwright.

This sense of theatricality rubs off on Antony as well. Philo recognizes that the Antony who exists for Cleopatra is not the real Antony but a stage lover who "comes too short of that great property / Which still should go with Antony" (1.1.58–59). Antony even speaks of his own decline in the phrase reminiscent of stage tragedies or tragic lives such as in *The Mirror for Magistrates:* "Alack, our terrene moon / Is now eclips'd, and it portends alone / The fall of Antony" (3.13.153–55). In his perspective both he and Cleopatra "strut" to their confusion (3.13.114); we may recall here Macbeth's use of that same verb (5.5.25) to describe a paltry actor playing his death scene. Though he is a man taking little delight in plays, as we would imagine, Octavius himself is concerned that his generosity to Cleopatra, his "nobleness," be "well acted." He wants a performance that her death would "never let come forth" (5.2.45–46).

In such an atmosphere of theatricality it is inevitable that the characters, and especially Cleopatra, be equally concerned with the performance or at least the surface appearance of others. Cleopatra wants to know, for example, if Antony appeared "sad or merry." When she is assured that he achieved some equipoise between the two moods, she appreciates the subtlety of the compromise by commending his response as a "well-divided disposition" (1.5.50–52). In acting poorly, in being too obvious or showing one's inexperience, one falls from the status of actor to a mere "dancer" (3.11.36). This is the term hurled at Octavius as Antony remembers his passive role in the deaths of Cassius and Brutus. One level below a dancer is a "puppet," Cleopatra's word for Dolabella when she accuses him of being manipulated by Octavius (5.2.208).

Recurrent allusions to the physical "tools" used by the actor as he practices his art are also used. Words uttered shallowly are deemed "mouth-made vows, / Which break themselves in swearing" (1.3.30–31). Octavius condemns Antony for breaking a previous oath, and then denies that Antony will ever have the "tongue" with which to make a similar charge against Caesar (2.2.82–83). One of the deepest curses Cleopatra can level against the Romans is that their "tongue rot" (3.7.16).

An oblique reference is even made to the practice on the Elizabethan stage of using all-male casts when Octavius condemns Antony for being "not more manlike" than Cleopatra (1.4.5). Antony himself makes an interesting allusion to role playing when he wishes that he "could be made so many men, / And all of you clapp'd up together in / An Antony." His immediate wish is that he could be multiplied so that his thanks to loyal followers would itself be magnified. At the same time all those to whom he is indebted would be neatly compressed into a single individual. Yet behind this is there not the awareness, at least on the playwright's part, that Antony in the play is not just an individual but a representative of mankind? He is a mirror for the triumphs and shortcomings of all men. Conversely, men in that macrocosm encompassing the stage are all potentially an Antony (4.2.16–19).

-ii-

Cleopatra's sexuality, which the Romans and many commentators find so degrading, is inseparable from her ability to put her unique stamp on anything falling within her sphere. This is an ability surpassing even her skills as an actress. Sex as creation and art as creation are correlatives here, and any encounter with Cleopatra's world involves a transformation. When he is with her, the soldier must change to a lover; he cannot play two roles at once. This is as true for Antony as it was for Caesar: "She made great Caesar lay his sword to bed" (2.2.232). Cleopatra is herself "transform'd" (1.1.12); depending on the speaker, that word is either magical or derogatory. Those who find her transforming abilities degrading because she debilitates Antony at the peak of an otherwise promising career find Egypt itself claustrophobic, a seamy nutshell affronting man's wider spirit. But to those like Antony who witness and are changed by Cleopatra's alchemy, the "space" surrounding embracing lovers is the macrocosm, as it is for Donne in "The Sun Rising." The macrocosm itself becomes a nutshell. With his optical shift in finding a world in Cleopatra's arms, Antony can let "Rome in Tiber melt, and the wide arch / Of the rang'd empire fall" (1.1.33–34).

The most complex statement regarding these powers of

transformation that are at one with Cleopatra's sexuality is made by Enobarbus as he describes her first meeting with Antony. There the queen's very presence transmuted sails and winds, the water and the ship's oars, her cheeks and the diver-colored fans, and flower-soft hands and silken tackle into love symbols of the receiving female and the aggressive male (2.2.196–223). The richness of her love is this power to change all objects and elements, even the wind itself, into something preeminently sexual.

Still, the description of the barge is a statement after the fact, a past event not witnessed by the audience. Cleopatra's "performance" at her death provides, instead, a direct and present example. As indicated in the Preface, in less than twenty lines (5.2.294–312) she manages to translate even the horrors of death into the pleasures of love. The asp's bite becomes a "lover's pinch," and then the asp is metamorphosed into a baby suckled at his mother's breast. Applying a second asp, the queen imagines it to be an Antony. Thus we have the almost sentimental tableau of the mother embracing her husband and their sleeping child. Even Charmian upon her mistress's death thinks of herself as part of a stage performance as she adjusts Cleopatra's crown and then readies herself to "play" (322) a part, to die like her queen before Octavius enters. The whore Cleopatra by the sheer force of her imagination has become a married woman. Antony will be her husband in death if she skillfully plays what remains of her earthly role, if "to that name [husband] my courage prove my title!" (290–91). Her next stage will be one of otherworldly dimensions, that pagan paradise to which a lonely wife hastens now that there is no good cause to "stay" (316) longer on this world's stage.

This transformation of what is literal or ugly into something symbolic and lovely has its beginning in pleasure. The dour Roman disposition, though advantageous for ruling, is hostile to such creation. To sustain an illusion

one must do the very thing Caesar cautions against, "Pawn
... experience to ... present pleasure" (1.4.32). The
function of Cleopatra's art itself is to transform past and
future into one immediate sensuous pleasure analogous to
that we receive as witnesses to the stage spectacle. When
Prospero announces his purpose in the Epilogue as being
"to please," we find behind this, surely, the Renaissance
equation of *utile et dulce*. We know that for the age pleasure
in art was a moral pleasure, the pleasure of instruction.
But Prospero may also imply something less instructive,
closer to that pleasure in illusion which he has relished and
then, like us on leaving the theater, been forced to abandon.
Both mysterious and short-lived, this pleasure clearly "lies"
in "th' East" (2.3.40).

Theseus charges that in giving himself to fantasies the
poet thereby ignores the demands of reality. This charge is
partially vindicated here. Those who share in Cleopatra's
art must forget public roles and "drown consideration"
(4.2.45). From this state or stupor nothing but "idleness"
may hatch (1.2.134).

And yet the same condition may lead to the Soothsayer's
ideal where "every of your wishes [has] a womb, / and
[fertile] every wish, a million" (1.2.38–39). She refers
specifically to Charmian's desire for children. Yet, having
already produced children, Cleopatra produces something
of a rarer order here as she peoples the stage with her
wish fulfillments. Hers is a transformation of the world as
public stage into a private ground of love and sex. Like the
Nile, she is the antithesis of restraint or chastity. From its
"o'erflowing" (1.2.50) the river that is her namesake de-
posits on its banks the ooze and slime that becomes the
fertile bed for crops (2.7.23–26).

Cleopatra has the same sort of "seething brains" that
Theseus would brand as excesses of the imagination
(5.1.4). To her, ideas are not abstractions but children; she
consistently makes the equation between thoughts and

creativity. One does not whisper an idea to her but rather is enjoined to "Ram thou thy fruitful tidings in mine ears" (2.5.24). For Cleopatra to "think," to come to logical conclusions based on evidence of the past, is also "to die" (3.13.1). For her, life offers a chance to envision and then create a reality above politics and public responsibility. As such, she is given to wine, love, fertility, visions, and, as we have seen in *A Midsummer Night's Dream,* sleep and the dreams of sleep. Even Octavius observes that in death she "looks like sleep, / As she would catch another Antony / In her strong toil of grace" (5.2.349–51).

Looking down at the supposedly dead body of Juliet and not knowing that she has been drugged, Romeo finds her loveliness preserved in spite of death:

> Death, that hath sucked the honey of thy breath,
> Hath no power yet upon thy beauty.
> Thou art not conquer'd; beauty's ensign yet
> Is crimson in thy lips and in thy cheeks,
> And death's pale flag is not advanced there.
>   (5.3.92–96)

We know he is deluded. A more rational man might have asked: Under what conditions can a woman seem to be dead and yet show no traces of rigor mortis? But deluded as he may be, Romeo is also richer for his denial of reality, for his imaginative leap at the expense of accuracy. He sees something we cannot. Yet in a curious sense he is correct: what Juliet represents *is* beyond death. She is a symbol greater than the body of the actress currently impersonating her. More literally, the actress playing Juliet is very much alive. Cleopatra similarly finds a triumph of love in death. Again, even her persecutor sees in her not a dead but a sleeping woman, caught in a moment of passionate embrace with her Antony.

Such an imaginative leap from pleasure through art to a reordering of reality is beyond philosophy, or Roman rationalism. It demands not this world but, to borrow the phrases introduced early in the play, "new heaven, new earth" (1.1.16–17). A solid discussion of political reality and the demands and dangers of the empire builder, the play also has room for its antithesis, an imaginative flight born of love serving as a correlative for the artist's creative powers. In this sense, Cleopatra and the Soothsayer are Shakespeare's surrogates. If the play holds a mirror up to a fascinating piece of history, it is also an evocation, nature wrought to a higher pitch. Even in that "realistic" Roman "half" of the play there are moments beyond reality. The soldiers on watch hear music in the air signaling "the god Hercules, whom Antony lov'd, / Now [leaving] him" (4.3.16–17). The laws of reality are invalid here, and the characters on leaving the stage conclude as one that " 'Tis strange.' "

-iii-

Again, Cleopatra's transformation in Act 5 is a mere illusion; souls less given to the theater are perfectly right in calling an asp an asp. And the moment we rhapsodize over Cleopatra's last scene we must remember the pettiness, the selfishness that accompanies her even to the end. For some scholars it remains a moot point whether she dies for the love of Antony or to avoid being led through the streets of Rome. Perhaps no more certain are Cleopatra's motives for hiding half of her wealth from Octavius.[4] Moreover, the clown with his cheap puns mocks not only concepts of immortality but the "worm" itself, Cleopatra's liberating instrument of death. Her imaginative world is a paradox since Cleopatra offers us not an empire, nothing as solid as Rome, but merely words, words, words. Antony speaks accurately when he finds her "cunning past man's thought" (1.2.150).

This power to control the audience's response as well as

one's own view of an otherwise grim situation is often thought of as "womanish" and unbecoming. Finding in Antony a similar power when he threatens to draw tears from hardened soldiers, Enobarbus begs his leader that he "Transform us not to women" (4.2.36). The transforming powers are like "enchanting" (1.2.132). There are sinister implications in that word; Cleopatra can be thought of as the black magician who would steal men from their true selves. Indeed, Pompey prays that Cleopatra's "witchcraft" will join with her beauty in ensnaring Antony and thereby render him helpless as a military leader (2.1.22–23). Enobarbus speaks of the "odd tricks which sorrow shoots / Out of the mind" (4.2.14–15) and thus negatively joins emotionalism and fancy. Yet this would-be rationalist will die of a broken heart, the result of his own violation of love.

One critic sees Antony developing a "poetic sensitivity"[5] like that of his mistress when he too speaks of death in pleasurable, sexual terms, calling it a "lover's bed" to which he as a "bridegroom" hastens (4.14.99–101). Yet we must also admit that this sensitivity demands an abdication of responsibility, and a loss of empire. On the negative side, then, the artist and the imagination are linked with what is a delusion, unbecomingly womanish, something dangerous. This same paradox also marked the Sonnets, where the poet is both artist and lover, stimulated and yet repulsed by his passion for a dark lady. He is alternatively confident that his verse will immortalize his love for the young man and yet cynical that his tongue-tied Muse will produce only a counterfeit art falling far short of its subject. If Shakespeare views love impartially, perhaps he may be equally impartial in viewing that imagination and actor's skill that distinguish Cleopatra no less than her patent sexuality.

To some degree, then, every aspect of Cleopatra's imagination is ironic. Robert Ornstein points out how it functions best in the remembrance of past events and how dormant it tends to be in the present.[6] Cleopatra's finest poetry, indeed, springs from memories of earlier affairs or from the sight of Antony dead before her; when the lovers are together and healthy they are more likely to quarrel and bicker. Even the most ardent admirers among the critics cannot overlook this fact. Moreover, the finest expression of their love in the play occurs as death approaches. Despite Cleopatra's wish to join Antony where souls couch on flowers, the basic stimulus and metaphor for love here is the very agent that separates and destroys the lovers. Conversely, Cleopatra's visions into the future are no less qualified. Diomedes speaks of the "prophesying fear" that drives the queen to lock herself in a monument (4.14.120), and Cleopatra shudders to see "In Fulvia's death" a grim portent of her own thankless end (1.3.64–65).

Perhaps this paradoxical attitude toward the poetic power is epitomized in her own line immediately following Iras's death: "Have I the aspic in my lips?" (5.2.296). There have been many references earlier in the play to the organ of speech: "mouth-made vows, / Which break themselves in swearing" (1.3.30–31), "wan'd lips" (2.1.21), gold melted and poured down ill-uttering throats (2.5.34–35), women who are "shrill-tongu'd" or "Dull of tongue" (3.3.15, 19), kisses laid upon lips (4.15.20–21). Like Yorick's skull the asp is the death symbol; yet the asp merges with Cleopatra's "lips," the very means by which her alchemic poetry was conveyed. And though she manages to metamorphose the asp into an Antony and their child, it also remains the agent that will literally stop her voice.

Yet once we have made such qualifications of Cleopatra's imagination, we must still admit that there is nothing comparable to her in Rome. This is not meant to place Rome and what is said or thought there at completely opposite ends from the poetry of Egypt. There is, in fact, a speech describing the entrance that should have been Octavia's that may put in a proper perspective the aesthetic dimensions of the two worlds:

> The wife of Antony
> Should have an army for an usher, and
> The neighs of horse to tell of her approach
> Long ere she did appear; the trees by th' way
> Should have borne men, and expectation fainted,
> Longing for what it had not; nay, the dust
> Should have ascended to the roof of heaven,
> Rais'd by your populous troops.
>
> (3.6.43–50)

This is not poetry for a Cleopatra, but it still has a special majestry, despite the irony of the occasion. Though not brilliantly erotic like the description of Cleopatra's barge, Octavius's speech is somehow triumphant and respectful. Cleopatra's messenger may have dismissed Octavia as "a statue [rather] than a breather" (3.3.24), but then a statue has a permanence and a loveliness to which the queen cannot lay claim.

However, it is fair to say that the Romans are somewhat deficient in the Egyptian gifts of imagination and acting. Octavia is reported to be of a "cold, and still conversation" (2.6.131), and even at moments of great emotion, as when she must part with a brother and a husband, there is a division between her "tongue" and her "heart" (3.2.47–50). As opposed to Cleopatra, who is nothing if not passionate, the Romans cultivate the art of separating "speech" from "passion" (2.2.12–13). And if wine is one stimulus for imaginative speech, as it is for the queen, Octavius himself wisely limits his drinking aboard Pompey's galley. The Roman way of talking is more given to "thought" (1.2.87), "judgment" (2.2.55), and "oath" (87)—words associated with reason and a sense of responsibility. In Egypt one takes pleasure in responding to what is immediate and sensuous, but in Rome, Antony is given to "a studied, not a present thought" (2.2.140). He later describes himself as "well studied" to express his debt to Pompey (2.6.48).

Still, if Rome is a world of solid achievement, something sure and masculine as opposed to something illusory and feminine, it is also an often graceless, unimaginative world. At the meeting between Antony and Octavius in Lepidus's house the conversation in the first half of the scene is formal, tensely polite, and, in that discussion about an expedient marriage, repulsively businesslike. Traversi's word for this Roman conversation is "witless,"[7] and in a very perceptive essay Michael Lloyd goes one step further, arguing that the Roman tongue is one "not merely of . . . self seeking but of . . . insensitiveness and incomprehension."[8] However, once the triumvirs depart, Enobarbus describes Cleopatra's barge and her first meeting with Antony in a speech that is surely the finest long piece of poetry in the play. The paradox of the situation mirrors that of the play's general aesthetic statement, for in Enobarbus's speech we have exquisite poetry spoken by a Roman, concerning a past rather than a present event, and all delivered by a soldier who has known but also condemns the splendors of Egypt.

If Cleopatra's remembrances and visions of the future remove or transform her from a sordid present reality, Rome is itself caught *in* time and has become, like its leader, "Fortune's knave" (5.2.3) and "Vassal" (29). And yet we may also think of Cleopatra as the victim of her own escapism, her role itself as a mere delusion. However degenerate and unimaginative, Rome represents the one hope for the future, Octavius himself the master bringing in a "time of universal peace" (4.6.5).

Shakespeare thus includes a great number of responses, not just toward art, Cleopatra, and the imagination, or love and politics, but toward theater generally. Words like "play," "act," "scene," and "stage" are alternately good or bad, fluctuating throughout the play with an array of meanings. The two dead lovers, however despicable, are in Octavius's view worth a "solemn show." They will receive a pageant comparable in dignity to that Fortinbras would offer Hamlet (5.2.367). But to "be stag'd to th' show" can also be a derogatory phrase when Enobarbus describes Antony's desperate stratagem to engage Octavius in a single duel (3.13.30–31).

The theater becomes truly dramatic when it arouses a variety of responses from its spectators, a variety richer than we could afford to have in the real world. The play is neutral not because it fails to present a viewpoint, or presents only hazy viewpoints, but rather because it presents sharply and brilliantly many viewpoints. All are confined in a work of art finite and unchanging in a way that life cannot be. Adapting the words of Octavius for our purposes here, things "left unshown" are "often left unlov'd," unappreciated by the audience (3.6.52–53). In the theater, one's "chronicle" (3.13.175) is earned not by the sword but by the playwright's pen. On stage, Antony, no less than Cleopatra, is large and significant in a way that echoes but ultimately does not parallel that historical figure who, when he died, really died. Even as it allows for an extraordinary variety of responses to the lovers,[9] the play itself offers extremes in the celebration and condemnation of art and the imagination—the very process that calls *Antony and Cleopatra* into being.

This road from *Hamlet* to *Antony and Cleopatra*, from death as a merciful end for the prince's fatal split between the theater and reality to death as an opportunity for Cleopatra to display her imaginative (albeit illusory) powers, is likely to leave one breathless. In this sense *The Tempest* allows us to catch our breath as it reviews the various dimensions of Shakespeare's aesthetic metaphor. A valediction of sorts, it also points our way out of the theater.

8

The Tempest: Release from the Theater

*T*he *Tempest* may represent not some new departure in Shakespeare's vision as a playwright but rather the clearest statement about the various dimensions of the aesthetic metaphor treated in this study. It comments most directly on the issue of our release from the theater, just as the first play, *The Shrew,* concerned our induction. But before turning to this question of our release, *The Tempest* is examined in terms of the seven general concerns defining the earlier chapters of this study. These were: the transformation of men into spectators and actors *(The Taming of the Shrew),* the relationship between language and speaker or actor *(Love's Labour's Lost),* the powers of the imagination *(A Midsummer Night's Dream),* the perversion of that imagination *(Othello),* the artist as controlling figure *(As You Like It* and *Measure for Measure),* the theatrical view of existence *(Hamlet),* and the divided response toward that vision *(Antony and Cleopatra).*

-i-

If that storm at sea is some sort of prelude or induction to the play proper, then *The Tempest* opens with an audience of one, Miranda in attendance for her father's recounting of events prior to the conspirators' landing. In-

192

deed, for some directors, the play opens with a theatrical failure. The question is: What to do with Miranda as she listens to Prospero's interminably long story of his life as Duke and subsequent overthrow? Whereas Sly wakes to a play, Miranda, after valiant efforts to remain conscious, and prodded by her father to do so, finally falls asleep. Does her falling asleep suggest that Prospero is a boring old man? Or is the action to be expected since Miranda is of that shallow younger generation? In this latter view Miranda is an inhabitant of a brave new world possible only because wiser individuals such as Prospero are bent on converting a corrupt past into a more honest and stable present. If his story bores her, it itself is not boring but a necessary account of a past that must be redeemed by present action on the magician's part. Prospero seems not disturbed but rather resigned and humane when he addresses his sleeping daughter: " 'tis a good dullness, / And give it way. I know thou canst not choose" (1.2.185–86).

Still, while Miranda is awake, Prospero seems particularly aware of her role as spectator of that earlier play tracing his decline and early life on the island. The play we observe is its sequel: "The hour's now come; / The very minute bids thee ope thine ear. / Obey, and be attentive" (36–38). As so often in this play words have both a thematic and a theatrical meaning. Here "hour" refers to the propitious landing of Prospero's enemies. Yet it is the very hour in which the actual play we observe begins. This hour of beginning so favorable for us is unfavorable for the characters caught in the mirror world of the drama. Earlier in the opening scene the Boatswain speaks of the "mischance of the hour" (27–28); their apparent loss is our gain.

Like *A Midsummer Night's Dream* or *Hamlet* or *Love's Labour's Lost*, *The Tempest* is replete with audiences. Besides the situation in the second scene, we observe the conspirators watching a dumb show, and later the young couple, attended by Prospero as presentor, watching a masque. Once the corrupt characters move toward some sort of salvation, they are allowed to watch the idyllic scene of lovers playing chess. We ourselves are part of the metaphor, an ever-present and silent audience watching this display of stage audiences.

The lowly audience of conspirators must be refined, however, before they can observe the blissful scene where human tensions are reduced to a playful lovers' spat over chess:

> *Miranda.* Sweet lord, you play me false.
> *Ferdinand.* No, my dearest love.
>   I would not for the world.
> *Miranda.* Yes, for a score of kingdoms you should wrangle,
>   And I would call it fair play.
>
> (5.1.172–75)

Earlier, when the conspirators are far from being reformed, the performance must be more direct. As they witness Prospero's dumb show (3.3.17–39), the conspirators momentarily forget their own sordid business and are inspired with something of a new faith. Sebastian is willing to believe in unicorns and in the phoenix; Antonio confesses that he will now trust in "what does else want credit"; and Alonzo cannot marvel enough at "Such shapes, such gesture, and such sound, expressing . . . a kind / Of excellent dumb discourse." Gonzalo knows that in Naples this miracle they witness might not be believed. The contrast between an unworthy audience astonished by the spectacle and its silent participants is particularly important. The "monstrous" shapes in the dumb show attest the artist's power of transformation for they have "manners . . . more gentle, kind" than those of the "human generation" watching them.

For purer individuals, such as Ferdinand, theatrical

spectacle is more a means of seduction than of moral reformation. Addicted to the splendid vision afforded by art, he seems to anticipate the Puritans' complaint that plays rob one of any desire to reenter life. Prospero's "fancies" would keep him in the "magic globe": "Let me live here ever; / So rare a wond'red father and a wise / Makes this place Paradise" (4.1.122–24).

No less pervasive is the sense of the conversion of men into actors. But in the context of *The Shrew* that conversion is even more splendid. There we saw a would-be shrew turned into a model wife, courtiers into Sly's attendants, or even visiting actors pressed unaware into service in the illusion cast over Sly. Here we have the extraordinary moment when supernatural deities or "spirits" (149) become "*certain* Reapers, *properly habited*." Prospero has gone not to the secular but the supernatural world for his players, changing them into a lower-class antithesis of their real selves, and from immortals to temporary mortals. This is surely a "translation," as Bottom or Sly would have it, of an extraordinary order.

Petruchio's transformation of Kate pales beside Prospero's conversion of bad men into good. Caliban is so humiliated that he vows to "be wise hereafter, / And seek for grace" (5.1.294–95). Once playing something beside their better selves, the conspirators now double back and promise to reform. His magic "charms . . . o'erthrown," Prospero becomes Burbage in his own person, asking for approval from the audience.

Sly's disappearance may raise serious questions about his reality, or our own relation to the play. But the epilogue here raises no such question at all. In its simple poetry it makes a literal statement about the situation. Burbage is no longer Prospero but himself, a man. The function of the play just past has been to please, possibly to instruct. The actors will be disconsolate if their efforts are not appreciated.

-ii-

The issue of language, which is so central to *Love's Labour's Lost,* is no less important in *The Tempest.* It is Prospero who has brought words and their concomitant order to the island; he has taught Caliban the names of the sun and moon. Devoted to "bettering . . . [the] mind" (1.2.90) rather than gratifying the body, he is both a powerful white magician and a word giver, a man offering, in the face of savagery, the hope of civilization and civilized communication. Caliban is wise enough to know that without his books Prospero is "but a sot, as I am, nor hath not / One spirit to command" (3.2.101–2). Words represent power here, because they are both prerequisites to vision and a way of bringing that order which complements true power. The Epilogue itself suggests the ultimate reaches of good words, such as those of prayer which "pierces so that it assaults / Mercy itself and frees all faults" (17–18).

Again, words possess both thematic and theatrical meanings, for they are at once the badge of Prospero's superiority over Caliban and also the means by which form is given to Shakespeare's own vision. The magnificent mature poetry of the play is itself testimony to this achievement. Prospero's control of language is almost indistinguishable from Shakespeare's; we may have the sense here that the play is a final bravado performance on the playwright's part. With no clear single source, *The Tempest* seems entirely Shakespeare's effort; every part therefore reflects on his success or failure.

The verbal and the physical here seem to be opposed. Prospero has Caliban as his antithesis. And it is words expressed as "sweet thoughts" that Ferdinand knows "do even refresh [his] labors" (3.1.14). Indeed, the meaning of "communication" seems to expand here to include any sound that is conducive to harmony. Even silent visions are

said to "speak." We know from other plays about the
speaking power of silence or of wordless vision: Cordelia's
tears more eloquent than words, and the statue of Her-
mione that communicates with the witnesses even before
she descends from her pedestal and breaks into direct
speech. There is in *The Tempest* a tendency, similar to that
G. Wilson Knight finds in *Cymbeline*,[1] to circumvent the
verbal for nonverbal arts. Prospero needs "heavenly
music" (5.1.52) to quiet his mind. And it is the dumb show
that moves its spectators to amazement. With the appropriate speaker even inarticulate words or sounds can serve
this higher function. Caliban speaks of the isle as "full of
noises," "Sounds and sweet airs, that give delight and hurt
not," a "thousand twanging instruments / Which hum
about" his ears, and "voices" that would make one sleep
again (3.2.144–49). If he is below the eloquent communication of Prospero and his daughter, Caliban is still
strangely attuned to sounds offering a sensation of
paradise more directly than language itself could suggest.

   As a boy in the Episcopal Church I had no idea of what
exactly the Book of Common Prayer meant when it said
that Christ was the "Propitiation for our sins," nor could I
supply the proper translation for that moment when the
communicants speak of themselves as the "very members
incorporate in the mystical body of thy Son." But the
positioning of the words, and the sounds themselves,
which were so appropriate to the mood of the service,
served to convey the message. Beyond words or music, the
dumb show moves Alonzo to ask: "What harmony is this?"
(3.3.18). Prospero, in fact, bids the lovers to stop talking as
they witness the masque: "No tongue! All eyes! Be silent"
(4.1.59).

   According to the early drafts of his poetry, Shelley first
wrote out the rhythms in form of musical notation and
only later supplied the actual words.[2] Shelley was quite the
opposite of Jonson who in *Timber* advises the young poet

first to write out his thoughts in prose and then to convert those thoughts into poetry.[3] *The Tempest* suggests a non-verbal harmony in language as the ultimate metaphor for the comic harmony sustained by Prospero's vision. If *Love's Labour's Lost* draws a distinction between a profound and a shallow use of language, *The Tempest* seems to ask that we grasp not just the direct meaning but the larger and yet more subtle, harmonious dimension of language itself. That harmony is our way of moving toward civilization, order, and vision.

That finer language and its harmony can be easily perverted. Ariel tells how he startled the conspirators with his tabor so that they pricked their ears "like unbacked colts, / Advanced their eyelids, lifted up their noses / As they smelt music." Their ears were so "charm'd" that they followed Prospero's spirit "calf-like" through "Tooth'd briers, sharp furzes, pricking [gorse] and thorns" (4.1.175–80). The confusion of the senses here may recall Bottom's own as he emerges from his night in the forest. Caliban, Stephano, and Trinculo are similarly driven out by the *"noise of hunters,"* with the *"divers Spirits, in the shape of dogs and hounds"* (4.1.255). Prospero and Ariel bellow at them like hunters giving commands to their dogs. Two of the animals mentioned, Fury and Tyrant, might suggest the end product when words are replaced by mere noise. Music of a low order, the "tune of our catch, played by the picture of Nobody" (3.2.135–36), is set against Prospero's own exquisite music. The movement from words to sounds to silence is thus double-edged, taking us to heaven or to hell. The possibilities include the upper refinements of civilization and comic synthesis, as well as humiliation and barbarism.

-iii-

Perhaps the play most called to mind by *The Tempest* is *A Midsummer Night's Dream,* for the latter play is also concerned with the imagination, the dimensions of the artist's vision, and that vision's relation to reality. In exile, Prospero has actually undergone an enlargement of vision. As Duke of Milan he was too bookish; by his own confession his "library / Was dukedom large enough" (1.2.109–10).

There is a suggestion in the play that his present condition, indeed the magic island itself, has issued out of a dream. Miranda confesses that her past life is "far off, / And rather like a dream" (1.2.44–45). Prospero recounts his past, but for us as audience that past exists only as words spoken to a daughter who falls asleep in the middle of such revelations. Caliban himself would reverse the movement from consciousness to unconsciousness; confronted by an extraordinary vision in which the clouds seemed to open and show forth riches, he desires upon waking only "to dream again" (3.2.150–52).

The larger reality represented by the forest in *A Midsummer Night's Dream* is dismissed by Theseus as a dream or mere fiction. With no one on stage up to the challenge, this judgment remains true for him. In *The Tempest* is the island some ideal commonwealth, a dream, or a reality? Is the island meant to be no more or no less a dream than Milan or the world encompassing the stage? The move from the sinking ship to the island seems dreamlike to the Boatswain: "On a trice, so please you, / Even in a dream, were we divided from them / And were brought moping hither" (5.1.238–40). In the midst of this one-day dream, this *play*, characters are continually falling asleep. Besides Miranda in scene 2, the mariners are cast into a deep trance by Prospero's magic. In Act 2 *"All sleep except Alon., Seb., and Ant."* (2.1.190). Prospero passes an even more general indictment over mankind in his remark that "We are such stuff / As dreams are made on, and our little life / Is rounded with a sleep" (4.1.156–58).

Hamlet's theatrical metaphor leads him to the rejection of this world. But whereas Prospero's sense of the world's stage or of life as a dream may deny him the thoughtless optimism of a Miranda, it still encourages him to make reforms. And with the world so reformed, he rejoins human society. If the movement through his art is from dream to a finer reality, or from one dream to a finer one, there is still progress. The play's resolution proves the reformative powers of the imagination. Like his daughter, Prospero suffers with those who suffer. At the end man emerges as nobler than he seemed or even than he was at first.

This expansive imagination, however, is parodied by the limited vision of the conspirators. If Ariel soars literally and figuratively, the direction of the conspirators' minds seems to be anticipated in the Boatswain's cry: "Shall we give o'er and drown? Have you a mind to sink" (1.1.41–42). If true imagination emerges out of sleep and dreams, Antonio appropriately stays awake while the others sleep. For him to be "waking" means to come to one's senses, to get on with the practical, hardly imaginative business of usurpation (2.1.217). "Waking" here is equated with political advancement, not with the artistic informing of a vision. The imaginative sleep of the artist is reversed in their case, and when Ariel casts them into a trance, the measure is protective, not procreative. The "state" that would emerge from their staying awake is a political state illegally won, not the ideal commonwealth envisioned by old Gonzalo.

The conspirators' imagination contrasts with Miranda's, for with her love of mankind, however indiscriminate, she can anticipate events in the play: "Would I might / But ever see that man!" (1.2.168–69). The first important word she uses is "art" (1.2.1), and, characteristically, she refers here to the art of her father. She uses the word itself in a plea to aid stricken sailors, to "allay" the "wild waters" that she suspects have been conjured up by Prospero.

The powers of the playwright are those of transformation from potential tragedy to comedy, from limited vision to an expanded one, from a dull or fatal reality to one finer and more symbolic. Surely the play contains one of the finest set descriptions of art's power in Ariel's lovely song "Full fathom five thy father lies" (1.2.396–402). The subject here is that alchemic force which can transform dead bones into coral, eyes into pearls, remaking a thing common and penetrable, such as the body, into something "rich and strange." The song is ironic, of course, since Ferdinand's father is alive. The son himself is ignorant of this fact. But this ability to transform, as illustrated by Ariel, perhaps comments on Prospero's own power. Whereas Cleopatra changes asps into lovers and babies, something deadly into something procreative, Ariel suggests that with art we can metamorphose something so unpromising as a body sunk at sea into something of grandeur.

In its highest form art celebrates life; the artist *is* a lover. In this sense the playwright is a creator taking pleasure in giving multiple births.

A colleague of mine holds that the director in the cinema is just such a lover: the movement of his camera corresponds to the eye and hands of one in the act of lovemaking.[4] One critic comments that even tragedy, the epitome of dramatic art, is not about death but is, instead, "a hymn to life." It is the artist's way of saying that the universe is not totally absurd, not so formless or meaningless as to be unworthy of being given the fictive form of the drama.[5] Miranda, who is not all-knowing, seems to celebrate life at the expense of the imagination when she says, "Nor can imagination form a shape, / Besides yourself, to like of" (3.1.56–57). But like Perdita of *The Winter's Tale*, who delivers a similarly misguided attack on art, Miranda herself is the product of art, of Shakespeare's vision. The same holds true for her Ferdinand, indeed, for the very line she utters. She cannot be "original," though Shakespeare seems incapable of being anything but so.

-iv-

None of the conspirators has the malignancy of an Iago. But though they are less complex as villains and under better control, like Iago the conspirators do stand as perversions or, at very least, parodies of the artist. For while they are on stage, the very concepts of art, the theater, and the imagination are bandied about in a sort of ugly counterpoint to those scenes involving Prospero and Ariel. The lovely poetry of Prospero's invocation, "Ye elves of hills" (5.1.33–57) and the songs of Ariel are twisted into the words that old Gonzalo would "cram" into Antonio's "ears against / The stomach of [his] sense" (2.1.105–6). And for the conspirators the word "prologue" signifies only the first step taken toward a foul purpose (253). This parody of art and language is even more elemental in the scenes involving the low-comedy characters Trinculo and Stephano. In place of Prospero's book of magic they substitute a bottle of "celestial liquor," that book on which Caliban swears to be a "true subject" (2.2.121–30). The instrument of heavenly music itself is sullied in Antonio's sarcastic line "His word is more than the miraculous harp" (2.1.86). And a mere mistake of Tunis for Carthage provokes his ugly witticism that Gonzalo has with his "word" rebuilt Carthage, a feat greater than the harp of Amphion, which only razed the walls of Thebes. The usurper himself is seen as a spurious artist, one who "new created," "chang'd," or "new formed" men (1.2.81–83) in the heinous sense that he converted Prospero's loyal subjects from friends to enemies. Clearly these were transformation for a selfish rather than a noble purpose.

Even Prospero himself is not immune to this destructive power of art. He knows that, if he wishes, he can punish Ariel cruelly: "If thou more murmur'st, I will rend an oak / And peg thee in his knotty entrails till / Thou hast howl'd away twelve winters" (1.2.294–96). But Prospero's potential for violence is itself transformed; he becomes a white magician rather than a black one, an Oberon instead of an Iago or a Richard III. This potential remains in others, however. If released, Caliban would use his power not to transform men already living but rather to stamp his own selfish kind on the island. If not checked, he would have "peopl'd else / This isle with Calibans" (1.2.305–51). Seeing that parody of creation in which Trinculo and Caliban, sharing the same garment, appear like some deformed creature, Stephano wonders if this aberration of nature can itself "vent Trinculos" (2.2.111). A parody of creation when he wears an ass's head, Bottom pales besides the bestiality suggested by these low-comedy characters. Thus, besides the nobler play there exists a "foul play" (1.2.62) that must be superseded.

-v-

The nobler play is managed by Prospero; he finds ancestors in Rosalind of *As You Like It* and the Duke of *Measure for Measure,* though ultimately he goes far beyond them in his power. Prospero's enemy Caliban knows best the degree of his magic, for his "art is of such power / It would control my dam's god, Setebos, / And make a vassal of him" (1.2.372–74). Though an allegorical reading touches at only one level of this play, Caliban's revolt from Prospero may bear analogies to man's own fall. In any case, Prospero's command by means of his "art" (1.2.1) is clearly beyond that of his former civil authority as Duke of Milan.

That present authority is not omnipotent; Anne Barton points out some events that exist independent of his art.[6] Prospero himself knows that he must also rely on a "bountiful Fortune" and an "auspicious star" (1.2.178–82) to effect his plans. It was by "Providence divine" (1.2.159) that he was rescued from what would otherwise have been sure death at sea.

Yet his authority is surely that of a controlling figure who must stand as surrogate for the playwright himself. His words alone possess this power; Miranda confesses that "The strangeness of your story put / Heaviness in me" (1.2.306–7). Through his angel Ariel Prospero literally controls everything, from the smallest to the largest, from the "still-closing waters" to "One dowle that's in [Ariel's] plume" (3.3.64–65).

Like Rosalind and Duke Vincentio, he is part of the story; however godlike, Shakespeare's controllers all have feet of clay. Still, Prospero is greater than they; the stakes seem larger here, or more immediate. Vincentio has the advantage of disguise over Angelo, and when he seems to falter, as when Barnadine refuses to give up his head for Claudio, lucky accidents happen. In *As You Like It,* Rosalind is so clearly superior to the others that we cannot really imagine a less than comic outcome. Prospero's own disguise includes invisibility and is more complex. His purpose in controlling the intruders is itself more serious. Even nature responds to Prospero's campaign; "The powers delaying, not forgetting, have / Incens'd the seas and shores, yea, all the creatures" against the peace of the conspirators (3.3.73–75). Prospero is able to move others to a state bordering on "ecstasy" (3.3.108). No less powerful than Oberon, he is only human. Human like Rosalind and the Duke, Prospero is also supernatural in his authority on the island. The most powerful controlling figure among many in the plays, he is also the most complex.

-vi-

Prospero's theatrical perspective is even more literal than Hamlet's. If the tragic hero is an interim scriptwriter, producer, actor, and presenter, the magician is more consistently all of these. More than just dominating the play as in *Hamlet*, the theatrical metaphor here *is* the play. Those who enter Prospero's world enter a world of stage magic, of illusions; a fictive world like the pageant staged for the lovers, it will itself fade and vanish.

Real in that it influences the lives of the spectators or the audience coming to the island, Prospero's world also dissolves once the playwright-director's purpose is fulfilled. Joyce talks about this transitory nature of the theater in his *Portrait of the Artist As a Young Man,* when Dedalus comments on the condition of the stage world during and after a college performance:

> A few moments after he found himself on the stage amid the garish gas and the dim scenery, acting before the innumerable faces of the void. It surprised him to see that the play which he had known at rehearsals for a disjointed lifeless thing had suddenly assumed a life of its own. It seemed now to play itself, he and his fellow actors aiding it with their parts. When the curtain fell on the last scene he heard the void filled with applause and, through a rift in the side scene, saw the simple body which before he had acted magically deformed, the void of faces breaking at all points and falling asunder into busy groups.[7]

In Shakespeare's play the metaphor becomes literal. Except for the opening scene controlled by (Shakespeare's) providence, *The Tempest* is in essence a play-within-a-play staged by Prospero. Prospero identifies the time in act 1, scene 2 as "At least two glasses" (239), that is, as two o'clock; his larger play about to unfold will take two hours, the approximate traffic of the stage noted in *Romeo and Juliet*. Rather than merely suspecting that his world is theatrical, Prospero knows this as a matter of course: all that happens is a "vanity" of his art (4.1.41). He must work to effect his vision, though in a sense he already knows the ending. When Alonso marvels at the dumb show, which is only a small part of Prospero's larger play, the magician in an aside wisely counsels the viewers to "Praise in departing" (3.3.40), that is, to save their praise for the end.

-vii-

And yet all this must perish. Bedimming the noontide sun, calling forth mutinous winds, setting war between the green sea and the azured vault, shaking the promontory, opening graves (5.1.40–50)—this grand review of Prospero's achievements may suggest Shakespeare's own achievement with the wars of the history plays, the return of the ghost as in *Hamlet,* the sheer intensity and geographical size of plays like *King Lear* and *Antony and Cleopatra*. Still, all of this the magician abjures (51); the fictive world dissolves upon the completion of his vision. Rather than resting on one or two successes, playwrights of Shakespeare's level "abandon" a play the moment it is finished, only to begin the next. Yet each play is reborn and reworked in the next. In this way *The Tempest* includes and goes beyond *A Midsummer Night's Dream; The Winter's Tale* carries the seemingly adulterous situation of *Othello* beyond tragedy to comic reunion; *Antony and Cleopatra* stands as a mature revisiting of the youthful love celebrated earlier in *Romeo and Juliet*. And once this larger vision has been consummated, the theater has served its purpose. As Shakespeare himself did, the playwright can return home. Shakespeare goes contented to Stratford, as Alfred Harbage has so eloquently said, because his audience had made him more than he would have been had he stayed there, and because he had elevated them by his high regard for the theater and its spectators.[8]

Yet, as in *Antony and Cleopatra,* this celebration of art must coexist with a skeptical, or at least more practical view of the craft. Prospero can deride his work as mere "vanity" (4.1.41), and in that speech where he discusses his revels (4.1.147–63), the wedding masque is passed off as a deceptive illusion which is like some "baseless fabric," an "insubstantial pageant" as uncertain and short-lived as life itself. Prospero himself is merely "such stuff / As dreams are made on." His magic is at last nothing but a "charm" that "dissolves apace" (5.1.64–65). Whatever his art's mystical directions, Prospero also talks of his work as "labours" (4.1.265), his magic as "rough magic" (5.1.50), and his play as a "project" (Epi., 12). In his closing remarks he confesses that his justification, as well as his own peace of mind, depends on the audience and its willingness to give approval to his art, whose aim stated simply and modestly "was to please" (13).

Yet even his "rejection" of his art must be qualified. For the moment we see a preference for nature over art, or think of Milan as representing the reality of Stratford and the island as the art world of Shakespeare's own Globe, we must acknowledge that Milan is only referred to in the play and therefore has, in a sense, even less claim to reality than the island. Moreover, if the play *is* a testament to life or conveys Shakespeare's ultimate rejection of the theater and its illusions, the fact that we are moved to make this sort of conclusion only recognizes the power of art which has so encouraged us. Even to see the play, along with the other three romances, as blurring the distinction between art and reality is perhaps to obscure the highly conscious artistry that allows for such philosophic readings. Surely the Globe audience did not consider what was happening on stage as a perfect correspondence with their own reality. They knew it was all a stage illusion, even though that illusion may have pointed to the uncertainty and dream-like state of life outside the theater.

-viii-

As suggested in the opening of this chapter, *The Tempest* seems to consider one issue more thoroughly than any of the plays previously discussed. This is the sense of release, the process by which we as an audience, having shared in the playwright's vision, are satisfied and then "returned" to our own reality. In this regard *The Tempest* complements *The Shrew,* whose chapter was entitled "Induction to the Theater."

The final act of *The Tempest,* appropriately, has as its first line Prospero's observation that his "project gather[s] to a head." On top of the play, he himself reminds us that his vision is nearing its culmination. The play proper has given us the experience of art issuing from sleep and dreams, and then taking form. That form itself has been threatened and then perfected, and now is about to be dissolved. Thematically, we have moved from a near-fatal storm, to near-fatal plotting, to the tension from the di-vided hierarchy of characters, to symbolic punishments, to the wished-for transformation of bad men into men promising something more than dissension and limited vision. This movement seems to be mirrored comically in the courtship of Ferdinand and Miranda; the wedding itself is the wished-for end, but also an end that must grow from the play, being sought by the characters rather than being imposed on them. Prospero wisely comments that he ordered labors and restraints on the young couple "lest the light winning / Make the prize light" (1.2.450–52). If the play were only a statement, and not an experience, we could bypass the theater and be handed a slip of paper inscribed with the moral of the drama. But theme is inseparable from structure; aesthetics includes observations not just on the end of art but on the process itself. How one gets there is part of the meaning in the journey's end.

Hence, after that necessary journey, there are numerous references to the notion of release, of ending. Again, that ending is defined by the time spent when imprisoned, whether in Shakespeare's power or Prospero's. Early in the play Ferdinand acknowledges that his spirits "as in a dream are all bound up" (1.2.486). The notion of release for the characters and for us is also anticipated in the masque, where the goddess Iris bids Ceres to leave her labors, her fields, forests and groves, and "Here on this grass plot, in this very place, / To come and sport" (4.1.73–74). Even Cupid can abandon his labors, for he "has broke his arrows, / Swears he will shoot no more, but play with sparrows / And be a boy right out" (4.1.99–101).

All the characters undergo some sort of release: Ariel from his semihuman form and from servitude to Prospero; Prospero from his supernatural role as controller; Ferdinand from his labors as woodcarrier; Miranda, though still innocent, from her ignorance of man and from the single-blessedness of her unmarried state; the conspirators from their worser selves; and Caliban from a half-beast. The movement, in effect, is downward for the supernatural characters, laterally for the young, and upward for those who have fallen too far. One thinks of a parallel movement in *The Merchant of Venice*, where characters too light and idealistic, such as Antonio and Bassanio, must be tested, humiliated, and then brought down from their lofty status. In his final scene, Shylock himself is given the chance for some upward ethical, if not financial, mobility, when he is asked by Portia to rejoin the human community.

The importance of magic, illusion, is diminished by Prospero's vow to break his staff and drown his book;

bestiality and human cruelty are mitigated. In the theater
itself the actors will be released, *discased* (5.1.85) from their
labors. We also will soon be on our way; the spell broken,
we are left to fend with that reality for which release means
not the end of a performance but of life itself. In this sense
the play is wide-ranging not just in its aesthetic commentary, but in its approach to existence itself. We are "born"
and then "die" as spectators; Shakespeare's own creation
and his actors themselves experience a similar cycle of
induction, existence, and release.

-ix-

The aesthetic commentary in *The Tempest* falls somewhere between the celebration of art such as that found
in *A Midsummer Night's Dream* and that denunciation of
acting and playwriting which Barton so carefully docu-
ments in the tragedies and dark comedies.[9] Its statement is
more inclusive in that it is more paradoxical; Prospero
represents both a semidivine power and a potential charlatan who, once he has had his vision, wisely renounces this
dangerous magic. Perhaps feeling in himself the same
desires and weaknesses that are so noticeable in his
enemies, knowing that he is ultimately "One of their kind,"
he breaks his staff. Having achieved by white magic a goal
normally beyond human capacity, Prospero puts aside
supernatural aid and, returning to the business of governing, proposes to deal with human problems as just
another human.

If, as some have suggested, the play *is* autobiographi-
cal,[10] perhaps its importance lies elsewhere than in the
possibility that it represents Shakespeare's farewell to the
London stage or his final thoughts about his profession.
Rather, *The Tempest* may comment not so much on the
playwright's life as on that general attitude toward his art
and his work. That healthy attitude gave him a balance

between the extremes of those practical, hack playwrights, whose work shows labor but not love, and the cloying aesthete, whose plays, though pleasing to a coterie, could not stand up to the more rigorous demands of both the Renaissance audience and time itself. If we can question to what extent *The Tempest* is valedictory, we may perhaps with more profit speculate to what extent it, as well as all of his plays, offers us the fullest flowering not only of the grand themes we associate with Shakespeare but also of those aesthetic principles that are the basis of his art.[11] For Shakespeare metaphors born of the theater serve the outside reality as window and the reality of his stage as mirror.

Afterword on Velázquez's
Las Meninas

Some time ago my colleague Alistair Duckworth volunteered to read the manuscript of this book. As always, I was the beneficiary of both his good judgment and his taste. Later, after that manuscript had been accepted for publication, I asked if he would choose an appropriate painting for the book jacket and frontispiece. This request was, ultimately, a matter of sentiment with me, and after I overrode Alistair's initial reluctance to assume a role he thought should be the author's own pleasure, he replied with a brief note: "What about Velázquez's *Las Meninas?*—just a suggestion, mind you." Surely, his was a splendid "suggestion."

Las Meninas is the perfect example of metadrama or, rather, meta-art, a moment, rare for Velázquez, when the artist, like Shakespeare in his theater, turns to himself and to his craft. The setting of the painting itself underscores this point: the main chamber of the apartment in the Royal Palace that Prince Baltasar Carlos had occupied until his death in 1646 and that was subsequently transformed into "the Court's painter's workshop," occupied first by Mazo (of whose forty paintings decorating the chamber only five were originals, the rest copies of Rubens and other Flemish painters), later by Velázquez until his death in 1660, and then by Luca Giordano who, posing before the masterpiece left behind by Velázquez, pronounced *Las Meninas* "the theology of Painting."[1]

Velázquez himself is to the left of the painting, at his easel. In the center is the infanta Margarita (born July 12, 1651), the only child of Philip IV of Spain and his second wife, Queen Mariana. Surrounding the infanta are two "meninas"—from the Portuguese "meninha" (young girl)—or maids of honor, Doña Isabel de Velasco and Doña María Sarmiento, the latter offering her mistress a drink of water from a "bucaro," or reddish earthen vessel. To the right foreground are a dwarf, Mari-Bárbola, and a midget, Nicholás de Pertusato, the latter poking with his foot at a mastiff on the floor. Halfway back and to the right are Doña Marcela de Ulloa, attendant to the ladies-in-waiting, and an anonymous male escort to the ladies. At the rear the palace marshall to the queen, Don José Nieto Velázquez, stands halfway up the steps, framed by light emanating from a doorway. Perhaps most intriguing is the mirror to the right of the painter, for reflected there, as they stand off-canvas, are the king and queen, half-length, a red curtain over their heads.

The painting itself shows the same "productive confusion" between art and life, illusion and reality, the same balance between art as a self-enclosed mirror world and, at the same time, as a window to the reality outside art's confines that is the subject of my book. Is Velázquez here an artist or a participant? A spectator or an actor? Scholars have speculated that he is painting the very scene we ourselves see, or that he had originally planned to paint only the royal couple but then, finding the chance arrangements of the infanta and her attendants more interesting, chose instead a group portrait, almost (but not quite) excluding the father and mother. A less likely suggestion is that he is painting the group through the mirror placed where the king had been sitting, though the perspective hardly seems to agree with this. The unseen canvas within the canvas must remain a mystery. Whatever its subject, the fact is that the artist looks upon the scene with the serenity of one in complete control.

And while the assemblage of artist, royalty, and attendants forms a clear unit somewhat unusual for a painter not given to such family portraits, each figure itself is highly individual, not only in terms of theme but also technique. The infanta, bathed in light coming from a window to the right, is the most conventional of the several figures, elongated by thin shadows and by what one critic calls "luminous strokes which make her hair weightless and shape her figure into a lucent image, the like of which the Master never painted again."[2] But the large, soft style of brushing used for the attendants and the midget and dwarf gives their figures at once a sense of movement and an effect of diffusion that are markedly different. The adults behind them are even less distinct, yet, paradoxically, more "natural" as they engage in conversation, seemingly oblivious to the young people or to the royalty just on the other side of the "fourth wall."

As one moves into the painting, toward the light coming from the rear door—that light itself stressing the indispensable ingredient for both the artist's coloring and form—human figures dissolve into the artificial stance of Don Nieto. The canvas itself is now overwhelmed by the room's insistent architectural symmetry, the sense of perspective afforded by the right-wall and back-wall paintings, the empty lamp hooks on the ceiling, and the squares in the back door. All of this, in turn, finds a parallel in the bare wooden horizontal and vertical lines of the painter's easel. If you will, as we move from the mastiff (a "natural" indifferent to the human drama and surely to the interpretation I am putting forth) to Don Nieto, and as the clearly defined human occupants are thinned out, the sense of conscious artifice is aggravated.

Except for that wonderful mirror! A third painting, in effect, it is an unusual touch for Velázquez, though he had used a portrait within a portrait in his 1618 *Christ in the House of Martha and Mary,* and much later in *The Tapestry Weavers* (about 1657–59). As a painting it pales beside the activity in the room, which one critic has called a "rounded vision" that avoids the "artificial elegancies of arrangement."[3] But when we think of the mirror as incorporating reality itself, a dimension ultimately outside art, then the mirror takes on a tremendous significance. As much as the painting includes—and its world spans the gamut from an animal to children to court figures to the artist-god himself—it stops short of reality. The eminence of the royal couple, on this occasion at least, is beyond art. The attention of almost everyone in the painting is directed to them, yet we viewers, standing like the royal couple on the other side of that stagelike fourth wall, cannot see them reproduced, except by a mechanical aid, with that mirror itself owing its existence to the painter's fancy. If he cannot include reality, and if the painting, like the mirror, is only a reproduction, the artist can at least give the *illusion* of reality. Like the world of Shakespeare's *A Midsummer Night's Dream,* Velázquez's seems large, "bursting with life," though we know it is at length only a lifeless illusion. The two doors of *Las Meninas,* therefore, suggest the range of art, from life itself, which insists on making its way into art, if only through a mirror, to the narrow door at the rear, incorporating the courtier in his theatrical pose. That second door, a conscious artifice, is correspondingly small, but it is also the opening for light, the life-source for both the painter and the creatures he paints, whether they exist in reality or on canvas.

Indeed, life or historical fact may have made its way into the painting. Legend has it that the red cross on Velázquez's doublet was added later, at Philip's command, when Velázquez became a knight of the Order of Santiago on November 28, 1659, less than a year before his death. In addition, the two large paintings on the back wall, albeit almost obscured, have been identified as Mazo's copies of Rubens's *Pallas and Arachne* and Jordaens's *Apollo and Marsyas.* Some critics have taken them as commentaries on *Las Meninas* itself, as symbolizing the "victory of divine art over human craftsmanship."[4] Perhaps this is stretching the issue. Still, I might point out that the source of the two paintings, Ovid's *Metamorphoses,* is itself a testament to the imagination, to the ability to transform. In my own commentary on *The Taming of the Shrew* I suggest a link between the references to Ovid in Shakespeare's early comedy and the larger issue of transformation, as the Lord converts Sly into an aristocrat and as Petruchio, with or without help from his subject, converts Kate from a shrew to a model wife. Years earlier Velázquez himself had painted *The Fable of Arachne* (1644–48).

Consider the easel itself: how dull it seems when juxtaposed with the human figures to the right. In a larger sense, the easel—art in potential—like the bare boards of the legitimate stage, contrasts with the finished product itself, even as the painting, however magnificent, gives way to the reality just outside the canvas proper. The painting at length is literally framed by its frame. And the legitimate stage, no matter how expansive its scenery or its language, no matter how much its stage is thrust upon the audience, is also framed by the larger room of the theater itself.

It is little wonder that the critics find in this late painting a curious combination of art and life, the artist himself aspiring to "immortalize man in the flesh, and to capture the poetry of the fleeting instance."[5] I translate this last parallelism as "the blending of art as mirror and as window." Shakespeare himself contends in the Sonnets that his art at once gives immortality to the young man, rescuing his essence from the devouring effects of time, even as it describes instances in time (Shakespeare's relations with the young man, the rival poet, and the dark mistress) that are, by definition, fleeting, albeit subjects for—let us drag out the sentimental phrase since Shakespeare can rescue it from banality—immortal poetry. When art turns to itself in this fashion, even as the theater turns to itself at the high level of a Shakespeare, the result is not aesthetic self-indulgence, not *ars pro gratia artis* (as the MGM motto would have it), but rather a profound comment on the interdependence of art and life. The canvas, the stage if you like, becomes both a metaphor for life and life itself. The microcosm/macrocosm duality is at once affirmed and productively blurred.

I believe that my colleague made an inspired, not to mention timely, choice in recommending *Las Meninas.*

Notes and Pertinent Sources

Preface: When the Theater Turns to Itself

1. The text used for Shakespeare is the New Cambridge edition, edited by William Allan Neilson and Charles Jarvis Hill (Cambridge, Mass.: Houghton Mifflin Company, 1942). For the most part I retain the editors' brackets when a quarto or folio reading was substituted in the basic text for a given play. On occasion I have used brackets when inserting a word or two so that a quotation would make more sense in the context of my own commentary.

I list in the notes themselves only those works directly cited in my text. This whole issue of Shakespeare's consciousness of his art has been a popular one among critics over the last two decades. But as I said in the Preface, I am not so much interested in Shakespeare's aesthetic commentary as a thing in itself as I am in using it as metaphor to approach the "world" of his plays. For me, aesthetics and thematics are not antithetical. And so the potential bibliography of relevant critical works is even larger than if I had confined myself to the playwright's thoughts about his art as art. I list, therefore, at the end of the notes for each chapter other works that were on my desk or in my mind at the time of writing, but which did not make their way into the text as direct citations. These lists are, to be sure, not impartial surveys but rather collections of "personal favorites."

Along with major studies of aesthetics, such as Lionel Abel's *Metatheatre* or Jackson Cope's more recent *The Theatre and the Dream*, some of the most impressive and meaningful commentary is to be found in the plays themselves. Surely the theater, at a very high level, is its own justification for being. This is as true for Renaissance playwrights as for those of our age. What Tamburlaine would do with language is at one with Marlowe's own purposes; and whatever its social bias, *The Knight of the Burning Pestle* talks about the relation of audience and actor in a way that anticipates Pirandello. Our age and theirs did not share, at least consciously, the same concept of the theater; conversely, all plays, whatever their date, are subject to some basic aesthetic

218

laws. What a play is doing is inseparable from how it is doing it. I would want, therefore, to supplement these references with the names of various playwrights, both ancient and modern, who are, however covertly, critics themselves—and scholars of the theater.

2. The text for *Six Characters* is that in *Naked Masks: Five Plays by Luigi Pirandello,* ed. Eric Bentley (New York: E. P. Dutton and Co., 1952), pp. 217, 224.

3. Lionel Abel, *Metatheatre: A New View of Dramatic Form* (New York: Hill and Wang, 1963): Anne Barton (née Righter), *Shakespeare and the Idea of the Play* (Baltimore, Md.: Penguin Books, 1967); Maynard Mack, "The World of *Hamlet*," *Yale Review* 41 (1952):502–23; James Calderwood, *Shakespearean Metadrama* (Minneapolis: University of Minnesota Press, 1971); Murray Krieger, *A Window to Criticism: Shakespeare's Sonnets and Modern Poetics* (Princeton: Princeton University Press, 1964); Francis Fergusson, *The Idea of a Theater: A Study of Ten Plays: The Art of Drama in Changing Patterns* (Princeton: Princeton University Press, 1949).

Abel speaks of "metatheatre" as giving us a "sense that the world is a projection of human consciousness," glorifying the imagination that is unwilling to "regard any image of the world as ultimate," and suggesting that our dreams are as "real" as our reality (p. 113). In his brilliant chapter on *Hamlet* ("Hamlet Q.E.D.," pp. 40–58) Abel comments on the prince's sense of improvisation, his essentially theatrical perspective on Denmark, his arms' length attitude toward any seriousness in the Claudius world. Anne Barton goes through the plays step by step, pointing out the theatrical metaphors, defining what she sees as a growing pessimism on Shakespeare's part toward his theater; she also links these aesthetic dimensions in Shakespearean and, more generally, Elizabethan drama with the moralities and the mystery plays. Most interesting for my purposes in Maynard Mack's essay—in addition to his fine analysis of the metaphoric "worlds" of *Hamlet*—is his section on the play's theatrical metaphor. James Calderwood speaks even more directly about Shakespeare's consciousness of his craft and his theater, seeing, for example, the early plays as "testing grounds," as Shakespeare's conversation with himself, his audience, and with us about the function of theater, about the movement from reality to illusion, and about the victories and the difficulties facing anyone trying to see reality through an imaginative act. I also frequently use in this book Murray Krieger's distinction between art as a mirror and as a window, between its being a self-enclosed, aesthetic world and its being a way of looking back out on reality. Francis Fergusson makes a particularly telling distinction between ritual and improvisation in *Hamlet,* between the prince's consciousness of the sterile formalities of Claudius's court and the narrow perspective, the thematic-mentality of his opponents.

For a very fine metadramatic study see Kirby Farrell's *Shakespeare's Creation: The Language of Magic and Play* (Amherst: University of Massachusetts Press, 1975). Over the last decade there have also been valuable studies that have wedded the findings of Shakespearean scholars with those of stage historians and, as well, the reactions of audiences. A seminal example of this effort is Normam Rabkin's edition, *Reinterpretations of Elizabethan Drama, Essays of the English Institute* (New York: Columbia University Press, 1969). See, especially, the essay by Robert Hapgood, "Shakespeare and the Included Spectator." I would also point out two important works, one a study of the challenges in bringing together the practices of scholarship and theatrical performance, the other an excellent example of this "hybrid" approach: J. L. Styan, *The Shakespeare Revolution: Criticism and Performance in the Twentieth Century* (Cambridge: At the University Press, 1977); and Alan C. Dessen's *Elizabethan Drama and the Viewer's Eye* (Chapel Hill: University of North Carolina Press, 1977). Writings linking audience and performers are not new, of course; one thinks immediately of Granville-Barker's important studies. In our decade, however, the process seems accelerated, and this is surely a good and natural state.

4. Morris Weitz in his closing remarks in *Hamlet and the Philosophy of Literary Criticism* (Chicago: University of Chicago Press, 1964).

5. Marshall McLuhan, "Roles, Masks, and Performances," *New Literary History* 2 (1971):221.

6. I take these terms "mirror" and "window" from Krieger, *Window to Criticism.*

SOURCES

1. Jackson Barry, *Dramatic Structure, the Shaping of Experience* (Berkeley and Los Angeles: University of California Press, 1970).

2. Eric Bentley, *The Life of the Drama* (New York: Atheneum Publishers, 1964).

3. Harry Berger, Jr., "Theater, Drama, and the Second World: A Prologue to Shakespeare," *Comparative Drama* 2 (1968): 3–20.

4. Ivor Brown, *Shakespeare and the Actors* (London: Bodley Head, 1970).

5. Kenneth Burke, *Counter-Statement* (New York: Harcourt, Brace, and World, 1931).

6. Augusto Centeno, ed., *The Intent of the Artist* (Princeton: Princeton University Press, 1941).

7. James Clay and Daniel Krempel, *The Theatrical Image* (New York: McGraw-Hill, 1967).

8. Wolfgang Clemen, *Shakespeare's Dramatic Art: Collected Essays* (London: Methuen and Co., 1972).

9. Jackson Cope, *The Theater and the Dream: From Metaphor to Form in Renaissance Drama* (Baltimore, Md.: Johns Hopkins University Press, 1973).

10. Edward Gordon Craig, *On the Art of Theatre* (London: Wm. Heinemann Limited, 1957).

11. Madeleine Doran, *Endeavors of Art: A Study of Form in Elizabethan Drama* (Madison: University of Wisconsin Press, 1953).

12. Tom Driver, *The Sense of History in Greek and Shakespearean Drama* (New York: Columbia University Press, 1960).

13. Una Ellis-Fermor, *Shakespeare the Dramatist*, Annual Lecture of the British Academy (London: Oxford University Press, 1948); and *The Frontiers of Drama* (London: Methuen and Co., 1945).

14. Harold Fisch, "Shakespeare and the Theatre of the World," in *The Morality of Art*, ed. D. W. Jefferson (London: Routledge and Kegan Paul, 1969), pp. 76–86.

15. Northrop Frye, *Anatomy of Criticism* (Princeton: Princeton University Press, 1957).

16. Marjorie Garber, *Dream in Shakespeare: From Metaphor to Metamorphosis* (New Haven, Conn.: Yale University Press, 1974).

17. Henri Gheon, *The Art of the Theater* (New York: Hill and Wang, 1961).

18. Michael Goldman, *Shakespeare and the Energies of Drama* (Princeton: Princeton University Press, 1972).

19. Robert B. Heilman, *The Iceman, the Arsonist, and the Troubled Agent: Tragedy and Melodrama on the Modern Stage* (Seattle: University of Washington Press, 1973); and *Tragedy and Melodrama: Versions of Experience* (Seattle: University of Washington Press, 1968).

20. Norman Holland, *The Shakespearean Imagination* (New York: Macmillan Publishing Co., 1964).

21. Benjamin Hunninger, *The Origin of the Theatre* (Amsterdam: Querido, 1961).

22. H. D. F. Kitto, *Form and Meaning in Drama: A Study of Six Greek Plays and of "Hamlet"* (London: Methuen and Co., 1956).

23. Susanne K. Langer, *Feeling and Form* (New York: Charles Scribner's Sons, 1953).

24. Clifford Lyons, "Stage Imagery in Shakespeare's Plays," *Essays in Shakespeare and Elizabethan Drama in Honor of Hardin Craig*, ed. Richard Hosley (Columbia: University of Missouri Press, 1962).

25. Jerome Mandel, "Dream and Imagination in Shakespeare," *Shakespeare Quarterly* 24 (1973): 61–68.

26. Kenneth Muir, "Shakespeare's Poets," *Shakespeare Survey* 23 (1970): 91–100.

27. Ruth Nevo, *Tragic Form in Shakespeare* (Princeton: Princeton University Press, 1972).

28. Elder Olson, *Tragedy and the Theory of Drama* (Detroit: Wayne State University Press, 1961).

29. E. C. Pettet, "Shakespeare's Conception of Poetry," *Essays and Studies* n.s. 3 (1950): 29–46.

30. L. E. Pinsky, *Shakespeare: Principles of His Dramatic Art* (Moscow: Khudozhestvennaya Literatura, 1972).

31. William Rosky, "Imagination in the English Renaissance: Psychology and Poetic," *Studies in the Renaissance* 5 (1958): 49–73.

32. L. G. Salingar, "Time and Art in Shakespeare's Romances," *Renaissance Drama* 9 (1966): 3–35.

33. Hallett Smith, *Shakespeare's Romances: A Study of Some Ways of the Imagination* (San Marino, Cal.: Huntington Library, 1972).

34. Thomas Stroup, *Microcosmos: The Shape of the Elizabethan Play* (Lexington: University of Kentucky Press, 1965).

35. J. L. Styan, *Shakespeare's Stagecraft* (Cambridge: At the University Press, 1967).

36. Naoe Takei, "Dreams as Metaphysical Vision: A Study of Shakespeare's Major Tragedies," *Shakespeare Studies* 8 (1969–1970): 18–47.

37. Karl F. Thompson, *Modesty and Cunning: Shakespeare's Use of Literary Tradition* (Ann Arbor: University of Michigan Press, 1971).

38. T. Weiss, *The Breadth of Clowns and Kings* (New York: Atheneum Publishers, 1971).

39. David Young, *The Heart's Forest: A Study of Shakespeare's Pastoral Plays* (New Haven, Conn.: Yale University Press, 1972).

Chapter 1. Induction to the Theater: **The Taming of the Shrew**

1. Irving Ribner in his Introduction to the edition of the play for the Kittredge Shakespeares series (Waltham, Mass.: Blaisdell Publishing Co., 1966) provides a good, concise review of the scholarship on the relationship between the two Shrew plays. I should also point out here J. Dennis Huston's " 'To Make a Puppet': Play and Play-Making in *The Taming of the Shrew*," *Shakespeare Studies* 9 (1976): 73–87. While our focus is not always the same, I continue to profit from Huston's fine analysis.

2. See Robert Heilman's discussion of the various explanations for Sly's disappearance in his Introduction to the play in the Signet Classic Shakespeare series (New York: New American Library, 1966), pp. xxvii–xxviii.

3. Peter Alexander in the *London Times Literary Supplement* for July 8, 1965, p. 588, cited by Ribner, Introduction to *The Shrew,* pp. x–xi.

4. The text for Ionesco is *Four Plays,* trans. Donald M. Allen (New York: Grove Press, 1958).

5. The text for Dekker is Fredson Bowers's edition to *The Dramatic Works of Thomas Dekker,* vol. 3 (Cambridge: At the University Press, 1958).

6. Stephen Gosson, *The School of Abuse,* Shakespeare Society Reprints (London: Shakespeare Society, 1841), p. 11.

7. Marshall McLuhan, "Roles, Masks, and Performances," *New Literary History* 2 (1971): 519–20.

8. In Fletcher's *Women Pleased;* the reference is probably a late insert.

9. In the edition for the Kittredge Shakespeares series (1966), p. 137.

10. See Maynard Mack, "Engagement and Detachment in Shakespeare's Plays," *Essays on Shakespeare and Elizabethan Drama in Honor of Hardin Craig,* ed. Richard Hosley (Columbia, Mo.: University of Missouri Press, 1962), pp. 279–80; Cecil C. Seronsy, " 'Supposes' as the Unifying Theme in *The Taming of the Shrew,*" *Shakespeare Quarterly* 14 (1963): 15–30; Richard Hosley in his Introduction to the play in the Pelican Shakespeare series (Baltimore, Md.: Penguin Books, 1964), pp. 24–25; and Thelma N. Greenfield, *The Induction in Elizabethan Drama* (Eugene, Oreg.: University of Oregon Books, 1969), pp. 99–104. The quote is from Heilman, Introduction to *The Shrew,* p. xxvi.

11. Richard Hosley, "Was There a 'Dramatic Epilogue' to *The Taming of the Shrew?*" *Studies in English Literature* 1 (1961): 17–34.

12. Printed in Geoffrey Bullough, *Narrative and Dramatic Sources of Shakespeare,* vol. 1 (New York: Columbia University Press, 1961), pp. 69–108.

SOURCES

1. Thelma N. Greenfield, "The Transformation of Christopher Sly," *Philological Quarterly* 33 (1954): 34–42 (later in her *The Induction in Elizabethan Drama,* cited in note 10 for this chapter).

2. Richard Henze, "Role Playing in *The Taming of the Shrew,*" *Southern Humanities Review* 4 (1970): 321–40.

3. Sears Jayne, "The Dreaming of *The Shrew,*" *Shakespeare Quarterly* 17 (1966): 147–61.

Chapter 2. Love's Labour's Lost: *Language for the Stage*

1. James Calderwood, "*Love's Labour's Lost:* A Wantoning with Words," *Studies in English Literature* 5 (1965). This article later becomes

the basis for a chapter in his *Shakespearean Metadrama,* pp. 52–84. I should also mention here the excellent thematic study of the play by Anne Barton, *"Love's Labour's Lost," Shakespeare Quarterly* 4 (1953): 411–26.

2. Calderwood, "A Wantoning with Words," p. 320.

3. Louis Zukofsky, *A Test of Poetry* (London: Routledge and Kegan Paul, 1952), p. vii.

See also:

1. Cyrus Hoy, *"Love's Labour's Lost* and the Nature of Comedy," *Shakespeare Quarterly* 13 (1962): 31–40.

2. John D. Hunt, "Grace, Art, and the Neglect of Time in *Love's Labour's Lost," Shakespearean Comedy, Stratford-upon-Avon Studies* 14 (New York: Crane, Russak, 1972): 75–96.

3. Joseph Westlund, "Fancy and Achievement in *Love's Labour's Lost," Shakespeare Quarterly* 18 (1967): 37–46.

4. Frances A. Yates, *A Study of "Love's Labour's Lost"* (Cambridge: At the University Press, 1936).

Chapter 3: The Celebration of Art: **A Midsummer Night's Dream**

1. David Young, *Something of Great Constancy: The Art of "A Midsummer Night's Dream"* (New Haven, Conn.: Yale University Press, 1966), p. 78. I am very much indebted to Mr. Young; he is the first critic, I believe, to discuss in detail Shakespeare's concept of the imagination in the play. However, in this present chapter I am concerned with stressing the singleness of the play's imaginary world, as opposed to the dualism perceived by both Theseus and some modern critics, besides making some points, such as the identification of the poet and the lover, that Mr. Young does not make. I review his book in the *Journal of English and Germanic Philology* 66 (1967): 578–82.

2. Paul Olsen, *"A Midsummer Night's Dream* and the Meaning of Court Marriage," *English Literary History* 24 (1957):113. And this is, with variations of course, basically the view of Peter F. Fisher, "The Argument of *A Midsummer Night's Dream," Shakespeare Quarterly* 8 (1957): 307–10; and of E. C. Pettet, *Shakespeare and the Romance Tradition* (London and New York: Staples Press, 1949), pp. 112–14.

3. Jan Kott, *Shakespeare Our Contemporary* (Garden City, N.Y.: Doubleday and Company, 1966), p. 234.

4. In *The Complete Poems and Stories of Edgar Allan Poe,* ed. Arthur Hobson Quinn and Edward H. O'Neill, vol. 1 (New York: Alfred A. Knopf, 1946), p. 24.

5. The best discussion of the relation of Bottom as artist and pro-

ducer to the larger play is, I believe, Robert Dent's "Imagination in *A Midsummer Night's Dream,*" in *Shakespeare 400,* ed. James G. McManaway (New York: Shakespeare Association of America, 1964), pp. 115–29.

6. Francis Bacon, *Advancement of Learning and Novum Organum,* ed. J. E. Crighton (London: Colonial Press, 1900), p. 133.

7. Robert Burton, *The Anatomy of Melancholy* (Philadelphia: J. B. Lippincott Company, 1869), pp. 102–103.

8. Geoffrey Bush, *Shakespeare and the Natural Condition* (Cambridge, Mass.: Harvard University Press, 1956), pp. 3–19.

9. In an edition of the play, under *dramatis personae,* for the Blackfriars Shakespeare series (Dubuque, Iowa: William C. Brown Company, 1970).

A recent and most excellent book on the play—with a title that speaks for itself—is that of my colleague T. Walter Herbert, *Oberon's Mazéd World: A Judicious Young Englishman Contemplates "A Midsummer Night's Dream," with a Mind Shaped by the Learning of Christendom Modified by the New Naturalist Philosophy and Excited by the Vision of a Rich, Powerful England* (Baton Rouge: Louisiana State University Press, 1977).

SOURCES

1. Georges A. Bonnard, "Shakespeare's Purpose in *A Midsummer Night's Dream,*" *Shakespeare-Jahrbuch* 92 (1956): 268–79.

2. Madeline Doran, "*A Midsummer Night's Dream:* A Metamorphosis," *Rice Institute Papers* 44 (1960): 113–35.

3. Harriet Hawkins, "Fabulous Counterfeits: Dramatic Construction and Dramatic Perspective in *The Spanish Tragedy, A Midsummer Night's Dream,* and *The Tempest,*" *Shakespeare Studies* 6 (1970): 51–65.

4. J. Dennis Huston, "Bottom Waking: Shakespeare's 'Most Rare Vision,' " *Studies in English Literature* 13 (1973): 208–22.

5. Robert A. Law, "The 'Pre-Conceived Pattern' of *A Midsummer Night's Dream,*" *Texas Studies in English* 23 (1943): 5–14.

6. Jerome Mandel, "Dream and Imagination in Shakespeare's *A Midsummer Night's Dream,*" *Shakespeare Quarterly* 24 (1974): 61–68.

7. James E. Robinson, "The Ritual and Rhetoric of *A Midsummer Night's Dream,*" *Publications of the Modern Language Association* 83 (1968): 380–91.

Chapter 4. Othello: *Art Perverted*

1. *Timber, or Discoveries,* in *Critical Essays of the Seventeenth Century,* ed. J. E. Spingarn, vol. 1 (Oxford: Clarendon Press, 1908), p. 50.

2. *Anacrisis,* in Spingarn, *Essays of the Seventeenth Century,* vol. 1, p. 185.

3. *Arte of English Poesie,* in *Elizabethan Critical Essays,* ed. G. G. Smith, vol. 2 (London: Oxford University Press, 1904), p. 8.

4. In discussing Kyd's character Revenge as a playwright, Barry Adams comments at greater length on the artist's antithetical divine and demonic natures in an article entitled "The Audiences of *The Spanish Tragedy,*" *Journal of English and Germanic Philology* 68 (1969): 221–36.

5. Anne Barton, *Shakespeare and the Idea of the Play,* (Baltimore: Penguin Books, 1967), pp. 87–88.

6. In the Kittredge Shakespeares series (Waltham, Mass.: Blaisdell Publishing Co., 1966), p. 3.

7. Robert Heilman, *Magic in the Web: Action and Language in "Othello"* (Lexington, Ky.: University of Kentucky Press, 1953), pp. 47, 56.

8. *A Discourse of English Poetrie,* in Smith, *Critical Essays,* vol. 1, p. 310.

9. This is T. S. Eliot's judgment in "Shakespeare and the Stoicism of Seneca," in *Elizabethan Essays* (London: Faber and Faber, 1942), p. 39. G. Wilson Knight, *Wheel of Fire* (London: Oxford University Press, 1930) is a good representative of the opposing view; and see Heilman's comments in "The End of the Case," *Magic in the Web,* pp. 160–68.

10. Webbe, *Of English Poetrie,* in Smith, vol. 1, *Critical Essays,* p. 234.

11. Stephen Gosson, *The School of Abuse,* Shakespeare Society Reprints (London: Shakespeare Society, 1841), p. 22.

I would like to point out three most valuable studies of this play: namely: G. R. Elliott's *Flaming Minister: A Study of "Othello" as Tragedy of Love and Hate* (Durham, N.C.: Duke University Press, 1953); Marvin Rosenberg's *The Masks of Othello* (Berkeley: University of California Press, 1971); and Bernard Spivack's *Shakespeare and the Allegory of Evil* (New York: Columbia University Press, 1958).

SOURCES

1. W. H. Auden, "The Dyer's Hand: Poetry and the Poetic Process," *The Anchor Review* 2 (1957): 255–301.

2. Francis Fergusson, *Shakespeare: The Pattern in His Carpet* (New York: The Delacorte Press, 1970).

3. Stanley E. Hyman, *Iago: Some Approaches to the Illusion of His Motivation* (New York: Atheneum Publishers, 1970); and "Portraits of the Artist: Iago and Prospero," *Shenandoah* 21 (1970): 18–42.

4. Hoover H. Jordan, "Dramatic Illusion in *Othello,*" *Shakespeare Quarterly* 1 (1950): 146–52.

5. E. E. Stoll, *Art and Artifice in Shakespeare: A Study in Dramatic Contrast and Illusion* (London: Cambridge University Press, 1934).

6. Richard B. Zacha, "Iago and the *Commedia dell'arte*," *Arlington Quarterly* 2 (1969): 98–116.

Chapter 5. The Art of the Controlling Figures: As You Like It *and* Measure for Measure

1. Helen Gardner, *"As You Like It,"* in *More Talking about Shakespeare*, ed. John Garrett (New York: Theatre Arts Books, 1959). But for an unqualified view of Arden as a paradise or thornless garden see: Edward Dowden, *Shakespeare: A Critical Study of his Mind and Art* (London: Henry S. King and Co., 1880), pp. 76–81; Donald A. Stauffer, *Shakespeare's World of Images* (New York: W. W. Norton and Co., 1949), p. 76; or Margaret Webster, *Shakespeare Without Tears* (Cleveland and New York: World Publishing Co., 1955), p. 200.

2. James Calderwood, *Shakespearean Metadrama* (Minneapolis: Univeristy of Minnesota Press, 1971), p. 103.

3. For good commentary on Touchstone see Robert Hills Goldsmith, "Touchstone: Critic in Motley," *Publications of the Modern Language Association* 68 (1953): 888 (where Mr. Goldsmith comments on the clown's satire of the bucolic characters).

4. I think the sanest commentary on Jaques remains O. J. Campbell's "Jaques," *Huntington Library Bulletin* 8 (1935): 71–102.

5. See Albert Gilman's Introduction to the Signet Classic Shakespeare edition (New York: New American Library, 1963), p. xxv.

6. See commentary on Genet in the Preface, p. 13.

7. John Palmer, *Comic Characters in Shakespeare* (London: Macmillan and Co., 1947), pp. 51–52.

8. C. L. Barber, *Shakespeare's Festive Comedy* (Princeton: Princeton University Press, 1959), p. 239.

9. My concern in the second half of this chapter is to talk about *Measure for Measure* in the context established by the comments on *As You Like It*. I therefore make no reference to specific critical arguments for the play, though there has been a wealth of commentary on this so-called "dark" or "problem" or "religious" comedy. I found particularly stimulating in the course of my own reading the following: R. W. Chambers, *"Measure for Measure,"* from *Man's Unconquerable Mind* (London: Jonathan Cape, 1939), pp. 277–310; M. C. Bradbrook, "Authority, Truth, and Justice in *Measure for Measure*," *Review of English Studies* 17 (1941): 385–99; G. Wilson Knight, *"Measure for Measure* and the Gospels," from *Wheel of Fire* (London: Oxford University Press, 1930), pp. 73–96; E. M. W. Tillyard, *"Measure for Measure,"* from *Shakespeare's Problem Plays* (London: Chatto and Windus, 1950), pp. 121–29; Ernest

Schanzer, *"Measure for Measure,"* from *The Problem Plays of Shakespeare* (New York: Schocken Books, 1963), pp. 106–31; Sir Arthur Quiller-Couch, Introduction to *Measure for Measure,* New Shakespeare edition (Cambridge: At the University Press, 1922), pp. xxii-xliii; W. M. T. Dodds, "The Character of Angelo in *Measure for Measure,"* *Modern Language Review* 41 (1946): 246–55.

10. In "Preface to Shakespeare," *Johnson on Shakespeare,* ed. Arthur Sherbo, intro. Bertrand Bronson, the Yale Edition of the Works of Samuel Johnson (New Haven: Yale University Press, 1968), vol. 7, pp. 71–72.

I would also point out David Stevenson's insightful study, *The Achievement of Shakespeare's "Measure for Measure"* (Ithaca, N.Y.: Cornell University Press, 1966).

SOURCES

1. Philip Edwards, *Shakespeare and the Confines of Art* (London: Methuen, 1968).

2. Francis Fergusson, "Philosophy and Theatre in *Measure for Measure,"* *Kenyon Review* 14 (1952): 103–20; and *The Human Image in Dramatic Literature* (New York: Doubleday and Co., 1957).

3. Hal Gelb, "Duke Vincentio and the Illusion of Comedy, or All's Not Well That Ends Well," *Shakespeare Quarterly* 22 (1971): 25–34.

4. William E. Godshalk, " 'The Devil's Horn': Appearance and Reality," *Shakespeare Quarterly* 23 (1972): 202–5.

5. Robert H. Hethman, "The Theatrical Design of *Measure for Measure,"* *Drama Survey* 1 (1962): 261–77.

6. Mary Lascelles, *Shakespeare's "Measure for Measure"* (London: Athlone Press, 1953).

7. D. J. Palmer, "Art and Nature in *As You Like It,"* *Philological Quarterly* 49 (1970): 30–40.

Chapter 6. **Hamlet**

1. Again, I am indebted to Maynard Mack's essay on the play, "The World of *Hamlet,"* *Yale Review* 41 (1952) cited earlier in the Preface; to Maurice Charney, *Style in "Hamlet"* (Princeton: Princeton University Press, 1969); and Charles R. Forker, "Shakespeare's Theatrical Symbolism and Its Function in *Hamlet,"* *Shakespeare Quarterly* 14 (1963): 215–29.

2. The last line in Virginia Woolf's novel *To the Lighthouse* (New York: Harcourt, Brace, and World, 1955) is "I have had my vision."

3. See Harry Levin, *The Question of Hamlet* (New York: Oxford University Press, 1959), p. 88.

4. T. S. Eliot, "Hamlet and His Problems," in *Selected Essays: 1917–1932* (New York: Harcourt, Brace and Co., 1932), p. 125.

5. See Robinson's essay, "The Visual Powers Denied and Coupled: *Hamlet* and *Fellini-Satyricon* as Narratives of Seeing," in my *Shakespeare's "More than Words Can Witness": Essays on Visual and Nonverbal Enactment in the Plays* (Lewisburg, Pa.: Bucknell University Press, 1980), pp. 177–206. The present paragraph and the one following are my paraphrase of Robinson's argument.

6. I am indebted here to Jack Jorgens's recent book *Shakespeare on Film* (Bloomington: University of Indiana Press, 1977), pp. 207–51.

7. Laurence Olivier, "An Essay on *Hamlet*," *The Film Hamlet: A Record of Its Production*, ed. Brenda Gross (London: Saturn, 1948), pp. 11–12, 15.

8. Geoffrey Bush, *Shakespeare the Natural Condition* (Cambridge, Mass.: Harvard University Press, 1956), p. 115.

SOURCES

1. Lee S. Cox, *Figurative Design in "Hamlet": The Significance of the Dumb Show* (Columbus: Ohio State University Press, 1973).

2. Charles A. Dawson, "Hamlet the Actor," *South Atlantic Quarterly* 47 (1948):522–33.

3. Leslie A. Fiedler, "The Defense of the Illusion and the Creation of Myth: Device and Symbol in the Plays of Shakespeare," *English Institute Essays* (New York: Columbia University Press, 1949), pp. 74–94.

4. Arthur Johnston, "The Player's Speech in *Hamlet*," *Shakespeare Quarterly* 13 (1962):21–30.

5. Joseph Katz, "Faith, Reason and Art," *American Scholar* 21 (1952): 151–60.

6. William W. Lawrence, "Hamlet and the Mouse Trap," *Publications of the Modern Language Association* 54 (1939):709–35.

7. C. S. Lewis, *Hamlet: The Prince or the Poem?* Annual Shakespeare Lecture of the British Academy, 1942 (London: H. Milford, 1942).

8. Carol Replogle, "Not Parody, Not Burlesque: The Play Within the Play in *Hamlet*," *Modern Philology* 67 (1969): 150–59.

9. Wendy C. Sanford, *Theater as Metaphor in "Hamlet,"* The LeBaron Russell Briggs Prize Honors Essay in English (Cambridge, Mass.: Harvard University Press, 1962).

10. Neille Shoemaker, "The Aesthetic Criticism of *Hamlet* from 1692–1699," *Shakespeare Quarterly* 16 (1965):99–103.

230 WHEN THE THEATER TURNS TO ITSELF

11. Theodore Spencer, "Hamlet and the Nature of Reality," *English Literary History* 5 (1938):253–77.

12. Sanford Sternlicht, *"Hamlet:* Six Characters in Search of a Play," *College English* 27 (1966):528–31.

13. David L. Stevenson, "Objective Correlative for T. S. Eliot's *Hamlet," Journal of Aesthetics and Art Criticism* 13 (1954):69–79.

14. C. G. Thayer, *"Hamlet:* Dream as Discovery and as Metaphor," *Shakespeare Newsletter* 28 (1956):118–29.

Chapter 7. *Love and the Imagination in* Anthony and Cleopatra

1. Barbara Everett, Introduction to her edition for the Signet Classic Shakespeare series (New York: New American Library, 1964), p. xxxvi.

2. Harley Granville-Barker, *Prefaces to Shakespeare,* vol. 1 (Princeton: Princeton University Press, 1946), p. 437.

3. Derek Traversi, *An Approach to Shakespeare* (Garden City, N.Y.: Doubleday and Company, 1956), p. 251.

4. Besides surveying Cleopatra's portrait in earlier works, Willard Farnham offers a detailed analysis of her motives in the last scene: *Shakespeare's Tragic Frontier* (Berkeley and Los Angeles: University of California Press, 1963), pp. 196–205.

5. Robert Ornstein, "The Ethic of the Imagination: Love and Art in *Antony and Cleopatra," Stratford-upon-Avon Studies,* vol. 8 (New York: St. Martin's Press, 1967), p. 40.

6. Ibid., pp. 35–36.

7. Traversi, *Approach to Shakespeare,* p. 245.

8. Michael Lloyd, "The Roman Tongue," *Shakespeare Quarterly* 10 (1956):461–68.

9. J. Leeds Barroll, for example, describes Antony as a man reduced to "nothing through his own vices," as one who dies "unreclaimed and deluded"; see "Antony and Pleasure," *Journal of English and Germanic Philology* 57 (1958):708–20. For Thomas Stroup, Cleopatra is a sort of Vice figure seducing her lover from his proper role as world leader; see *Microcosmos: The Shape of the Elizabethan Play,* (Lexington: University of Kentucky Press, 1965), pp. 194–95. Yet Jan Kott in *Shakespeare Our Contemporary* can argue that the political world is ultimately inferior to Egypt because it is "small, because one cannot escape it" (p. 173). To S. L. Bethell, Cleopatra is Antony's "good, and not his evil genius, rescuing him from an undue preoccupation with the world, which is a snare and a delusion": *Shakespeare and the Popular Dramatic Tradition* (London: King and Staples, 1944), p. 131.

SOURCES

1. Anne Barton, *Nature's Piece 'Gainst Fancy: The Divided Catastrophe in "Antony and Cleopatra": An Inaugural Lecture* (London: Bedford College, 1974).
2. R. A. Foakes, "Vision and Reality in *Antony and Cleopatra*," *Durham University Journal* 25 (1964):66–76.
3. Julian Markels, *The Pillar of the World: "Antony and Cleopatra" in Shakespeare's Development* (Columbus: Ohio State University Press, 1969).
4. Arnold Stein, "The Image of Antony: Lyric and Tragic Imagination," *Kenyon Review* 21 (1959):586–606.
5. W. K. Wimsatt, Jr., "Poetry and Morals," *Thought* 23 (1948):281–99.

Chapter 8. The Tempest: *Release from the Theater*

1. G. Wilson Knight, *The Crown of Life* (New York: Barnes and Noble, 1966), pp. 174–75.
2. Bennett Weaver, "Shelley Works Out the Rhythms of 'A Lament,'" *Publications of the Modern Language Association* 47 (1932):570–76.
3. *Timber,* in Spingarn, vol. 1, *Essays of the Seventeenth Century,* pp. 31–32.
4. My colleague W. R. Robinson has maintained this point in our conversations and in a series of articles: particularly, "The Movies, Too, Will Make You Free," *Man and the Movies* (Baton Rouge: Louisiana State University Press, 1967), pp. 112–36; and "*2001* and the Literary Sensibility," *The Georgia Review* 26 (1972):21–37.
5. Norbert Fuerst, *The Victorian Age of German Literature: Eight Essays* (University Park: Pennsylvania State University Press, 1966), p. 25.
6. Anne Barton, *Shakespeare and the Idea of the Play* (Baltimore: Penguin Books, 1967), p. 180.
7. James Joyce, *Portrait of the Artist As a Young Man* (New York: Viking Press, 1968), p. 85.
8. See Harbage's remarks in the final chapter of *Shakespeare and the Rival Traditions* (New York: Macmillan Publishing Co., 1952).
9. Barton, *Idea of the Play,* pp. 154–71.
10. For example, John Masefield in *William Shakespeare* (Greenwich, Conn.: 1964), p. 135, invites us to "suppose (however wrongly) that Shakespeare, as Prospero, with a plumed hat and a rapier, spoke the Epilogue and bade farewell at art, audience and the bare boards that he had so often shaken with passion."
11. I return here to the terms Murray Krieger uses in his influential book *A Window to Criticism.* He argues that a work of art is at once a

window opening out to the world, allowing us to perceive those factors in our existence which, without art, would go undetected, and also a *mirror,* a self-enclosed world running by its own principles, separable from the encompassing reality.

SOURCES

For a provocative aesthetic approach to Shakespeare, from a somewhat different perspective, see my colleague Tommy Ruth Waldo's *Musical Terms as Rhetoric: the Complexity of Shakespeare's Dramatic Style,* Salzburg Studies in English Literature (Salzburg: Institut für Englische Sprache und Literatur, Universität Salzburg, 1974).

1. Richard Abrams, *"The Tempest* and the Concept of the Machiavellian Playwright," *English Literary Renaissance* 8 (1978):43–66.

2. Harry Berger, "Miraculous Harp: A Reading of Shakespeare's *Tempest," Shakespeare Studies* 5 (1970):253–83.

3. Stephen E. Bluestone, "William Shakespeare and the Circles of the Imagination: A Study of the Art of *Pericles, Cymbeline, The Winter's Tale,* and *The Tempest,"* Dissertation Abstracts 33 (Ann Arbor: University of Michigan 6301A, 1973).

4. H. E. Bowen, " 'I'll Break My Staff . . . I'll Drown My Book,' " *Renaissance Papers,* The Southeastern Renaissance Conference (1961):47–56.

5. Philip Brockbank, *"The Tempest:* Conventions of Art and Empire," *Stratford-upon-Avon Studies,* vol. 8 (New York: St. Martin's Press, 1967), pp. 183–202.

6. Ruben Arthur Brower, *The Fields of Light: An Experiment in Critical Reading* (New York: Oxford University Press, 1951).

7. Robert G. Egan, "This Rough Magic: Perspectives of Art and Morality in *The Tempest," Shakespeare Quarterly* 23 (1972):171–82.

8. Harry Epstein, "The Divine Comedy of *The Tempest," Shakespeare Studies* 8 (1975):279–96.

9. D. G. James, *The Dream of Prospero* (Oxford: Clarendon Press, 1967).

10. Jacqueline E. M. Latham, " 'The Tempest' and King James's 'Daemonology,' " *Shakespeare Survey* 28 (1975):118.

11. Cary Nelson, *The Incarnate Word: Literature As Verbal Space* (Urbana, Ill.: University of Illinois Press, 1973).

12. Mary M. Nilan, *"The Tempest* at the Turn of the Century: Cross-Currents in Production," *Shakespeare Survey* 25 (1972):120.

13. Douglas L. Peterson, *Time, Tide, and Tempest: A Study of Shakespeare's Romances* (San Marino, Cal.: Huntington Library, 1972).

14. Mary Ellen Rickey, "Prospero's Living Drolleries," *Renaissance Papers,* the Southeastern Renaissance Conference (1964):35–42.

15. Hanns Sacks, "Aesthetics and Psychology of the Artist," *International Journal of Psychoanalysis* 2 (1921):98–100.

16. Irvin Smith, "Ariel and the Masque in *The Tempest,*" *Shakespeare Quarterly* 21 (1970):213–22.

17. Joseph H. Summers, "The Anger of Prospero," *Michigan Quarterly Review* 12 (1973):135.

18. Theodore Weiss, "Caliban Remembers," in *The Last Day and the First* (New York: Macmillan 1968).

19. David Young, *The Heart's Forest: A Study of Shakespeare's Pastoral Plays* (New Haven: Yale University Press, 1972).

Afterword on Velázquez's Las Meninas

1. Quoted by José López-Rey, *Velázquez' Work and World* (Greenwich, Conn.: New York Graphic Society, 1968), p. 134.

2. Ibid., p. 136.

3. Theodore Crombie, *Velázquez* (London: G. Bell and Sons, 1962), pp. 69, 100.

4. See Charles de Tolnay, "Velázquez's 'Las Hilanderas' and 'Las Meninas,' " *Gazette des Beaux-Arts* 35 (1949): 21–38; and Karl M. Birkmeyer, "Realism and Realities in the Painting of Velázquez," *Gazette des Beaux-Arts* 52 (1958): 63–80. Cited by López-Rey, p. 137.

5. Enrique Lafuente Ferrari, *Velázquez,* trans. James Emmons, The Taste of Our Time series, vol. 33 (Lusanne, Switzerland: Editions d'Art Albert Stiura, n.d.), p. 114.

Index